RED DUSK
AND THE MORROW

PAUL DUKES

RED DUSK

AND THE MORROW

ADVENTURES AND INVESTIGATIONS IN SOVIET RUSSIA

Biteback Publishing

First published in Great Britain in 1922 by Doubleday, Page & Company

This edition published in 2012 by
Biteback Publishing Ltd
Westminster Tower
3 Albert Embankment
London SE1 7SP
Copyright © Paul Dukes 1922

ISBN 978-1-84954-218-0

10 9 8 7 6 5 4 3 2 1

A CIP catalogue record for this book is available from the British Library.

Set in Garamond
Cover design by Namkwan Cho

Printed and bound in Great Britain by
CPI Group (UK) Ltd, Croydon CR0 4YY

Nothing is more vital to national progress than the spontaneous development of individual character... Independence of thought was formerly threatened by monarchs who feared the disaffection of their subjects. May it not again be threatened by other forms of intolerance, possible even in a popular government? – Bryce, *Modern Democracies*

Contents

Introduction

The activities of Britain's Secret Intelligence Service, the organisation we now know as MI6, have always been shrouded in mystery, and no more so than in its first few decades between 1909 and 1939. Former secret service officers who sought to publicise their work were treated like pariahs and pursued through the courts. The prime example being Compton Mackenzie, whose book *Greek Memories,* still officially banned, we published in this series last year. There was one major exception to the rule. The activities of Paul Dukes inside Russia in the wake of the 1917 Bolshevik revolution were publicised by the British government in order to justify its military intervention in northern Russia.

'We understand that Mr Dukes, who recently returned to England after a stay of several months at Petrograd and Moscow, has placed at the disposal of the Government valuable information upon the situation and outlook in Bolshevist Russia,' *The Times* reported. 'In some official quarters, it is felt that this information should not be withheld from the public. The issues involved are held to be far too grave to justify final decisions by the Government without the support of an accurately informed public opinion.'

The newspaper subsequently published a series of reports from Dukes on the dire situation inside Russia where the Bolsheviks had launched the 'Red Terror', summarily executing thousands of 'counter-revolutionaries' and imprisoning many more. It was not the last time, of course, that a British government would resort to revealing secret intelligence to justify a foreign military escapade, but it was nevertheless remarkable given how important Dukes's mission had been. He was smuggled into Russia to take over the British spy networks from an expatriate British businessman, John Merrett, who had been left in charge when the British secret service officers were forced to withdraw in the late summer of 1918. Merrett, surely one of Britain's lost heroes, was something of a Scarlet Pimpernel figure. He not only took charge of the British espionage networks when the embassy withdrew but also smuggled potential victims of the Red Terror out of Russia along the courier lines. He was on the run from the Cheka, a predecessor of the KGB, when Dukes arrived.

Having already encouraged him to describe his role as a British spy inside Russia, where he operated under cover as a member of the Ukrainian Cheka, both the government and SIS were scarcely in a position to prevent the publication of this book a few years later. Dukes does not disclose his real role inside Russia, but he does mention the main players. He took over the networks from Merrett – referred to here as Mr Marsh – and then smuggled him out of Russia. Dukes then put his own mistress Nadezhda Ivanovna Petrovskaya in charge of the networks. Petrovskaya was a doctor and former revolutionary who was a personal friend of the Russian leader Vladimir Lenin. Her covername was Mariya Smirnova and she is referred to here misleadingly as Merrett's housekeeper 'Maria'. Petrovskaya was assisted by a journalist, Kurz-Gedroitz, named in this book as Dmitri Konstantinovitch.

Petrovskaya did not last long after Dukes left. She was arrested a few months later and sentenced to death but released in 1922, ironically around the time that *Red Dusk* was first published. The main two networks however lasted until 1927 when the main agents were put on trial, in what the British claimed were Stalinist show trials but were in fact the genuine trials of British spies. The work of Merrett, Dukes and Petrovskaya was therefore extremely productive in maintaining a vital source of secret intelligence for SIS.

Despite his understandable reticence over the true purpose of his mission, Dukes describes his real-life adventures in gripping detail and might be reasonably credited with inventing what was to become a standard piece of tradecraft for the secret agent as depicted in the movies. Dukes recalls, with some humour, placing incriminating evidence in a condom and hiding it in a lavatory cistern. 'I wrote mostly at night, in minute handwriting on tracing-paper, with a small caoutchouc [latex] bag about four inches in length, weighted with lead, ready at my side,' he recalled. 'In case of alarm all my papers could be slipped into this bag and within thirty seconds be transferred to the bottom of the cistern of the water-closet... I have seen pictures, carpets, and book shelves removed and everything turned topsy-turvy by diligent searchers, but it never occurred to anybody to ... thrust his hand into the water-closet cistern.'

Michael Smith
Editor of the Dialogue Espionage Classics
March 2012

Foreword

If ever there was a period when people blindly hitched their wagons to shibboleths and slogans instead of stars it is the present. In the helter-skelter of events which constantly outrun mankind, the essential meaning of commonly used words is becoming increasingly confused. Not only the abstract ideas of liberty, equality, and fraternity, but more concrete and more recently popularized ones such as proletariat, bourgeois, soviet, are already surrounded with a sort of fungus growth concealing their real meaning, so that every time they are employed they have to be freshly defined.

The phenomenon of Red Russia is a supreme example of the triumph over reason of the shibboleth, the slogan, and the political catchword. War-weary and politics-weary, the Russian people easily succumbed to those who promised wildly what nobody could give, the promisers least of all. Catchwords such as 'All Power to the Soviets', possessing cryptic power before their coiners seized the reins of government, were afterwards discovered either to have no meaning whatsoever, or else to be endowed with some arbitrary, variable, and quite unforeseen sense. Similarly, words such as 'workers', 'bourgeois', 'proletariat', 'imperialist', 'socialist', 'cooperative', 'soviet', are endowed by mob orators everywhere, with arbitrary significations, meaning one thing one day and another the next as occasion demands.

The extreme opponents of Bolshevism, especially amongst Russians, have sinned in this respect as greatly as the extreme proponents, and with no advantage to themselves even in their own class. For to their unreasoning immoderation, as much as to the distortion of ideas by ultra-radicals, is due the appearance, amongst a certain class of people of inquiring minds but incomplete information, of that oddest of anomalies, the 'parlour Bolshevik'. Clearness of vision and understanding will never be restored until precision in terminology is again re-established, and that will take years and years.

It was the discrepancy between the actualities of Bolshevist Russia and the terminology employed by the Red leaders that impressed me beyond all else. I soon came to the conclusion that this elaborate catch-phraseology was designed primarily for propagandist purposes in foreign countries, for the Bolsheviks in their home press indulge at times in unexpected spurts of candour, describing their own failures in terms that vie with those of their most inveterate foes. But they still cling to anomalous terms, such as 'workers' and peasants 'government' and 'dictatorship of the proletariat'.

It is to such discrepancies that I have sought to draw attention in the following pages. My point of view was neither that of the professional politician, nor of the social reformer, nor of the stunt-journalist, but simply that of the ordinary human individual, the 'man in the street'. As an official of the intelligence service the Soviet Government has charged me with conspiracies and plots to overthrow it. But I went to Russia not to conspire but to inquire. The Soviet Government's references to me have not been felicitous and I may be pardoned for recalling one or two of the most striking. At the close of 1920 I received an intimation from the Foreign Office that on January 16, 1920, a certain Mr Charles Davison had been executed in Moscow and that to the British Government's demand for an explanation the Soviet Government had replied that Mr Davison was shot as an accomplice of my 'provocative activities'. The letter from the British Foreign Office was, however, my first intimation that such a person as Mr Davison had ever existed. Again, on the occasion of the last advance of General Yudenich on Petrograd the Bolshevist Government asserted that I was the instigator of a 'White' Government which should seize power upon the fall of the city, and a list of some dozen or so ministers was published who were said to have been nominated by me. Not only had I no knowledge of or connection with the said government, but the prospective ministers with one exception were unknown to me even by name, the exception being a gentleman I had formerly heard of but with whom I had never had any form of communication.

It would be tedious to recount the numerous instances of which these are examples. I recognize but few of the names with which the Bolshevist Government has associated mine. The majority are of people I have never met or heard of. Even of the Englishmen and women, of whom the Bolsheviks arrested several as my 'accomplices', holding them in prison in some cases for over twelve months, I knew but few. With only one had I had any communication as an intelligence officer. Some of the others, whom I met subsequently, gave me the interesting information that their arrest and that of many innocent Russians was attributed by the Bolsheviks to a 'diary' which I was supposed to have kept and in which I was said to have noted their names. This 'diary' has apparently also been exhibited to sympathetic foreign visitors as conclusive evidence of the implication of the said Russians and Britishers in my numerous 'conspiracies'! I barely need say that, inexperienced though I was in the art and science of intelligence work, I made it from the outset an invariable rule in making notes never to inscribe any name or address except in a manner intelligible to no living soul besides myself, while the only "diary" I ever kept was the chronicle from which this book is partly compiled, made during those brief visits to Finland which the reader will find described in the following pages.

It goes without saying that this book is not designed to rectify this record of inaccuracies on the part of the Soviet Government. It was impossible in writing my story to combine precision of narrative with effective camouflage of individuals and places. The part of this book which deals with my personal experiences is therefore not complete, but is a selection of episodes concerning a few individuals, and I have endeavoured to weave these episodes into a more or less consecutive narrative, showing the peculiar chain of circumstances which led to my remaining in charge of the intelligence service in Russia for the best part of a year, instead of a month or two, as I had originally expected. To my later travels in Belorussia, the northern Ukraine and Lithuania I make but little reference, since my observations there merely confirmed the conclusions I had already arrived at as to the attitude of the Russian peasantry. In writing, I believe I have achieved what I was bound to regard as a fundamental condition, namely, the masking of the characters by confusing persons and places (except in one or two instances which are now of small import) sufficiently to render them untraceable by the Bolshevist authorities.

'Even when one thinks a view unsound or a scheme unworkable,' says Viscount Bryce in *Modern Democracies*, 'one must regard all honest efforts to improve this unsatisfactory world with a sympathy which recognizes how many things need to be changed, and how many doctrines once held irrefragable need to be modified in the light of supervenient facts.' This is true no less of Communist experiments than of any others. If in this book I dwell almost entirely on the Russian people's point of view, and not on that of their present governors, I can only say that it was the people's point of view that I set out to study. The Bolshevist revolution will have results far other than those anticipated by its promoters, but in the errors and miscalculations of the Communists, in their fanatical efforts to better the lot of mankind, albeit by coercion and bloodshed, lessons are to be learned which will be of incalculable profit to humanity. But the greatest and most inspiring lesson of all will be the ultimate example of the Russian people, by wondrous patience and invincible endurance overcoming their present and perhaps even greater tribulation, and emerging triumphant through persevering belief in the truths of that philosophy which the Communists describe as 'the opium of the people'.

Acknowledgements

Portions of this book first appeared, in slightly different form, in *Harper's Magazine*, *The Atlantic Monthly* and *The World's Work*.

PART 1

PART I

Chapter I

One of the Crowd

The snow glittered brilliantly in the frosty sunshine on the afternoon of March 11, 1917. The Nevsky Prospect was almost deserted. The air was tense with excitement and it seemed as if from the girdling faubourgs of the beautiful city of Peter the Great rose a low, muffled rumbling as of many voices. Angry, passionate voices, rolling like distant thunder, while in the heart of the city all was still and quiet. A mounted patrol stood here or there, or paced the street with measured step. There were bloodstains on the white snow, and from the upper end of the Prospect still resounded the intermittent crack of rifles.

How still those corpses lay over there! Their teeth grinned ghastily. Who were they and how did they die? Who knew or cared? Perhaps a mother, a wife... The fighting was in the early morning. A crowd – a cry – a command – a volley – panic – an empty street – silence – and a little group of corpses, hideous, motionless in the cold sunshine!

Stretched across the wide roadway lay a cordon of police disguised as soldiers, prostrate, firing at intervals. The disguise was an attempt to deceive, for it was known that the soldiers sided with the people. 'It is coming,' I found myself repeating mechanically, over and over again, and picturing a great cataclysm, terrible and overwhelming, yet passionately hoped for. 'It is coming, any time now – tomorrow – the day after—'.

What a day the morrow was! I saw the first revolutionary regiments come out and witnessed the sacking of the arsenal by the infuriated mob. Over the river the soldiers were breaking into the Kresty Prison. Crushing throngs surged round the Duma building at the Tauride Palace, and toward evening, after the Tsarist police had been scattered in the Nevsky Prospect, there rose a mighty murmur, whispered in awe on a million lips: 'Revolution!' A new era was to open. The revolution, so thought I, would be the Declaration of Independence of Russia! In my imagination I figured to myself a huge pendulum, weighted with the pent-up miseries and woes of a hundred and eighty millions of people, which had suddenly been set in motion. How far would it swing? How many times? When and where would it come to rest, its vast, hidden store of energy expended?

Late that night I stood outside the Tauride Palace, which had become the centre of the revolution. No one was admitted through the great gates without a pass. I sought a place midway between the gates and, when no one was looking, scrambled up, dropped over the railings, and ran through the bushes straight to the main porch. Here I soon met folk I knew – comrades of student days, revolutionists. What a spectacle within the palace, lately so still and dignified! Tired soldiers lay sleeping in heaps in every hall and corridor. The vaulted lobby, where Duma members had flitted silently, was packed almost to the roof with all manner of truck, baggage, arms and ammunition. All night long and the next I laboured with the revolutionists to turn the Tauride Palace into a revolutionary arsenal.

Thus began the revolution. And after? Everyone knows now how the hopes of freedom were blighted. Truly had Russia's foe, Germany, who despatched the proletarian dictator Lenin and his satellites to Russia, discovered the Achilles' heel of the Russian revolution! Everyone now knows how the flowers of the revolution withered under the blast of the Class War, and how Russia was replunged into starvation and serfdom. I will not dwell on these things. My story relates to the time when they were already cruel realities.

My reminiscences of the first year of Bolshevist administration are jumbled into a kaleidoscopic panorama of impressions gained while journeying from city to city, sometimes crouched in the corner of crowded box-cars, sometimes travelling in comfort, sometimes riding on the steps, and sometimes on the roofs or buffers. I was nominally in the service of the British Foreign Office, but the Anglo-Russian Commission (of which I was a member) having quit Russia, I attached myself to the American YMCA, doing relief work. A year after the revolution I found myself in the eastern city of Samara, training a detachment of boy scouts. As the snows of winter melted and the spring sunshine shed joy and cheerfulness around, I held my parades and together with my American colleagues organized outings and sports. The new proletarian lawgivers eyed our manoeuvres askance but were too preoccupied in dispossessing the 'bourgeoisie' to devote serious attention to the 'counter-revolutionary' scouts, however pronounced the anti-Bolshevik sympathies of the latter. 'Be prepared!' the scouts would cry, greeting each other in the street. And the answer, 'Always prepared!', had a deep significance, intensified by their boyish enthusiasm.

Then one day, when in Moscow, I was handed an unexpected telegram. 'Urgent' – from the British Foreign Office. 'You are wanted at once in London,' it ran. I set out for Archangel without delay. Moscow, with its turbulences, its political wranglings, its increasing hunger, its counter-revolutionary conspiracies, with Count Mirbach and his German designs, was left behind. Like a bombshell followed the news that Mirbach was murdered. Leaning over the side of the White Sea steamer, a thousand kilometres from Moscow, I cursed my luck that I was not in the capital. I stood and watched the sun dip low to the horizon; hover, an oval mass of fire, on the edge of the blazing sea; merge with the water; and, without disappearing, mount again to celebrate the triumph over darkness of the nightless Arctic summer. Then, Murmansk and perpetual day, a destroyer to Petchenga, a tug to the Norwegian frontier, a ten-day journey round the North Cape and by the fairy-land of Norwegian fjords to Bergen, with finally a zigzag course across the North Sea, dodging submarines, to Scotland.

At Aberdeen the control officer had received orders to pass me through by the first train to London. At King's Cross a car was waiting, and knowing neither my destination nor the cause of my recall I was driven to a building in a side street in the vicinity of Trafalgar Square. 'This way,' said the chauffeur, leaving the car. The chauffeur had a face like a mask. We entered the building and the elevator whisked us to the top floor, above which additional superstructures had been built for war-emergency offices.

I had always associated rabbit-warrens with subterranean abodes, but here in this building I discovered a maze of rabbit-burrow-like passages, corridors, nooks, and alcoves, piled higgledy-piggledy on the roof. Leaving the elevator my guide led me up one flight of steps so narrow that a corpulent man would have stuck tight, then down a similar flight on the other side, under wooden archways so low that we had to stoop, round unexpected corners, and again up a flight of steps which brought us out on the roof. Crossing a short iron bridge we entered another maze, until just as I was beginning to feel dizzy I was shown into a tiny room about ten feet square where sat an officer in the uniform of a British colonel. The impassive chauffeur announced me and withdrew.

'Good afternoon, Mr Dukes,' said the colonel, rising and greeting me with a warm handshake. 'I am glad to see you. You doubtless wonder that no explanation has been given you as to why you should return to England. Well, I have to inform you, confidentially, that it has been proposed to offer you a somewhat responsible post in the Secret Intelligence Service.'

I gasped. 'But,' I stammered, 'I have never – May I ask what it implies?'

'Certainly,' he replied. 'We have reason to believe that Russia will not long continue to be open to foreigners. We wish someone to remain there to keep us informed of the march of events.'

'But,' I put in, 'my present work? It is important, and if I drop it—'

'We foresaw that objection,' replied the colonel, 'and I must tell you that under war regulations we have the right to requisition your services if need be. You have been attached to the Foreign Office. This office also works in conjunction with the Foreign Office, which has been consulted on this question. Of course,' he added, bitingly, 'if the risk or danger alarms you—'

I forget what I said but he did not continue.

'Very well,' he proceeded, 'consider the matter and return at 4:30 tomorrow. If you have no valid reasons for not accepting this post we will consider you as in our service and I will tell you further details.' He rang a bell. A young lady appeared and escorted me out, threading her way with what seemed to me marvellous dexterity through the maze of passages.

Burning with curiosity and fascinated already by the mystery of this elevated labyrinth I ventured a query to my young female guide. 'What sort of establishment is this?' I said. I detected a twinkle in her eye. She shrugged her shoulders and without replying pressed the button for the elevator. 'Good afternoon,' was all she said as I passed in.

Next day another young lady escorted me up and down the narrow stairways and ushered me into the presence of the colonel. I found him in a fair-sized apartment with easy chairs and walls hidden by bookcases. He seemed to take it for granted that I had nothing to say. 'I will tell you briefly what we desire,' he said. 'Then you may make any comments you wish, and I will take you up to interview – er – the Chief. Briefly, we want you to return to Soviet Russia and to send reports on the situation there. We wish to be accurately informed as to the attitude of every section of the community, the degree of support enjoyed by the Bolshevist Government, the development and modification of its policy, what possibility there may be for an alteration of regime or for a counter-revolution, and what part Germany is playing. As to the means whereby you gain access to the country, under what cover you will live there, and how you will send out reports, we shall leave it to you, being best informed as to conditions, to make suggestions.'

He expounded his views on Russia, asking for my corroboration or correction, and also mentioned the names of a few English people I might come into contact with. 'I will see if – er – the Chief is ready,' he said finally, rising, 'I will be back in a moment.'

The apartment appeared to be an office but there were no papers on the desk. I rose and stared at the books on the bookshelves. My attention was arrested by an edition of Thackeray's works in a decorative binding of what looked like green morocco. I used at one time to dabble in bookbinding and am always interested in an artistically bound book. I took down *Henry Esmond* from the shelf. To my bewilderment the cover did not open, until, passing my finger accidentally along what I thought was the edge of the pages, the front suddenly flew open of itself, disclosing a box! In my astonishment I almost dropped the volume and a sheet of paper slipped out on to the floor. I picked it up hastily and glanced at it. It was headed *Kriegsministerium, Berlin*, had the German Imperial arms imprinted on it, and was covered with minute handwriting in German. I had barely slipped it back into the box and replaced the volume on the shelf when the colonel returned.

'A – the – er – Chief is not in,' he said, 'But you may see him tomorrow. You are interested in books?' he added, seeing me looking at the shelves. 'I collect them. That is an interesting old volume on Cardinal Richelieu, if you care to look at it. I picked it up in Charing Cross Road for a shilling.' The volume mentioned was immediately above *Henry Esmond*. I took it down warily, expecting something uncommon to occur, but it was only a musty old volume in French with torn leaves and soiled pages. I pretended to be interested. 'There is not much else there worth looking at, I think,' said the colonel, casually. 'Well, goodbye. Come in tomorrow.'

I wondered mightily who 'the Chief' of this establishment

could be and what he would be like. The young lady smiled enigmatically as she showed me to the elevator. I returned again next day after thinking overnight how I should get back to Russia – and deciding on nothing. My mind seemed to be a complete blank on the subject in hand and I was entirely absorbed in the mysteries of the roof-labyrinth.

Again I was shown into the colonel's sitting room. My eyes fell instinctively on the bookshelf. The colonel was in a genial mood. 'I see you like my collection,' he said. 'That, by the way, is a fine edition of Thackeray.' My heart leaped! 'It is the most luxurious binding I have ever yet found. Would you not like to look at it?'

I looked at the colonel very hard, but his face was a mask. My immediate conclusion was that he wished to initiate me into the secrets of the department. I rose quickly and took down *Henry Esmond*, which was in exactly the same place as it had been the day before. To my utter confusion it opened quite naturally and I found in my hands nothing more than an *edition de luxe* printed on Indian paper and profusely illustrated! I stared bewildered at the shelf. There was no other *Henry Esmond*. Immediately over the vacant space stood *The Life of Cardinal Richelieu* as it had stood yesterday. I replaced the volume, and trying not to look disconcerted turned to the colonel. His expression was quite impassive, even bored. 'It is a beautiful edition,' he repeated, as if wearily. 'Now if you are ready we will go and see – er – the Chief.'

Feeling very foolish I stuttered assent and followed. As we proceeded through the maze of stairways and unexpected passages which seemed to me like a miniature House of Usher, I caught glimpses of treetops, of the Embankment Gardens, the Thames, the Tower Bridge, and Westminster. From the suddenness with which the angle of view changed I concluded that in reality we were simply gyrating in one very limited space, and when suddenly we entered a spacious study – the sanctum of '– er – the Chief' – I had an irresistible sentiment that we had moved only a few yards and that this study was immediately above the colonel's office.

It was a low, dark chamber at the extreme top of the building. The colonel knocked, entered, and stood at attention. Nervous and confused I followed, painfully conscious that at that moment I could not have expressed a sane opinion on any subject under the sun. From the threshold the room seemed bathed in semi-obscurity. The writing desk was so placed with the window behind it that on entering everything appeared only in silhouette. It was some seconds before I could clearly distinguish things. A row of half-a-dozen extending telephones stood at the left of a big desk littered with papers. On a side table were numerous maps and drawings, with models of aeroplanes, submarines, and mechanical devices, while a row of bottles of various colours and a distilling outfit with a rack of test tubes bore witness to chemical experiments and operations. These evidences of scientific investigation only served to intensify an already overpowering atmosphere of strangeness and mystery.

But it was not these things that engaged my attention as I stood nervously waiting. It was not the bottles or the machinery that attracted my gaze. My eyes fixed themselves on the figure at the writing table. In the capacious swing desk-chair, his shoulders hunched, with his head supported on one hand, busily writing, there sat in his shirt sleeves —

Alas, no! Pardon me, reader, I was forgetting! There are still things I may not divulge. There are things that must still remain shrouded in secrecy. And one of them is – who was the figure in the swing desk-chair in the darkened room at the top of the roof-labyrinth near Trafalgar Square on this August day in 1918. I may not describe him, nor mention even one of his twenty-odd names. Suffice it to say that, awe-inspired as I was at this first encounter, I soon learned to regard 'the Chief' with feelings of the deepest personal regard and admiration. He was a British officer and an English gentleman of the finest stamp, absolutely fearless and gifted with limitless resources of subtle ingenuity, and I count it one of the greatest privileges of my life to have been brought within the circle of his acquaintanceship.

In silhouette I saw myself motioned to a chair. The Chief wrote for a moment and then suddenly turned with the unexpected remark, 'So I understand you want to go back to Soviet Russia, do you?' as if it had been my own suggestion. The conversation was brief and precise. The words Archangel, Stockholm, Riga, Helsingfors recurred frequently, and the names were mentioned of English people in those places and in Petrograd. It was finally decided that I alone should determine how and by what route I should regain access to Russia and how I should despatch reports.

'Don't go and get killed,' said the Chief in conclusion, smiling. 'You will put him through the ciphers,' he added to the colonel, 'and take him to the laboratory to learn the inks and all that.'

We left the Chief and arrived by a single flight of steps at the door of the colonel's room. The colonel laughed. 'You will find your way about in course of time,' he said. 'Let us go to the laboratory at once...'

And here I draw a veil over the roof-labyrinth. Three weeks later I set out for Russia, into the unknown.

I resolved to make my first attempt at entry from the north, and travelled up to Archangel on a troopship of American soldiers, most of whom hailed from Detroit. But I found the difficulties at Archangel to be much greater than I had anticipated. It was 600 miles to Petrograd and most of this distance would have to be done on foot through unknown moorland and forest. The roads were closely watched, and before my plans were ready autumn storms broke and made the moors and marshes impassable. But at Archangel, realizing that to return to Russia as an Englishman was impossible, I let my beard grow and assumed an appearance entirely Russian.

Failing in Archangel I travelled down to Helsingfors to try my luck from the direction of Finland. Helsingfors, the capital of Finland, is a busy little city bristling with life and intrigue. At the time of which I am writing it was a sort of dumping-ground for every variety of conceivable and inconceivable rumour, slander, and scandal, repudiated elsewhere but swallowed by the gullible scandalmongers, especially German and *ancien régime* Russian, who found in this city a haven of rest. Helsingfors was one of the unhealthiest spots in Europe. Whenever mischance brought me there I lay low, avoided society, and made it a rule to tell everybody the direct contrary of my real intentions, even in trivial matters.

In Helsingfors I was introduced at the British Consulate to an agent of the American Secret Service who had recently escaped from Russia. This gentleman gave me a letter to a Russian officer in Viborg, by the name of Melnikoff. The little town of Viborg, being the nearest place of importance to the Russian frontier, was a hornet's nest of Russian refugees, counter-revolutionary conspirators, German agents, and Bolshevist spies, worse if anything than Helsingfors. Disguised now as a middle-class commercial traveller I journeyed on to Viborg, took a room at the same hotel as I had been told Melnikoff stayed at, looked him up, and presented my note of introduction. I found him to be a Russian naval officer of the finest stamp and intuitively conceived an immediate liking for him. His real name, I discovered, was not Melnikoff, but in those parts many people had a variety of names to suit different occasions. My meeting with him was providential, for it appeared that he had worked with Captain Crombie, late British Naval Attaché at Petrograd. In September, 1918, Captain Crombie was murdered by the Bolsheviks at the British Embassy and it was the threads of his shattered organization that I hoped to pick up upon arrival in Petrograd. Melnikoff was slim, dark, with stubbly hair, blue eyes, short and muscular. He was deeply religious and was imbued with an intense hatred of the Bolsheviks – not without reason, since both his father and his mother had been brutally shot by them, and he himself had only escaped by a miracle. 'The searchers came at night,' he related the story to me. 'I had some papers referring to the insurrection at Yaroslavl which my mother kept for me. They demanded access to my mother's room. My father barred the way, saying she was dressing. A sailor tried to push past, and my father angrily struck him aside. Suddenly a shot rang out and my father fell dead on the threshold of my mother's bedroom. I was in the kitchen when the Reds came and through the door I fired and killed two of them. A volley of shots was directed at me. I was wounded in the hand and only just escaped by the back stairway. Two weeks later my mother was executed on account of the discovery of my papers.'

Melnikoff had but one sole object left in life – to avenge his parents' blood. This was all he lived for. As far as Russia was concerned he was frankly a monarchist, so I avoided talking politics with him. But we were friends from the moment we met, and I had the peculiar feeling that somewhere, long, long ago, we had met before, although I knew this was not so.

Melnikoff was overjoyed to learn of my desire to return to Soviet Russia. He undertook not only to make the arrangements with the Finnish frontier patrols for me to be put across the frontier at night secretly, but also to precede me to Petrograd and make arrangements there for me to find shelter. Great hostility still existed between Finland and Soviet Russia. Skirmishes frequently occurred, and the frontier was guarded jealously by both sides. Melnikoff gave me two addresses in Petrograd where I might find him, one at a hospital where he had formerly lived, and the other of a small café which still existed in a private flat unknown to the Bolshevist authorities.

Perhaps it was a pardonable sin in Melnikoff that he was a toper. We spent three days together in Viborg making plans for Petrograd while he drank up all my whisky except a small medicine bottle full which I hid away. When he had satisfied himself that my stock was really exhausted he announced himself ready to start. It was a Friday and we arranged that

I should follow two days later on Sunday night, the 24th of November. Melnikoff wrote out a password on a slip of paper. 'Give that to the Finnish patrols,' he said, 'at the third house, the wooden one with the white porch, on the left of the frontier bridge.'

At six o'clock he went into his room, returning in a few minutes so transformed that I hardly recognized him. He wore a sort of seaman's cap that came right down over his eyes. He had dirtied his face, and this, added to the three-days-old hirsute stubble on his chin, gave him a truly demoniacal appearance. He wore a shabby coat and trousers of a dark colour, and a muffler was tied closely round his neck. He looked a perfect *apache* as he stowed away a big Colt revolver inside his trousers.

'Goodbye,' he said, simply, extending his hand; then stopped and added, 'let us observe the good old Russian custom and sit down for a minute together.' According to a beautiful custom that used to be observed in Russia in the olden days, friends sit down at the moment of parting and maintain a moment's complete silence while each wishes the others a safe journey and prosperity. Melnikoff and I sat down opposite each other. With what fervour I wished him success on the dangerous journey he was undertaking for me! Suppose he were shot in crossing the frontier? Neither I nor would anyone know! He would just vanish – one more good man gone to swell the toll of victims of the revolution. And I? Well, I might follow! 'Twas a question of luck, and 'twas all in the game!

We rose. 'Goodbye,' said Melnikoff again. He turned, crossed himself, and passed out of the room. On the threshold he looked back. 'Sunday evening,' he added, 'without fail.' I had a curious feeling I ought to say something, I knew not what, but no words came. I followed him quickly down the stairs. He did not look round again. At the street door he glanced rapidly in every direction, pulled his cap still further over his eyes, and passed away into the darkness – to an adventure that was to cost him his life. I only saw him once more after that, for a

brief moment in Petrograd, under dramatic circumstances –
but that comes later in my story.

I slept little that night. My thoughts were all of Melnikoff,
somewhere or other at dead of night risking his life, outwitting
the Red outposts. He would laugh away danger, I was sure, if
caught in a tight corner. His laugh would be a devilish one – the
sort to allay all Bolshevist suspicions! Then, in the last resort,
was there not always his Colt? I thought of his past, of his
mother and father, of the story he had related to me. How his
fingers would itch to handle that Colt!

I rose early next day but there was not much for me to
do. Being Saturday the Jewish booths in the usually busy little
market-place were shut and only the Finnish ones were open.
Most articles of the costume which I had decided on were
already procured, but I made one or two slight additions on this
day and on Sunday morning when the Jewish booths opened.
My outfit consisted of a Russian shirt, black leather breeches,
black knee boots, a shabby tunic, and an old leather cap with
a fur brim and a little tassel on top, of the style worn by the
Finns in the district north of Petrograd. With my shaggy black
beard, which by now was quite profuse, and long unkempt hair
dangling over my ears I looked a sight indeed, and in England or
America should doubtless have been regarded as a thoroughly
undesirable alien!

On Sunday an officer friend of Melnikoff's came to see
me and make sure I was ready. I knew him by the Christian
name and patronymic of Ivan Sergeievitch. He was a pleasant
fellow, kind and considerate, like many other refugees from
Russia he had no financial resources and was trying to make a
living for himself, his wife and his children by smuggling Finnish
money and butter into Petrograd, where both were sold at a high
premium. Thus he was on good terms with the Finnish patrols
who also practised this trade and whose friendship he cultivated.

'Have you any passport yet, Pavel Pavlovitch?' Ivan
Sergeievitch asked me.

'No,' I replied, 'Melnikoff said the patrols would furnish me with one.'

'Yes, that is best,' he said; 'they have the Bolshevist stamps. But we also collect the passports of all refugees from Petrograd, for they often come in handy. And if anything happens remember you are a "speculator".'

All were stigmatized by the Bolsheviks as speculators who indulged in the private sale or purchase of foodstuffs or clothing. They suffered severely, but it was better to be a speculator than what I was.

When darkness fell Ivan Sergeievitch accompanied me to the station and part of the way in the train, though we sat separately so that it should not be seen that I was travelling with one who was known to be a Russian officer.

'And remember, Pavel Pavlovitch,' said Ivan Sergeievitch, 'go to my flat whenever you are in need. There is an old housekeeper there who will admit you if you say I sent you. But do not let the house porter see you – he is a Bolshevik – and be careful the house committee do not know, for they will ask who is visiting the house.'

I was grateful for this offer which turned out to be very valuable.

We boarded the train at Viborg and sat at opposite ends of the compartment, pretending not to know each other. When Ivan Sergeievitch got out at his destination he cast one glance at me but we made no sign of recognition. I sat huddled up gloomily in my corner, obsessed with the inevitable feeling that everybody was watching me. The very walls and seats seemed possessed of eyes! That man over there, did he not look at me – twice? And that woman, spying constantly (I thought) out of the corner of her eye! They would let me get as far as the frontier, then they would send word over to the Reds that I was coming! I shivered and was ready to curse myself for my fool adventure. But there was no turning back! *Forsan et haec olim meminisse iuvabit* wrote Virgil. (I used to write that on my

Latin books at school – I hated Latin.) 'Perhaps someday it will amuse you to remember even these things' – cold comfort, though, in a scrape and with your neck in a noose. Yet these escapades *are* amusing – afterward.

At last the train stopped at Rajajoki, the last station on the Finnish side of the frontier. It was a pitch-dark night with no moon. Half a mile remained to the frontier, and I made my way along the rails in the direction of Russia and down to the wooden bridge over the little frontier river Sestro. I looked curiously across at the gloomy buildings and the dull, twinkling lights on the other bank. That was my Promised Land over there, but it was flowing not with milk and honey but with blood. The Finnish sentry stood at his post at the bar of the frontier bridge and twenty paces away, on the other side, was the Red sentry. I left the bridge on my right and turned to look for the house of the Finnish patrols to whom I had been directed.

Finding the little wooden villa with the white porch I knocked timidly. The door opened, and I handed in the slip of paper on which Melnikoff had written the password. The Finn who opened the door examined the paper by the light of a greasy oil lamp, then held the lamp to my face, peered closely at me, and finally signalled to me to enter.

'Come in,' he said. 'We were expecting you. How are you feeling?' I did not tell him how I was really feeling, but replied cheerily that I was feeling splendid.

'That's right,' he said. 'You are lucky in having a dark night for it. A week ago one of our fellows was shot as we put him over the river. His body fell into the water and we have not yet fished it out.'

This, I suppose, was the Finnish way of cheering me up. 'Has anyone been over since?' I queried, affecting a tone of indifference. 'Only Melnikoff.' 'Safely?' The Finn shrugged his shoulders. "We put him across all right – *a dalshe ne znayu* ... what happened to him after that I don't know.'

The Finn was a lean, cadaverous looking fellow. He led me into a tiny eating-room, where three men sat round a smoky oil lamp. The window was closely curtained and the room was intolerably stuffy. The table was covered with a filthy cloth on which a few broken lumps of black bread, some fish, and a samovar were placed. All four men were shabbily dressed and very rough in appearance. They spoke Russian well, but conversed in Finnish amongst themselves. One of them said something to the cadaverous man and appeared to be remonstrating with him for telling me of the accident that had happened to their colleague a week before. The cadaverous Finn answered with some heat. 'Melnikoff is a chuckle-headed scatterbrain,' persisted the cadaverous man who appeared to be the leader of the party. 'We told him not to be such a fool as to go into Petrograd again. The Redskins are searching for him everywhere and every detail of his appearance is known. But he *would* go. I suppose he loves to have his neck in a noose. With you, I suppose, it is different. Melnikoff says you are somebody important – but that's none of our business. But the Redskins don't like the English. If I were you I wouldn't go for anything. But it's your affair, of course.'

We sat down to the loaves and fishes. The samovar was boiling and while we swilled copious supplies of weak tea out of dirty glasses the Finns retailed the latest news from Petrograd. The cost of bread, they said, had risen to about 800 or 1,000 times its former price. People hacked dead horses to pieces in the streets. All the warm clothing had been taken and given to the Red army. The Tchrezvichaika (the Extraordinary Commission) was arresting and shooting workmen as well as the educated people. Zinoviev threatened to exterminate all the bourgeoisie if any further attempt were made to molest the Soviet Government. When the Jewish Commissar Uritzky was murdered Zinoviev shot more than 500 at a stroke; nobles, professors, officers, journalists, teachers, men and women, and a list of a further 500 was published who would be shot at the next attempt on a Commissar's life. I listened patiently, regarding the bulk of these stories as the product of Finnish imagination. 'You will be held up frequently to be examined,' the cadaverous man warned me, 'and do not carry parcels – they will be taken from you in the street.'

After supper we sat down to discuss the plans of crossing. The cadaverous Finn took a pencil and paper and drew a rough sketch of the frontier.

'We will put you over in a boat at the same place as Melnikoff,' he said. 'Here is the river with woods on either bank. Here, about a mile up, is an open meadow on the Russian side. It is now 10 o'clock. About 3 we will go out quietly and follow the road that skirts the river on this side till we get opposite the meadow. That is where you will cross.'

'Why at the open spot?' I queried, surprised. 'Shall I not be seen there most easily of all? Why not put me across into the woods?'

'Because the woods are patrolled, and the outposts change their place every night. We cannot follow their movements. Several people have tried to cross into the woods. A few succeeded, but most were either caught or had to fight their way back. But this meadow is a most unlikely place for anyone to cross, so the Redskins don't watch it. Besides, being open we can see if there is any one on the other side. We will put you across just here,' he said, indicating a narrow place in the stream at the middle of the meadow.

'At these narrows the water runs faster, making a noise, so we are less likely to be heard. When you get over run up the slope slightly to the left. There is a path which leads up to the road. Be careful of this cottage, though,' he added, making a cross on the paper at the extreme northern end of the meadow. 'The Red patrol lives in that cottage, but at 3 o'clock they will probably be asleep.'

There remained only the preparation of 'certificates of identification' which should serve as passport in Soviet Russia.

Melnikoff had told me I might safely leave this matter to the Finns who kept themselves well informed of the kind of papers it was best to carry to allay the suspicions of Red guards and Bolshevik police officials. We rose and passed into another of the three tiny rooms which the villa contained. It was a sort of office, with paper, ink, pens, and a typewriter on the table.

'What name do you want to have?' asked the cadaverous man.

'Oh, any,' I replied. 'Better, perhaps, let it have a slightly non-Russian smack. My accent—'

'They won't notice it,' he said, 'but if you prefer—'

'Give him a Ukrainian name,' suggested one of the other Finns, 'he talks rather like a Little Russian.' Ukrainia, or Little Russia, is the southwest district of European Russia, where a dialect with an admixture of Polish is talked.

The cadaverous man thought for a moment. '"Afirenko, Joseph Ilitch",' he suggested, 'that smacks of Ukrainia.'

I agreed. One of the men sat down to the typewriter and carefully choosing a certain sort of paper began to write. The cadaverous man went to a small cupboard, unlocked it, and took out a box full of rubber stamps of various sizes and shapes with black handles.

'Soviet seals,' he said, laughing at my amazement. 'We keep ourselves up to date, you see. Some of them were stolen, some we made ourselves, and this one,' he pressed it on a sheet of paper leaving the imprint *Commissar of the Frontier Station Bielo'ostrof*, 'we bought from over the river for a bottle of vodka.' Bielo'ostrof was the Russian frontier village just across the stream.

I had had ample experience earlier in the year of the magical effect upon the rudimentary intelligence of Bolshevist authorities of official 'documents' with prominent seals or stamps. Multitudinous stamped papers of any description were a great asset in travelling, but a big coloured seal was a talisman that levelled all obstacles. The wording and even language of the document were of secondary importance. A friend of mine

once travelled from Petrograd to Moscow with no other passport than a receipted English tailor's bill. This 'certificate of
identification' had a big printed heading with the name of the
tailor, some English postage stamps attached, and a flourishing
signature in red ink. He flaunted the document in the face of
the officials, assuring them it was a diplomatic passport issued
by the British Embassy! This, however, was in the early days
of Bolshevism. The Bolsheviks gradually removed illiterates
from service and in the course of time restrictions became very
severe. But seals were as essential as ever.

When the Finn had finished writing he pulled the paper out
of the typewriter and handed it to me for perusal. In the top
left-hand corner it had this heading:

Extraordinary Commissar of the Central Executive Committee
of the Petrograd Soviet of Workers' and Red Army-men's
Deputies.

Then followed the text:

CERTIFICATE

This is to certify that Joseph Afirenko is in the service of
the Extraordinary Commissar of the Central Executive
Committee of the Petrograd Soviet of Workers' and Red
Army-men's Deputies in the capacity of office clerk, as the
accompanying signatures and seal attest.

'In the service of the Extraordinary Commission?' I gasped,
taken aback by the amazing audacity of the thing.

'Why not?' said the cadaverous man coolly, 'what could
be safer?'

What, indeed? What could be safer than to purport to be
in the service of the institution whose duty it was to hound
down all – old or young, rich or poor, educated or illiterate – who ventured to oppose and sought to expose the

pseudo-proletarian   Bolshevist   administration?   Nothing, of course, could be safer! *S volkami zhitj, po voltchi vitj*, as the Russians say. 'If you must live amongst wolves, then howl, too, as the wolves do!'

'Now for the signatures and seal,' said the Finn. 'Tihonov and Friedmann used to sign these papers, though it don't matter much, it's only the seal that counts.' From some Soviet papers on the table he selected one with two signatures from which to copy. Choosing a suitable pen he scrawled beneath the text of my passport in an almost illegible slanting hand, 'Tihonov.' This was the signature of a proxy of the Extraordinary Commissar. The paper must also be signed by a secretary, or his proxy. 'Sign for your own secretary,' said the Finn, laughing and pushing the paper to me. 'Write upright this time, like this. Here is the original "Friedmann" is the name.' Glancing at the original I made an irregular scrawl, resembling in some way the signature of the Bolshevist official.

'Have you a photograph?' asked the cadaverous man. I gave him a photograph I had had taken at Viborg. Cutting it down small he stuck it at the side of the paper. Then, taking a round rubber seal, he made two imprints over the photograph. The seal was a red one, with the same inscription inside the periphery as was at the head of the paper. The inner space of the seal consisted of the five-pointed Bolshevist star with a mallet and a plough in the centre.

'That is your certificate of service,' said the Finn, 'we will give you a second one of personal identification.' Another paper was quickly printed off with the words, 'The holder of this is the Soviet employee, Joseph Ilitch Afirenko, aged 36 years.' This paper was unnecessary in itself, but two 'documents' were always better than one.

It was now after midnight and the leader of the Finnish patrol ordered us to lie down for a short rest. He threw himself on a couch in the eating-room. There were only two beds for the remaining four of us and I lay down on one of them with one of the Finns. I tried to sleep but couldn't. I thought of all sorts of things – of Russia in the past, of the life of adventure I had elected to lead for the present, of the morrow, of friends still in Petrograd who must not know of my return – if I got there. I was nervous, but the dejection that had overcome me in the train was gone. I saw the essential humour of my situation. The whole adventure was really one big exclamation mark! *Forsan et haec olim...*

The two hours of repose seemed interminable. I was afraid of 3 o'clock and yet I wanted it to come quicker, to get it over. At last a shuffling noise approached from the neighbouring room and the cadaverous Finn prodded each of us with the butt of his rifle. 'Wake up,' he whispered, 'we'll leave in a quarter of an hour. No noise. The people in the next cottage mustn't hear us.'

We were ready in a few minutes. My entire baggage was a small parcel that went into my pocket, containing a pair of socks, one or two handkerchiefs, and some dry biscuits. In another pocket I had the medicine bottle of whiskey I had hidden from Melnikoff, and some bread, while I hid my money inside my shirt. One of the four Finns remained behind. The other three were to accompany me to the river. It was a raw and frosty November night, and pitch-dark. Nature was still as death. We issued silently from the house, the cadaverous man leading. One of the men followed up behind, and all carried their rifles ready for use.

We walked stealthily along the road the Finn had pointed out to me on paper overnight, bending low where no trees sheltered us from the Russian bank. A few yards below on the right I heard the trickling of the river stream. We soon arrived at a ramshackle villa standing on the river surrounded by trees and thickets. Here we stood stock-still for a moment to listen for any unexpected sounds. The silence was absolute. But for the trickling there was not a rustle.

We descended to the water under cover of the tumble-down villa and the bushes. The stream was about twenty paces wide at this point. Along both banks there was an edging of ice. I looked across at the opposite side. It was open meadow, but the trees loomed darkly a hundred paces away on either hand in the background. On the left I could just see the cottage of the Red patrol against which the Finns had warned me.

The cadaverous man took up his station at a slight break in the thickets. A moment later he returned and announced that all was well. 'Remember,' he enjoined me once in an undertone, 'run slightly to the left, but – keep an eye on that cottage.' He made a sign to the other two and from the bushes they dragged out a boat. Working noiselessly they attached a long rope to the stem and laid a pole in it. Then they slid it down the bank into the water.

'Get into the boat,' whispered the leader, 'and push yourself across with the pole. And good luck!'

I shook hands with my companions, pulled at my little bottle of whiskey, and got into the boat. I started pushing, but with the rope trailing behind it was no easy task to punt the little bark straight across the running stream. I was sure I should be heard, and had amid streams the sort of feeling I should imagine a man has as he walks his last walk to the gallows. At length I was at the farther side, but it was impossible to hold the boat steady while I landed. In jumping ashore I crashed through the thin layer of ice. I scrambled out and up the bank. And the boat was hastily pulled back to Finland behind me.

'Run hard!' I heard a low call from over the water.

Damn it, the noise of my splash had reached the Red patrol! I was already running hard when I saw a light emerge from the cottage on the left. I forgot the injunctions as to direction and simply bolted away from that lantern. Halfway across the sloping meadow I dropped and lay still. The light moved rapidly along the river bank. There was shouting, and then suddenly shots, but there was no reply from the Finnish side. Then the light began to move slowly back toward the cottage of the Red patrol, and finally all was silent again.

I lay motionless for some time, then rose and proceeded

cautiously. Having missed the right direction I found I had to negotiate another small stream that ran obliquely down the slope of the meadow. Being already wet I did not suffer by wading through it. Then I reached some garden fences over which I climbed and found myself in the road.

Convincing myself that the road was deserted I crossed it and came out on to the moors where I found a half-built house. Here I sat down to await the dawn – blessing the man who invented whiskey, for I was very cold. It began to snow, and half-frozen I got up to walk about and study the locality as well as I could in the dark. At the cross-roads near the station I discovered some soldiers sitting round a bivouac fire, so I retreated quickly to my half-built house and waited till it was light. Then I approached the station with other passengers. At the gate a soldier was examining passports. I was not a little nervous when showing mine for the first time, but the examination was a very cursory one. The soldier seemed only to be assuring himself the paper had a proper seal. He passed me through and I went to the ticket office and demanded a ticket.

'One first class to Petrograd,' I said, boldly.

'There is no first class by this train, only second and third.'

'No first? Then give me a second.' I had asked the Finns what class I ought to travel, expecting them to say, third. But they replied. First of course, for it would be strange to see an employee of the Extraordinary Commission travelling other than first class. Third class was for workers and peasants.

The journey to Petrograd was about twenty-five miles, and stopping at every station the train took nearly two hours. As we approached the city the coaches filled up until people were standing in the aisles and on the platforms. There was a crush on the Finland Station at which we arrived. The examination of papers was again merely cursory. I pushed out with the throng and looking around me on the dirty, rubbish-strewn station I felt a curious mixture of relief and apprehension. A flood of strange thoughts and recollections rushed through my mind. I saw my whole life in a new and hitherto undreamt-of perspective. Days of wandering in Europe, student days in Russia, life amongst the Russian peasantry, and three years of apparently aimless war work all at once assumed symmetrical proportions and appeared like the sides of a prism leading to a common apex at which I stood. Yes, my life, I suddenly realized, *had* had an aim – it was to stand here on the threshold of the city that was my home, homeless, helpless, and friendless, one of the common crowd. That was it – *one of the common crowd!* I wanted not the theories of theorists, nor the doctrines of doctrinaires, but to see what the greatest social experiment the world has ever witnessed did for the common crowd. And strangely buoyant, I stepped lightly out of the station into the familiar streets.

Chapter II

Five Days

One of the first things that caught my eye as I emerged from the station was an old man, standing with his face to the wall of a house, leaning against a protruding gutter-pipe. As I passed him I noticed he was sobbing. I stopped to speak to him.

'What is the matter, little uncle?' I said.

'I am cold and hungry,' he whimpered without looking up and still leaning against the pipe. 'For three days I have eaten nothing.' I pushed a twenty-rouble note into his hand. 'Here, take this,' I said.

He took the money but looked at me, puzzled. 'Thank you,' he mumbled, 'but what is the good of money? Where shall I get bread?' So I gave him a piece of mine and passed on.

There was plenty of life and movement in the streets, though only of foot-passengers. The roadway was dirty and strewn with litter. Strung across the street from house to house were the shreds of washed-out red flags, with inscriptions that showed they had been hung out to celebrate the anniversary of the Bolshevist *coup d'état* a few weeks earlier. Occasionally one came across small groups of people, evidently of the educated class, ladies and elderly gentlemen in worn-out clothes, shovelling away the early snow and slush under the supervision of a workman, who as taskmaster stood still and did nothing.

Crossing the Liteiny Bridge on my way into the city I stopped, as was my wont, to contemplate the marvellous view of the river Neva. No capital in Europe possesses so beautiful an expanse of water as this city of Peter the Great. Away on the horizon the slender gilded spire of the cathedral of St. Peter and St. Paul rose from the gloomy fortress. By force of habit I wondered who was now incarcerated in those dark dungeons. Years ago, before the revolution, I used to stand and look at the 'Petropavlovka' as the fortress is popularly called, thinking of those who pined in its subterranean cells for seeking the liberty of the Russian people.

My first destination was the house of an English gentleman, to whom I shall refer as Mr Marsh. Marsh was a prominent business man in Petrograd. I did not know him personally, but he had been a friend of Captain Crombie and until recently was known to be at liberty. He lived on the quay of the Fontanka, a long, straggling branch of the Neva flowing through the heart of the city. Melnikoff knew Marsh and had promised to prepare him for my coming. I found the house and, after assuring myself the street was clear and I was not observed, I entered. In the hall I was confronted by an individual, who might or might not have been the house-porter — I could not tell. But I saw at once that this man was not disposed to be friendly. He let me in, closed the door behind me, and promptly placed himself in front of it.

'Whom do you want?' he asked.

'I want Mr Marsh,' I said. 'Can you tell me the number of his flat?' I knew the number perfectly well, but I could see from the man's manner that the less I knew about Marsh, the better for me.

"Marsh is in prison,' replied the man, 'and his flat is sealed up. Do you know him?'

Devil take it, I thought, I suppose I shall be arrested, too, to see what I came here for! The idea occurred to me for a moment to flaunt my concocted passport in his face and make myself out to be an agent of the Extraordinary Commission, but as such I should have known of Marsh's arrest, and I should still have to explain the reason of my visit. It wouldn't do. I thought rapidly for a plausible pretext.

'No, I don't know him,' I replied. 'I have never seen him in my life. I was sent to give him this little parcel.' I held up the packet containing my *trousseau* of socks, biscuits, and handkerchiefs. 'He left this in a house at Alexandrovsky the other night. I am an office clerk there. I will take it back.'

The man eyed me closely. 'You do not know Mr Marsh?' he said again, slowly.

'I have never seen him in my life,' I repeated, emphatically, edging nearer the door.

'You had better leave the parcel, however,' he said.

'Yes, yes, certainly,' I agreed with alacrity, fearful at the same time lest my relief at this conclusion to the incident should be too noticeable.

I handed him over my parcel. 'Good morning,' I said civilly, 'I will say that Mr Marsh is arrested.' The man moved away from the door, still looking hard at me as I passed out into the street.

Agitated by this misfortune, I turned my steps in the direction of the hospital where I hoped to find Melnikoff. The hospital in question was at the extreme end of the Kamenostrovsky Prospect, in the part of the city known as The Islands because it forms the delta of the river Neva. It was a good four-mile walk from Marsh's house. I tried to get on to a street-car, but there were very few running and they were so crowded that it was impossible to board them. People hung in bunches all round the steps and even on the buffers. So, tired as I was after the night's adventure, I footed it.

Melnikoff, it appeared, was a relative of one of the doctors of this hospital, but I did not find him here. The old woman at the lodge said he had been there one night and not returned since. I began to think something untoward must have occurred, although doubtless he had several other night-shelters besides this one. There was nothing to do but wait for the afternoon and go to the clandestine café to which he had directed me.

I retraced my steps slowly into town. All around was shabbiness. Here and there in the roadway lay a dead horse. The wretched brutes were whipped to get the last spark of life and labour out of them and then lay where they fell, for the ladies

who were made to sweep the streets were not strong enough
to remove dead horses. Every street, every building, shop, and
porch spoke to me of bygone associations, which with a pang
I now realized were dead. A few stores remained open, notably
of music, books, and flowers, but Soviet licenses were required
to purchase anything, except propagandist literature, which was
sold freely at a cheap price, and flowers, which were fabulously
dear. Hawkers with trucks disposed of second-hand books,
obviously removed from the shelves of private libraries, while
a tiny basement store, here and there peeping shamefacedly up
from beneath the level of the street, secreted in semi-obscurity
an unappetizing display of rotting vegetables or fruits and the
remnants of biscuits and canned goods. But everything spoke
bitterly of the progressive dearth of things and the increasing
stagnation of normal life.

I stopped to read the multifarious public notices and
announcements on the walls. Some bore reference to Red army
mobilization, others to compulsory labour for the bourgeoisie,
but most of them dealt with the distribution of food. I bought
some seedy-looking apples, and crackers that tasted several years
old. I also bought all the newspapers and a number of pamphlets
by Lenin, Zinoviev and others. Finding a cab with its horse still
on four legs, I hired it and drove to the Finland Station, where
upon arrival in the morning I had noticed there was a buffet. The
condiments exhibited on the counter, mostly bits of herring on
microscopic pieces of black bread, were still less appetizing than
my crackers, so I just sat down to rest, drank a weak liquid made
of tea-substitute, and read the Soviet papers.

There was not much of news, for the ruling Bolshevist* class
had already secured a monopoly of the press by closing down

---

*   In March, 1918, the Bolsheviks changed their official title from
    'Bolshevist Party' to that of 'Communist Party of Bolsheviks'.
    Throughout this book, therefore, the words Bolshevik and
    Communist are employed, as in Russia, as interchangeable terms.

all journals expressing contrary opinions, so that all that was
printed was propaganda. While the press of the Western world
was full of talk of peace, the Soviet journals were insisting on
the creation of a mighty Red army that should set Europe and
the globe aflame with world-revolution.

At three o'clock I set out to look for Melnikoff's café a
clandestine establishment in a private flat on the top floor of a
house in one of the streets off the Nevsky Prospect. When I
rang the bell the door was opened just a wee bit and I espied a
keen and suspicious eye through the chink. Seeing it was immediately about to close again I slid one foot into the aperture and
asked quickly for Melnikoff.

'Melnikoff?' said the voice accompanying the eagle eye.
'What Melnikoff?'

'N—,' I said, giving Melnikoff's real name. At this point the
door was opened a little wider and I was confronted by two
ladies, the one (with the eagle eye) elderly and plump, the other
young and good-looking.

'What is his first name and patronymic?' asked the younger
lady. 'Nicolas Nicolaevitch,' I replied. 'It is all right,' said the
younger lady to the elder. 'He said someone might be coming
to meet him this afternoon. Come in,' she went on, to me.
'Nicolas Nicolaevitch was here for a moment on Saturday and
said he would be here yesterday but did not come. I expect him
any minute now.'

I passed into a sitting room fitted with small tables, where
the fair young lady, Vera Alexandrovna, served me to my
surprise with delicious little cakes which would have graced any
Western tea-table. The room was empty when I arrived, but
later about a dozen people came in, all of distinctly bourgeois
stamp, some prepossessing in appearance, others less so. A few
of the young men looked like ex-officers of dubious type. They
laughed loudly, talked in raucous voices, and seemed to have
plenty of money to spend, for the delicacies were extremely
expensive. This café, I learned later, was a meeting-place for

conspirators, who were said to have received funds for counter-revolutionary purposes from representatives of the Allies.

Vera Alexandrovna came over to the table in the corner where I sat alone. 'I must apologize,' she said, placing a cup on the table, 'for not giving you chocolate. I ran out of chocolate last week. This is the best I can do for you. It is a mixture of cocoa and coffee – an invention of my own in these hard times.' I tasted it and found it very nice.

Vera Alexandrovna was a charming girl of about twenty summers, and with my uncouth get-up and general aspect I felt I was a bad misfit in her company. I was painfully conscious of attracting attention and apologized for my appearance.

'Don't excuse yourself,' replied Vera Alexandrovna, 'we all look shabby nowadays.' (She herself, however, was very trim.) 'Nicolas Nicolaevitch told me you were coming and that you were a friend of his – but I shall ask no questions. You may feel yourself quite safe and at home here and nobody will notice you.' (But I saw four of the loud-voiced young officers at the next table looking at me very hard.)

'I scarcely expected to find these comforts in hungry Petrograd,' I said to Vera Alexandrovna. 'May I ask how you manage to keep your café?'

'Oh, it is becoming very difficult indeed,' complained Vera Alexandrovna. 'We have two servants whom we send twice a week into the villages to bring back flour and milk, and we buy sugar from the Jews in the Jewish market. But it is getting so hard. We do not know if we shall be able to keep it going much longer. Then, too, we may be discovered. Twice the Reds have been to ask if suspicious people live in this house, but the porter put them off because we give him flour.'

Vera Alexandrovna rose to attend to other guests. I felt extremely ill at ease, for it was clear I was attracting attention and I did not at all like the looks of some of the people present.

'Ah, *ma chère* Vera Alexandrovna!' exclaimed a fat gentleman in spectacles who had just come in, kissing her hand effusively.

'Here we are again! Well, our Redskins haven't long to last now, I'll be bound. The latest is that they are going to mobilize. Mobilize, indeed! Just a little push from outside, and pouf! Up they'll go like a bubble bursting!'

At once one of the four young men rose from the next table and approached me. He was tall and thin, with sunken eyes, hair brushed straight up, and a black moustache. There was a curious crooked twitch about his mouth.

'Good afternoon,' he said. 'Allow me to introduce myself. Captain Zorinsky. You are waiting for Melnikoff, are you not? I am a friend of his.'

I shook hands with Zorinsky, but gave him no encouragement to talk. Why had Melnikoff not told me I should meet this 'friend of his'? Had this Zorinsky merely guessed I was waiting for Melnikoff, or had Vera Alexandrovna told him – Vera Alexandrovna, who assured me no one would notice me?

'Melnikoff did not come here yesterday,' Zorinsky continued, 'but if I can do anything for you at any time I shall be glad.'

I bowed and he returned to his table. Since it was already six I resolved I would stay in this café no longer. The atmosphere of the place filled me with indefinable apprehension.

'I am so sorry you have missed Nicolas Nicolaevitch,' said Vera Alexandrovna as I took my leave. 'Will you come in tomorrow?' I said I would, fully determined that I would not. 'Come back at any time,' said Vera Alexandrovna, with her pleasant smile; 'and remember,' she added, reassuringly, in an undertone, 'here you are perfectly safe.'

Could anybody be more charming than Vera Alexandrovna? Birth, education and refinement were manifested in every gesture. But as for her café, I had an ominous presentiment, and nothing would have induced me to re-enter it.

I resolved to resort to the flat of Ivan Sergeievitch, Melnikoff's friend who had seen me off at Viborg. The streets were bathed in gloom as I emerged from the café. Lamps burned only at rare intervals. And suppose, I speculated, I find

no one at Ivan Sergeievitch's home? What would offer a night's
shelter – a porch, here or there, a garden, a shed? Perhaps one
of the cathedrals, Kazan, for instance, might be open. Ah, look,
there was a hoarding round one side of the Kazan Cathedral!
I stepped up and peeped inside. Lumber and rubbish. Yes, I
decided, that would do splendidly!

Ivan Sergeievitch's house was in a small street at the end of
Kazanskaya, and like Vera Alexandrovna's his flat was on the
top floor. My experience of the morning had made me very
cautious, and I was careful to enter the house as though I were
making a mistake, the easier to effect an escape if necessary.
But the house was as still as death. I met nobody on the stairs,
and for a long time there was no reply to my ring. I was just
beginning to think seriously of the hoarding round the Kazan
Cathedral when I heard footsteps, and a female voice said
querulously behind the door, 'Who is there?'

'From Ivan Sergeievitch,' I replied, speaking just loud
enough to be heard through the door.

There was a pause. 'From which Ivan Sergeievitch?' queried
the voice.

I lowered my tone. I felt the other person was listening
intently. 'From *your* Ivan Sergeievitch, in Viborg,' I said in a low
voice at the keyhole.

There was another pause. 'But who are you?' came the query.

'Do not be alarmed,' I said in the same tone. 'I have a
message to you from him.'

The footsteps receded. I could hear voices conferring. Then
two locks were undone, and the door was partially opened on a
short chain. I saw a middle-aged woman peering at me with fear
and suspicion through the chink.

I repeated what I had already said, adding in a whisper
that I myself had just come from Finland and would perhaps
be going back shortly. The chain was then removed and I
passed in.

The woman who opened the door, and who proved to be

the housekeeper spoken of by Ivan Sergeievitch, closed it again hastily, locked it securely, and stood before me, a trembling little figure with keen eyes that looked me up and down with uncertainty. A few paces away stood a girl, the nurse of Ivan Sergeievitch's children who were in Finland.

'Ivan Sergeievitch is an old friend of mine,' I said, not truthfully, but very anxious to calm the suspicions of my humble hostesses. 'I knew him long ago and saw him again quite recently in Finland. He asked me, if I found it possible, to come round and see you.'

'Come in, come in, please,' said the housekeeper, whom I shall call Stepanovna, still very nervously. 'Excuse our showing you into the kitchen, but it is the only room we have warmed. It is so difficult to get firewood nowadays.'

I sat down in the kitchen, feeling very tired. 'Ivan Sergeievitch is well and sends his greetings,' I said. 'So are his wife and the children. They hope you are well and not suffering. They would like you to join them but it is impossible to get passports.'

'Thank you, thank you,' said Stepanovna. 'I am glad they are well. We have not heard from them for so long. May we offer you something to eat—?'

'Ivan Pavlovitch is my name,' I interpolated, catching her hesitation.

'May we offer you something to eat, Ivan Pavlovitch?' said Stepanovna kindly, busying herself at the stove. Her hands still trembled. 'Thank you,' I said, 'but I am afraid you have not much yourself.'

'We are going to have some soup for supper,' she replied. 'There will be enough for you, too.'

Stepanovna left the kitchen for a moment, and the nursing maid, whose name was Varia, leaned over to me and said in a low voice, 'Stepanovna is frightened today. She nearly got arrested this morning at the market when the Reds came and took people buying and selling food.'

I saw from Varia's manner that she was a self-possessed and

intelligent girl and I resolved to speak to her first regarding my staying the night, lest I terrified Stepanovna by the suggestion.

'When I went to my home this afternoon,' I said, 'I found it locked. I expect the housekeeper was out. It is very far, and I wonder if I may stay the night here. A sofa will do to lie on, or even the floor. I am dreadfully tired and my leg is aching from an old wound. Ivan Sergeievitch said I might use his flat whenever I liked.'

'I will ask Stepanovna,' said Varia. 'I do not think she will mind.' Varia left the room and, returning, said Stepanovna agreed – for one night.

The soup was soon ready. It was cabbage soup, and very good. I ate two big platefuls of it, though conscience piqued me in accepting a second. But I was very hungry. During supper a man in soldier's uniform came in by the kitchen door and sat down on a box against the wall. He said nothing at all, but he had a good-natured, round, plump face, with rosy cheeks and twinkling eyes. With a jack-knife he hewed square chunks off a loaf of black bread, one of which chunks was handed to me.

'This is my nephew Dmitri,' said Stepanovna. 'He has just become a volunteer so as to get Red army rations, so we are better off now.'

Dmitri smiled at being mentioned, but said nothing. After two platefuls of soup I could scarcely keep my eyes open. So I asked where I might spend the night and was shown into the study, where I threw myself on the couch and fell fast asleep.

When I awoke I had such a strange sensation of unaccustomed surroundings that I was completely bewildered, and was only brought to my senses by Varia entering with a glass of tea – real tea, from Dmitri's Red rations.

Then I recalled the previous day, my adventurous passage across the frontier, the search for Marsh and Melnikoff, the secret café, and my meeting with my present humble friends. With disconcerting brusqueness I also recollected that I had as yet no prospects for the ensuing night. But I persuaded myself that much might happen before nightfall and tried to think no more about it.

Stepanovna had quite got over her fright, and when I came into the kitchen to wash and drink another glass of tea she greeted me kindly. Dmitri sat on his box in stolid silence, munching a crust of bread.

'Been in the Red army long?' I asked him, by way of conversation.

'Three weeks,' he replied.

'Well, and do you like it?'

Dmitri pouted and shrugged his shoulders disparagingly.

'Do you have to do much service?' I persisted.

'Done none yet.'

'No drill?'

'None.'

'No marching?'

'None.'

Sounds easy, I thought. 'What *do* you do?'

'I draw rations.'

'So I see,' I observed.

Conversation flagged. Dmitri helped himself to more tea and Stepanovna questioned me further as to how Ivan Sergeievitch was doing.

'What were you in the old army?' I continued at the first opportunity to Dmitri.

'An orderly.'

'What are you now?'

'A driver.'

'Who are your officers?'

'We have a commissar.' A commissar in the army is a Bolshevist official attached to a regiment to supervise the actions of the officer staff.

'Who is he?'

'Who knows?' replied Dmitri. 'He is one like the rest,' he added, as if all commissars were of an inferior race.

'What *is* the Red army?' I asked, finally.

'Who knows?' replied Dmitri, as if it were the last thing in the world to interest any one.

Dmitri typified the mass of the unthinking proletariat at this time, regarding the Bolshevist Government as an accidental, inexplicable, and merely temporary phenomenon which was destined at an early date to decay and disappear. As for the thinking proletariat they were rapidly dividing into two camps, the minority siding with the Bolsheviks for privilege and power, the majority becoming increasingly discontented with the suppression of liberties won by the revolution.

'Have you a Committee of the Poor in this house?' I asked Stepanovna. 'Yes,' she said, and turning to Dmitri added, 'Mind, Mitka, you say nothing to them of Ivan Pavlovitch.'

Stepanovna told me the committee was formed of three servant girls, the yard-keeper and the house-porter. The entire house with forty flats was under their administration. 'From time to time,' said Stepanovna, 'they come and take some furniture to decorate the apartments they have occupied on the ground floor. That is all they seem to think of. The house-porter is never in his place in the hall' (for this I was profoundly thankful), 'and when we need him we can never find him.'

Varia accompanied me to the door as I departed. 'If you want to come back,' she said, 'I don't think Stepanovna will mind.' I insisted on paying for the food I had eaten and set out to look again for Melnikoff.

The morning was raw and snow began to fall. People hurried along the streets huddling bundles and small parcels. Queues, mostly of working women, were waiting outside small stores with notices printed on canvas over the lintel 'First-Communal Booth', 'Second Communal Booth', and so on, where bread was being distributed in small quantities against food cards. There was rarely enough to go round, so people came and stood early, shivering in the biting wind. Similar queues formed later in the day outside larger establishments marked 'Communal Eating

House, Number so-and-so'. One caught snatches of conversation from these queues. 'Why don't the "comrades" have to stand in queues?' a woman would exclaim indignantly. 'Where are all the Jews? Does Trotzky stand in a queue?' and so on. Then, receiving their modicum of bread, they would carry it hastily away, either in their bare hands, or wrapped up in paper brought for the purpose, or shielded under the shawls which they muffled round their ears and neck.

Again I tracked across the river and up the long Kamenostrovsky Prospect to Melnikoff's hospital, but again he had not returned and they knew nothing of him. Wandering irresolutely about the city I drifted into the district where I had formerly lived, and here in a side-street I came unexpectedly upon a window on which a slip of paper was pasted with the word 'Dinners', written in pencil. This, I could see, was no 'communal eating-house'. Without a ticket I could not go to a communal eating-house, so I peered cautiously into the door of the little establishment and found that a single room on the ground floor, probably once a store, had been cleared out and fitted with three tiny tables, large enough to accommodate half a dozen people in all. Everything was very simple, clearly a temporary arrangement but very clean. The room being empty, I entered.

'Dinner?' queried a young lady, appearing from behind a curtain. 'Yes, please.'

'Will you sit down a moment?' she said. 'It is rather early, but it will be ready soon.'

Presently she brought a plate of gruel, small in quantity but good. 'Bread, I am afraid, is extra,' she observed when I asked for it. 'Can I get dinner here every day?' I enquired. 'As long as they do not close us down,' she replied with a shrug. I drew her into conversation. 'We have been here a week,' she explained. 'People come in who have no food cards or who want something better than the communal eating-houses. My father used to keep a big restaurant in Sadovaya Street and when the Bolsheviks shut it he went into a smaller one in the backyard. When that was closed too, we moved in here, where one of father's cooks used to live. We cannot put up a sign, that would attract attention, but you can come as long as the paper is in the window. If it is not there, do not enter; it will mean the Reds are in possession.'

For second course she brought carrots. Three other people came in during the meal and I saw at once that they were persons of education and good station, though they all looked haggard and worn. All ate their small portions with avidity, counting out their payment with pitiful reluctance. One of them looked a typical professor, and of the others, both ladies, I guessed one might be a teacher. Though we sat close to each other there was no conversation.

Purchasing three small white loaves to take with me I returned in the afternoon to Stepanovna's. My humble friends were delighted at this simple contribution to the family fare, for they did not know white bread was still procurable. I telephoned to Vera Alexandrovna, using a number she had given me, but Melnikoff was not there and nothing was known of him.

So with Stepanovna's consent to stay another night I sat in the kitchen sipping Dmitri's tea and listening to their talk. Stepanovna and Varia unburdened their hearts without restraint, and somehow it was strange to hear them abusing their house committee, or Committee of the Poor, as it was also called, composed of people of their own station. 'Commissars' and 'Communists' they frankly classed as *svolotch*, which is a Russian term of extreme abuse.

It was a prevalent belief of the populace at this time that the Allies, and particularly the British, were planning to invade Russia and relieve the stricken country. Hearing them discussing the probability of such an event, and the part their master Ivan Sergeievitch might take in it, I told them straight out that I was an Englishman, a disclosure the effect of which was electric. For a time they would not credit it, for in appearance I might be any nationality but English. Stepanovna was a little frightened, but Dmitri sat still and a broad smile gradually spread over his good-natured features. When we sat down about nine I found quite a good supper with meat and potatoes, prepared evidently chiefly for me, for their own dinner was at midday.

'However did you get the meat?' I exclaimed as Stepanovna bustled about to serve me.

'That is Dmitri's army ration,' she said, simply. Dmitri sat still on his box against the kitchen wall, but the smile never departed from his face.

That night I found Varia had made up for me the best bed in the flat, and lying in this unexpected luxury I tried to sum up my impressions of the first two days of adventure. For two days I had wandered round the city, living from minute to minute and hour to hour, unnoticed. I no longer saw eyes in every wall. I felt that I really passed with the crowd. Only now and again someone would glance curiously and perhaps enviously at my black leather breeches. But the breeches themselves aroused no suspicions for the commissars all wore good leather clothes. None the less, I resolved I would smear my breeches with dirt before sallying forth on the morrow, so that they would not look so new. How shabbily everyone was dressed, I mused drowsily. But the peasants looked the same as ever in their sheepskin coats and bast shoes. One of the pamphlets I had bought was an address to the peasantry, entitled *Join the Communes*, urging the peasants to labour not for pecuniary gain but for the common weal, supplying bread to the town workers who would in turn produce for the peasantry. The idea was a beautiful one, but the idealistic conception was completely submerged in the welter of rancour and incitement of class-hatred. I recalled my talk with the cabman who told me it cost him two hundred roubles a day to feed his horse because the peasantry refused to bring provender to the cities. Two hundred roubles, I reflected dreamily as I dozed off, was half my monthly wages of the previous year and twice as much as I earned before the war teaching English. I reheard snatches of conversation at the railway station, at the little dining

room, and with Stepanovna. Was everyone really so bitter as
Stepanovna said they were? Stepanovna and Varia were devoted
to their master and thought in their simplicity Ivan Sergeievitch
would return with the English. Anyway, it was nice of them to
give me this bed. There were no sheets, but the blankets were
warm and they had even found me an old pair of pyjamas. I
nestled cosily into the blankets; the streets, Stepanovna and the
room faded away in a common blur, and I passed into the silent
land of no dreams.

‡

I was awakened rudely by a loud ring at the belly and sprang
up, all alert. It was quarter to eight. Who, I asked myself, could
the callers be? A search? Had the house committee heard
of the unregistered lodger? What should I say? I would say
Stepanovna was a relative, I would complain rudely of being
disturbed, I would bluster, I would flaunt my passport of the
Extraordinary Commission. Or perhaps Stepanovna and Varia
would somehow explain away my presence, for they knew the
members of the committee. I began dressing hastily. I could
hear Stepanovna and Varia conferring in the kitchen. Then
they both shuffled along the passage to the door. I heard the
door opened, first on the chain, and then a moment's silence.
At last the chain was removed. Someone was admitted and the
door closed. I heard men's voices and boots tramping along
the passage. Convinced now that a search was to be made I
fished feverishly in my pockets to get out my passport for
demonstration, when – into the room burst Melnikoff! Never
was I so dumbfounded in my life! Melnikoff was dressed in
other clothes than I had seen him in when we last parted and
he wore spectacles which altered his appearance considerably.
Behind him entered a huge fellow, a sort of Ilya Muromets,
whose stubble-covered face brimmed over with smiles beaming

good-nature and jollity. This giant was dressed in a rough and ragged brown suit and in his hand he squeezed a dirty hat.

'Marsh,' observed Melnikoff, curtly, by way of introduction, smiling at my incredulity. We shook hands heartily all round while I still fumbled my passport. 'I was about to defy you with that!' I laughed, showing them the paper. 'Tell me, how the—, I thought you were in prison!'

'Not quite!' Marsh exclaimed, dropping into English at once. 'I had a larky get-away! Slithered down a drainpipe outside the kitchen window into the next yard as the Reds came in at the front door. Shaved my beard at once.' He rubbed his chin. 'About time, by the way, I saw the barber again. The blighters are looking for me everywhere. I was held up one evening by one of their damned spies under a lamp-post. I screwed my face into a freak and asked him for a light. Then I knocked him down. And yesterday evening I was going into a yard on Sadovaya Street when under the arch I heard someone behind me say, "Marsh!" I sprang round, just about to administer the same medicine, when I saw it was Melnikoff!'

'But how did you find me here?' I said.

'Ask Melnikoff.' I asked Melnikoff in Russian. He was nervous and impatient.

'Luck,' he replied. 'I guessed you might possibly be in Sergeievitch's flat and so you are. But listen, I can't stay here long. I'm being looked for, too. You can meet me safely at three this afternoon at the 15th communal eating-house in the Nevsky. You don't need a ticket to enter. I'll tell you everything then. Don't stay more than two nights in one place.'

'All right,' I said, 'three o'clock at the 15th eating-house.'

'And don't go to Vera's any more,' he added as he hurried away. 'Something is wrong there. Goodbye.'

'Get dressed,' said Marsh when Melnikoff had gone, 'and I'll take you straight along to a place you can go to regularly. But rely mainly on Melnikoff, he's the cleverest card I ever saw.'

Stepanovna, beaming with pleasure and pride at having two Englishmen in her flat, and nervous at the same time on account of the circumstances, brought in tea, and I told Marsh of my mission to Russia. Though he had not been connected with intelligence organizations, he knew people who had, and mentioned the names of a number of persons whose aid might be re-enlisted. One or two occupied high positions in the ministry of war and the admiralty.

But there was a more pressing task on hand than intelligence. The Bolsheviks suspected Marsh of complicity, together with other Englishmen, in assisting allied citizens who were refused passports to escape from the country secretly. Numerous arrests amongst foreigners were being made and Marsh had had a hair-breadth escape. But his wife had been seized in his stead as hostage, and this calamity filled him with concern.

Mrs Marsh was imprisoned at the notorious *No. 2 Goróhovaya* Street, the address of the Extraordinary Commission, and Marsh was awaiting the report of a man who had connections with the Commission as to the possibilities of effecting her escape. 'This man,' explained Marsh, 'was, I believe, an official of the *ohrana* (the Tsar's personal secret police) before the revolution, and is doing some sort of clerical work in a Soviet institution now. The Bolsheviks are re-engaging Tsarist police agents for the Extraordinary Commission, so he has close connections there and knows most of what goes on. He is a liar and it is difficult to believe what he says, but,' (Marsh paused and rubbed his forefinger and thumb together to indicate that finance entered into the transaction), 'if you outbid the Bolsheviks, this fellow can do things, understand?'

Marsh put me up to the latest position of everything in Petrograd. He also said he would be able to find me lodging for a few nights until I had some settled mode of living. He had wide acquaintance-ship in the city and many of his friends lived in a quiet, unobtrusive manner, working for a living in Soviet offices.

'Better be moving along now,' he said when we had finished tea. 'I'll go ahead because we mustn't walk together. Follow me in about five minutes, and you'll find me standing by the hoarding round the Kazan Cathedral.'

'The hoarding round the Kazan Cathedral? So you know that hoarding, too?' I asked, recalling my intention of hiding in that very place.

'I certainly do,' he exclaimed. 'Spent the first night there after my get-away. Now I'll be off. When you see me shoot off from the hoarding follow me as far behind as you can. So long.'

'By the way,' I said, as he went out, 'that hoarding – it doesn't happen to be a regular shelter for – for homeless and destitute Englishmen or others, does it?'

'Not that I know of,' he laughed, 'Why?'

'Oh, nothing. I only wondered.'

I let Marsh out and heard his steps echoing down the stone staircase.

'I shall not be back tonight, Stepanovna,' I said, preparing to follow him. 'I can't tell you how grateful—'

'Oh, but Ivan Pavlovitch,' exclaimed the good woman, 'you can come here any time you like. If anything happens,' she added in a lower tone, 'we'll say you belong to us. No one need know.'

'Well, well,' I said, 'but not tonight. Goodbye, goodbye.' While Stepanovna and Varia let me out I had a vision of Dmitri standing at the kitchen door, stolidly munching a crust of black bread.

Outside the hoarding of the Kazan Cathedral I espied the huge figure of Marsh sitting on a stone. When he saw me over the way he rose and slouched along with his collar turned up, diving into side streets and avoiding the main thoroughfares. I followed at a distance. Eventually we came out to the Siennaya market, crossed it, and plunged into the maze of streets to the south. Marsh disappeared under an arch and, following his steps, I found myself in a dark, filthy, reeking yard with a back stair entrance on either hand. Marsh stood at the stairway on the left. 'Flat No. 5 on the second floor,' he said. 'We can go up together.'

The stairway was narrow and littered with rubbish. At a door with '5' chalked on it Marsh banged loudly three times with his fist, and it was opened by a woman, dressed plainly in black, who greeted Marsh with exclamations of welcome and relief.

'Aha, Maria,' he shouted boisterously, 'here we are, you see – not got me yet. And *won't* get me, unless I've got a pumpkin on my shoulders instead of a head!'

Maria was his housekeeper. She looked questioningly at me, obviously doubtful whether I ought to be admitted. Marsh howled with laughter. 'All right, Maria,' he cried, 'let him in. He's only my comrade – comrades in distress, and ha! ha! ha! "comrades" in looks, eh, Maria?'

Maria smiled curiously. 'Certainly "comrades" in looks,' she said, slowly.

'By the way,' asked Marsh, as we passed into an inner room, 'what name are you using?'

'Afirenko,' I said. 'But that's official. Tell Maria I'm called "Ivan Ilitch".'

Maria set the samovar and produced some black bread and butter.

'This flat,' said Marsh, with his mouth full, 'belonged to a business colleague of mine. The Reds seized him by mistake for someone else. Silly fool, nearly (here Marsh used a very unparliamentary expression) with funk when he got arrested. Sat in chokey three days and was told he was to be shot, when luckily for him the right man was collared. Then they let him out and I shipped him over the frontier. They'll forget all about him. In the daytime this is one of the safest places in town.'

The flat was almost devoid of furniture. A bare table stood in one room and a desk in another. An old couch and a few chairs made up the outfit. The windows were so dirty that they were quite opaque and admitted very little light from the narrow street. Although it was nearly midday an oil lamp burned on the table of the room we sat in. Electric light was becoming rarer and rarer and only burned for a few hours every evening.

Marsh sat and talked of his adventures and the work he had been doing for the allied colonies. His country farm had been seized and pillaged, his city business was ruined, he had long been under suspicion. and yet he refused to leave. But the arrest of his wife bore constantly on his mind. From time to time his boisterous flow of talk would suddenly cease. He would pass his hand over his brow, a far-away troubled look coming into his eyes.

'If only it were an ordinary prison,' he would say, 'if only they were human beings. But these—! By the way, will you come with me to see the Policeman? I am going to meet him in half an hour.' The 'Policeman' was the nickname by which we referred to the Tsarist official of whom Marsh had spoken in the morning. I reflected for a moment. Perhaps the Policeman might be useful to me later. I consented.

Telling Maria to look out for us both about that time next morning, we left the flat by the back entrance as we had entered it. Again Marsh walked ahead, and I followed his slouching figure at a distance as he wound in and out of side streets. The dwelling we were going to, he told me, was that of an ex-journalist, who was now engaged as a scribe in the Department of Public Works, and it was at the journalist's that he had arranged to meet the Policeman.

The journalist lived all alone in a flat in the Liteiny Prospect. I watched Marsh disappear into the entrance and waited a moment to convince myself he was not being tracked. From the opposite sidewalk I saw him look back through the glass door, signalling that all was well within, so giving him time to mount the stairs I followed.

He rang the bell at a door covered with oilcloth and felt. After a moment's silence there was a shuffling of slippers, an inner door opened, and a voice said, 'Who's there?'

'He expects me to say who's here, the silly fool,' growled Marsh under his breath, adding just loud enough to be heard through the door, 'I.'

'Who? I?' persisted the voice.

'I, Peter Sergeievitch' (aloud), 'blithering idiot' (undertone), said Marsh.

There was much undoing of bars and bolts, and finally, the door opening slightly on the chain, a pair of nervous, twinkling eyes peered through the chink.

'Ah!' said the nervous face, breaking into a smile, 'Ivan Petrovitch!' The door closed again and the chain was removed. Then it reopened and we passed in.

'Why the devil couldn't you open at once?' grumbled Marsh. 'You knew I was coming. "Who's there", indeed! Do you want me to bawl "Marsh" at the top of my voice outside your door?' At this the nervous man looked terrified. 'Well, then why don't you open? "Ivan Petrovitch" or "Peter Sergeievitch" – can't anyone be Ivan Petrovitch? Isn't that just why I *am* "Ivan Petrovitch"?'

'Yes, yes,' answered the nervous man, 'but nowadays one never knows who may be at the door.'

'Well, then, open and look, or next time I *will* shout "Marsh".' The nervous man looked more terrified than ever. 'Well, well,' laughed Marsh, 'I am only joking. This is my friend – er—'

'Michael Mihailovitch,' I put in.

'Very glad to see you, Michael Mihailovitch,' said the nervous man, looking anything but glad.

The journalist was a man of thirty-five years of age, though his thin and pale features, dishevelled hair, and ragged beard, gave him the appearance of being nearly fifty. He was attired in an old greenish overcoat with the collar turned up, and dragged his feet about in a pair of worn-out carpet slippers. The flat was on the shady side of the street, the sun never peered into its gloomy precincts, it was dark and musty, and icy cold.

'Well, how go things, Dmitri Konstantinovitch?' asked Marsh.

'Poorly, poorly, Ivan Petrovitch,' said the journalist, coughing.

'This is the third day I have not been to work. You will excuse my proceeding with business, I'm having lunch. Come into the kitchen, it is the least cold of all rooms.'

The journalist, preparing his noonday meal, was engaged in boiling a few potatoes over a stick fire in a tiny portable oven. 'Two days' rations,' he remarked, ironically, holding up a salt herring. 'How do they expect us to live, indeed? And half a pound of bread into the bargain. That's how they feed the bourgeois in return for sweating for them. And if you *don't* sweat for them, then you get nothing. "He who toileth not, neither let him eat", as they say. But it's only "toil" if it is to *their* advantage. If you toil to your own advantage, then it is called "speculation", and you get shot. Ugh! A pretty state our Russia has come to, indeed! Do we not rightly say we are a herd of sheep?'

Continuing in this strain the journalist scraped his smelly herring and began eating it with his potatoes ravenously and yet gingerly, knowing that the quicker he finished the scanty repast the sooner he would realize there was nothing more. Picking the skeleton clean, he sucked the tail and dug his fork into the head for the last scraps of meat.

'Plus 1,000 roubles a month,' he went on. 'Here I eat two days' rations at a single meal, and what can I buy with 1,000 roubles? A few pounds of potatoes, a pound or two of bread and butter? Then there's nothing left for fuel, when wood that used to cost 5 roubles a sazhen now costs 500!'

From his overcoat pocket Marsh produced half a pound of bread. 'Here, Dmitri Konstantinovitch,' he said, thrusting it toward him, 'your health!'

The journalist's face became transfigured. Its haggard look vanished. He glanced up, his mouth fixed in a half-laugh of delight and incredulity, his sunken eyes sparkling with childlike pleasure and gratitude.

'For me?' he exclaimed, scarcely believing his eyes. 'But what about yourself? Surely you do not get sufficient, especially since—'

'Don't worry about me,' said Marsh, with his good-natured smile. 'You know Maria? She is a wonder! She gets everything. From my farm she managed to save several sacks of potatoes and quite a lot of bread, and hide it all here in town. But listen, Dmitri Konstantinovitch, I'm expecting a visitor here soon, the same man as the day before yesterday. I will take him into the other room, so that he need not see you.'

The journalist, I could see, was overcome with fear at being obliged to receive Marsh's unwelcome visitor, but he said nothing. He wrapped the bread carefully up in paper and put it away in a cupboard. A moment later there were three sharp rings at the bell. Marsh hurried to the door, admitted his visitor, and led him into the journalist's cabinet.

'You may as well come in, too,' he said to me, looking into the kitchen. 'Michael Ivanitch,' I whispered, pointing at myself, as we passed in. Marsh introduced me. 'My friend, Michael Ivanitch Schmit,' he said.

My first impulse when I saw the individual Marsh nicknamed 'the Policeman' was to laugh, for any one less like a policeman than the little man who rose and bowed I have seldom seen. I will not describe him too precisely, but he was short, red-faced, and insignificant-looking. In spite of this, however, his manner showed that he had a very high opinion of his own importance. He shook hands and reseated himself with comical dignity.

'Go on, Alexei Fomitch,' said Marsh. 'I want my friend to know how matters stand. He may be able to help.'

'Madame Marsh, as I was saying,' proceeded the Policeman, 'is incarcerated in chamber No. 4 with 38 other women of various station, including titled personages, servant girls, and prostitutes. The chamber is not a large one and I fear the conditions are far from pleasant. My informants tell me she is cross-examined several hours every day with the object of eliciting the hiding-place of Monsieur Marsh, which they believe she knows. Unfortunately her case is complicated by the confused replies she has given, for after several hours' interrogation it often becomes difficult to retain clarity of mind. Confused or incoherent replies, even though accidental, lead to further and still more exacting interpellation.'

Marsh followed every word with a concern that was not lost upon the Policeman. 'But can we not get round the interrogators?' he asked, 'they all have their price, damn it.'

'Yes, that is often so,' continued the Policeman in a tone of feigned consolation. 'The investigator can frequently be induced to turn the evidence in favour of the accused. But in this case it is unfortunately useless to offer the usual bribe, for even if Madame Marsh's innocence is proven to the hilt, she will still be detained as a hostage until the discovery of Monsieur Marsh.'

Marsh's face twinged. 'I feared so,' he said in a dull voice. 'What are the chances of flight?'

'I was coming to that,' said the Policeman, suavely. 'I am already making inquiries on the subject. But it will take some days to arrange. The assistance of more than one person will have to be enlisted. And I fear – I hesitate,' he added in unctuous tones of regret, 'I hesitate to refer to such a matter – but I am afraid this method may be a little more – er – costly. Pardon me for—'

'Money?' cried Marsh. 'Damn it all, man, don't you realize it is my wife? How much do you want?'

'Oh, Monsieur Marsh,' expostulated the Policeman, raising his palm, 'you are well aware that I take nothing for myself. I do this out of friendship to you – and our gallant Allies. But there is a prison janitor, I must give him 5,000, two warders 10,000, a go-between 2,000, odd expenses—'

'Stop!' put in Marsh, abruptly, 'tell me how much it will cost.'

The Policeman's face assumed a pained expression. 'It may cost,' he said, 'twenty-five, possibly thirty thousand roubles.'

'Thirty thousand. You shall have it. I gave you ten thousand, here are another ten thousand; you shall have the third ten thousand the day my wife leaves prison.'

The Policeman took the notes, and with a look of offended

dignity, as though the handling of money were altogether beneath him, hid them in an inner pocket.

'When will you be able to report again?' asked Marsh.

'I expect the day after tomorrow. If you like to come to my house it is quite safe.'

'Very well, we will meet there. And now, if you are not in a hurry, I'll see if I can raise some tea. It's damned cold in this room.'

When Marsh had gone into the kitchen the little Policeman ventured to open conversation.

'Such times, such times,' he sighed. 'Who would have thought it possible? You live in Petrograd, Michael Ivanitch?'

'Yes.'

'You are in service, perhaps?'

'Yes.'

There was a pause.

'Yours must have been an interesting occupation,' I remarked, 'in days gone by.'

'You mean?'

'You were connected with the police, were you not?'

I saw at once I had made a *faux pas*. The little man turned very red. 'I beg your pardon,' I hastened to add, 'I understood you were an official of the *ohrana*.'

This apparently was still worse. The little Policeman sat up very straight, flushing deeply and looking rather like a turkey-cock.

'No, sir,' he said in what were intended to be icy tones, 'you have been grossly misinformed. I have never been connected either with the police or the *ohrana*. Under the Tsar, sir, I moved in Court circles. I had the ear of his late Imperial Majesty, and the Imperial Palace was open to me at any time.'

At this point, fortunately for me. Marsh returned with three glasses of tea, apologizing for not providing sugar, and the conversation turned to the inevitable subject of famine. At length the Policeman rose to go.

'By the way, Alexei Fomitch,' said Marsh, 'can you find me a lodging for tonight?'

'A lodging for tonight? I shall be honoured, Monsieur Marsh, if you will accept such hospitality as I myself can offer. I have an extra bed, though my fare I am afraid will not be luxurious. Still, such as it is—'

'Thank you. I will come as near nine o'clock as possible.'

'Give three short rings, and I will open the door myself,' said the Policeman. When he had gone I told Marsh of our conversation and asked what the little man meant by 'moving in Court circles'. Marsh was greatly amused.

'Oh, he was a private detective or something,' he said. 'Conceited as hell about it. "Ear of the Tsar", indeed! What he's after is money. He'll pocket most of the 30,000. But he's afraid of us, too. He's cocksure the Allies are coming into Petrograd, so if you have anything to do with him tell him you're an Englishman and he'll grovel. By the way, we had better let Dmitri Konstantinovitch into the secret, too, because you will find this flat very useful. The journalist is a damned old coward, but buy him some grub or, still better, pay for his fuel and he will let you use the flat as much as you like.'

So the nervous ex-journalist was initiated into the great secret, and when Marsh said, 'You don't mind if he comes in occasionally to sleep on the sofa, do you?' Dmitri Konstantinovitch nearly died with fear. His thin lips vibrated, and clearer than any words his twitching smile and tear-filled eyes implored, 'Oh, for God's sake, leave me alone! – until I said boldly, 'But I don't like sleeping in the cold, Dmitri Konstantinovitch. Perhaps you could get some wood in for me. Here is the price of a sazhen of logs; we will share the wood, of course.' Then his care-worn, troubled face again became suddenly transfigured as it had when Marsh gave him bread. 'Ah, splendid, splendid,' he cried in delight, his fears completely obliterated by the anticipation of coming warmth. 'I will get the wood in this very afternoon, and you shall have sheets and blankets and I will make you comfortable.'

So it was arranged that unless Melnikoff found me a more suitable place I should return to the journalist's that night.

It was now time for me to be thinking of keeping my appointment with Melnikoff at the communal eating-house. So I left Marsh arranging to meet him at the empty flat 'No. 5' next morning. Musing on the events of the day I made my way down the staircase and came out again into the Liteiny Prospect. It seemed ages since, but two days ago, I walked along this same street on the day of my arrival in Petrograd, after running across the frontier. What would Melnikoff now have to tell me, I wondered?

As I rounded the corner of the Nevsky Prospect I noticed a concourse of people outside the communal eating-house toward which I was directing my steps. I followed the people, who were moving hurriedly across the street to the other side. At the entrance to the eating-house stood two sailors on guard with fixed bayonets, while people were being filed out of the building singly, led by militiamen. In the dark lobby within one could dimly discern individuals being searched. Their documents were being examined and, standing in their shirt sleeves, their clothing was being subjected to strict investigation.

I waited to see if Melnikoff would emerge from the building. After a moment I felt a tap on my arm and looking round I was confronted by Zorinsky, the officer who had accosted me in the café of Vera Alexandrovna on the day of my arrival. Zorinsky signalled to me to move aside with him.

'Were you to meet Melnikoff here?' he asked. 'It is lucky for you you did not enter the restaurant. The place is being raided. I was about to go in myself, but came a little late, thank God. Melnikoff was one of the first to be arrested and has already been taken away.'

'What is the cause of the raid?' I asked, dismayed by this news.

'Who knows?' replied Zorinsky. 'These things are done spasmodically. Melnikoff has been tracked for some days, I believe, and it may have been on his account. Anyway, it is serious, for he is well known.'

People were beginning to move away and the search was clearly nearing its end.

'What are you going to do?' said my companion.

'I do not know,' I replied, not wishing to confide any of my movements to Zorinsky.

'We must begin to think of some way of getting him out,' he said. 'Melnikoff was a great friend of mine, but you are, I expect, as interested in his release as I am.'

'Is there any chance?' I exclaimed. 'Of course I am interested.'

'Then I suggest you come home with me and we will talk it over. I live quite near.'

Anxious to learn of any possibility of saving Melnikoff, I consented. We passed into Troitzkaya Street and entered a large house on the right.

'How do you wish me to call you?' asked Zorinsky as we mounted the staircase. I was struck by the considerateness of his question and replied, 'Pavel Ivanitch.'

The flat in which Zorinsky lived was large and luxuriously furnished, and showed no signs of molestation. 'You live comfortably,' I remarked, sinking into a deep leather arm-chair. 'Yes, we do pretty well,' he replied. 'My wife, you see, is an actress. She receives as many provisions as she wants and our flat is immune from requisition of furniture or the obtrusion of workmen. We will go round some evening, if you like, and see her dance. As for me, my wife has registered me as a sub-manager of the theatre so that I receive additional rations also. These things, you know, are not difficult to arrange! Thus I am really a gentleman at large, and living like many others at the expense of a generous proletarian regime. My hobby,' he added, idly, 'is *contre-espionage*.'

'What?' I cried, the exclamation escaping me inadvertently.

'*Contre-espionage*,' he repeated, smiling. When he smiled one end of his crooked mouth remained stationary, while the other seemed to jut right up into his cheek. 'Why should you be surprised? *Tout le monde est contre-revolutionnaire*: it is merely a question of whether one is actively or passively so.' He took from a drawer a typewritten sheet of paper and handed it to me. 'Does that by any chance interest you?'

I glanced at the paper. The writing was full of uncorrected orthographical errors, showing it had been typed by an unpractised hand in extreme haste. Scanning the first few lines I at once became completely absorbed in the document. It was a report, dated two days previously, of confidential negotiations between the Bolshevist Government and the leaders of non-Bolshevist parties with regard to the possible formation of a coalition Government. Nothing came of the negotiations, but the information was of great importance as showing the nervousness of the Bolshevist leaders at that time and the clearly defined attitude of the Socialist-Revolutionary and Menshevist parties toward the military counter-revolution.

'Is it authentic?' I inquired, dubiously.

'That report,' replied Zorinsky, 'is at this moment being considered by the central committee of the Menshevist party in this city. It was drawn up by a member of the Menshevist delegation and despatched secretly to Petrograd, for the Bolsheviks do not permit their opponents to communicate freely with each other. I saw the original and obtained a copy two hours before it reached the Menshevist committee.'

The suspicion of forgery immediately arose, but I could see no reason for concocting the document on the off-chance of somebody's being taken in by it. I handed it back.

'You may as well keep it,' said Zorinsky. 'I should have given it to Melnikoff and he would doubtless have given it to you. I am expecting a further report shortly. Yes,' he added, nonchalantly, tapping the arm of the desk-chair in which he sat, 'it is an amusing game – *contre-espionage*. I used to provide your Captain

Crombie with quite a lot of information. But I'm not surprised you have not heard of me for I always preferred to keep in the background.'

He produced a large box of cigarettes and, ringing a bell, ordered tea.

'I don't know what you Allies propose doing with regard to Russia,' he observed, offering me a light. 'It seems to me you might as well leave us alone as bungle about in the way you are doing. Meanwhile, all sorts of people are conducting, or think they are conducting, espionage underground in Russia, or planning to overthrow the Reds. Are you interested?'

'Very.'

'Well, have you heard of General F.?' Zorinsky launched into an exposition of the internal counter-revolutionary movement, of which he appeared to know extensive details. There existed, he said, belligerent 'groups', planning to seize army stores, blow up bridges, or raid treasuries. 'They will never do anything,' he said, derisively, 'because they all organize like idiots. The best are the S. R.'s (Socialist-Revolutionaries): they are fanatics, like the Bolsheviks. None of the others could tell you what they want.'

The maid, neatly attired in a clean white apron, brought in tea, served with biscuits, sugar, and lemon. Zorinsky talked on, displaying a remarkable knowledge of everybody's movements and actions.

'Crombie was a fine fellow,' he said, referring to the British. 'Pity he got killed. Things went to pieces. The fellows who stayed after him had a hard time. The French and Americans have all gone now except (he mentioned a Frenchman living on the Vasili Island) but he doesn't do much. Marsh had hard luck, didn't he?'

'Marsh?' I put in. 'So you know him, too?'

'*Of* him,' corrected Zorinsky. All at once he seemed to become interested and leaned over the arm of his chair toward me. 'By the way,' he said, in a curious tone, 'you don't happen to know where Marsh is, do you?'

For a moment I hesitated. Perhaps this man, who seemed to know so much, might be able to help Marsh. But I checked myself. Intuitively I felt it wiser to say nothing.

'I have no idea,' I said, decisively.

'Then how do you know about him?'

'I heard in Finland of his arrest.'

Zorinsky leaned back again in his chair and his eyes wandered out of the window.

'I should have thought,' I observed, after a pause, 'that knowing all you do, you would have followed his movements.'

'Aha,' he exclaimed, and in the shadow his smile looked like a black streak obliterating one half of his face, 'but there is one place I avoid, and that is *No. 2 Goróhovaya*! When any one gets arrested I leave him alone. I am wiser than to attempt to probe the mysteries of that institution.'

Zorinsky's words reminded me abruptly of Melnikoff.

'But you spoke of the possibility of saving Melnikoff,' I said. 'Is he not in the hands of *No. 2 Goróhovaya?*'

He turned round and looked me full in the face. 'Yes,' he said, seriously, 'with Melnikoff it is different. We must act at once and leave no stone unturned. I know a man who will be able to investigate and I'll get him on the job tonight. Will you not stay to dinner? My wife will be delighted to meet you, and she understands discretion.'

Seeing no special reason to refuse, I accepted the invitation. Zorinsky went to the telephone and I heard him ask someone to call about nine o'clock 'on an urgent matter'.

His wife, Elena Ivanovna, a jolly little creature, but very much of a spoilt child, appeared at dinner dressed in a pink Japanese kimono. The table was daintily set and decked with flowers. As at Vera Alexandrovna's café, I again felt myself out of place, and apologized for my uncouth appearance.

'Oh! Don't excuse yourself,' said Elena Ivanovna, laughing. 'Everyone is getting like that nowadays. How dreadful it is to think of all that is happening! Have the olden days gone forever, do you think? Will these horrid people never be overthrown?'

'You do not appear to have suffered much, Elena Ivanovna,' I remarked.

'No, of course, I must admit our troupe is treated well,' she replied. 'Even flowers, as you see, though you have no idea how horrible it is to have to take a bouquet from a great hulking sailor who wipes his nose with his fingers and spits on the floor. The theatre is just full of them, every night.'

'Your health, Pavel Ivanitch,' said Zorinsky, lifting a glass of vodka. 'Ah!' he exclaimed with relish, smacking his lips, 'there are places worse than Bolshevia, I declare.'

'You get plenty of vodka?' I asked.

'You get plenty of everything if you keep your wits about you,' said Zorinsky. 'Even without joining the Communist Party. I am not a Communist,' he added (somehow I had not suspected it), 'but still I keep that door open. What I am afraid of is that the Bolsheviks may begin to make their Communists *work*. That will be the next step in the revolution unless you Allies arrive and relieve them of that painful necessity. Your health, Pavel Ivanitch.'

The conversation turned on the Great War and Zorinsky recounted a number of incidents in his career. He also gave his views of the Russian people and the revolution. 'The Russian peasant,' he said, 'is a brute. What he wants is a good hiding, and unless I'm much mistaken the Communists are going to give it to him. Otherwise the Communists go under. In my regiment we used to smash a jaw now and again on principle. That's the only way to make Russian peasants fight. Have you heard about the Red army? Comrade Trotzky, you see, has already abolished his Red officers, and is inviting – inviting, if you please – *us*, the "counter-revolutionary Tsarist officer swine", to accept posts in his new army. Would you ever believe it? By God, I've half a mind to join! Trotzky will order me to flog the peasants to my heart's content. Under Trotzky, mark my words, I would make a career in no time.'

The dinner was a sumptuous banquet for the Petrograd of the period. There was nothing that suggested want. Coffee was served in the drawing room, while Zorinsky kept up an unceasing flow of strange and cynical but entertaining conversation.

I waited till nearly ten for the call from Zorinsky's friend with regard to Melnikoff, and then, in view of my uncertainty as to whether the journalist's house would still be open, I accepted Zorinsky's invitation to stay overnight. 'There is no reason,' he said, 'why you should not come in here whenever you like. We dine every day at six and you are welcome.'

Just as I was retiring Zorinsky was called to the telephone and returned explaining that he would only be able to begin the investigation of Melnikoff's case next day. I was shown to the spare bedroom, where I found everything provided for me. Zorinsky apologized that he could not offer me a hot bath. 'That rascal dvornik downstairs,' he said, referring to the yard keeper whose duty it was to procure wood for the occupants, 'allowed an extra stock of fuel that I had my eyes on to be requisitioned for somebody else, but next week I think I shall be able to get a good supply from the theatre. Goodnight – and don't dream of *No. 2 Goróhovaya.*

‡

The Extraordinary Commission, spoken of with such abhorrence by Zorinsky, is the most notorious of all Bolshevist institutions. It is an instrument of terror and inquisition designed forcibly to uproot all anti-Bolshevist sentiment through Lenin's dominions. Its full title is the *Extraordinary Commission for the Suppression of the Counter-Revolution and Speculation*, 'speculation' being every form of private commerce – the bugbear of Communism. The Russian title of this institution is *Tchrezvitchainaya Kommissia*, popularly spoken of as the

Tchrezvitchaika, or still shorter the *Tche-Ka*. The headquarters of the *Tche-Ka* in Petrograd are situated at No. 2 of the street named *Goróhovaya*, the seat of the Prefecture of Police during the Tsar's regime, so that the popular mode of appellation of the Prefecture by its address – '*No. 2 Goróhovaya*' – has stuck to the Extraordinary Commission and will go down as a by-word in Russian history.

At the head of *No. 2 Goróhovaya* there sits a *soviet* or council, of some half-dozen revolutionary fanatics of the most vehement type. With these lies the final word as to the fate of prisoners. Recommendations are submitted to this *soviet* by 'Investigators' whose duty it is to examine the accused, collect the evidence and report upon it. It is thus in the hands of the 'Investigators' that power over prisoners' lives actually lies, since they are in a position to turn the evidence one way or the other, as they choose.

Investigators vary considerably. There are some who are sincere and upright, though demoniacal visionaries, cold as steel, cruel, unpolluted by thirst for filthy lucre, who see the dawn of proletarian liberty only through mists of non-proletarian blood. Such men (or women) are actuated by malignant longing for revenge for every wrong, real or imaginary, suffered in the past. Believing themselves to be called to perform a sacred task in exterminating the 'counter-revolution', they can upon occasion be civil and courteous, even chivalrous (though that is rare), but never impartial. There are other investigators who are merely corrupt, ready to sacrifice any proletarian interest for a price, regarding their job purely as a means of amassing a fortune by the taking of bribes.

Every responsible official of the Extraordinary Commission must be a member of the Communist Party. The lower staff, however, is composed of hirelings, frequently of foreign origin, and many of them re-engaged agents of the Tsarist police. The latter, who lost their jobs as the result of the revolution which overthrew the Tsarist autocracy, have been re-enlisted as

specialists by the Bolsheviks, and find congenial occupation
in spying, eavesdropping, and hounding down rebellious or
suspected workmen just as they did when the government was
the Tsar's instead of Lenin's. It is this fact which renders it
almost impossible for the Russian workers to organize a revolt
against their new taskmasters. It is thus that arose the *sobriquet*
applied to the Red regime of 'Tsarism inside out'. The faintest
signs of sedition are immediately reported to the *Tche-Ka* by
its secret agents disguised as workers, the ringleaders are then
'eliminated' from the factory under pretext of being conscripted
elsewhere, and they are frequently never heard of afterward.

The Extraordinary Commission overshadows all else in
Red Russia. No individual is free from its all-perceiving eye.
Even Communists stand in awe of it, one of its duties being to
unearth black sheep within the Party ranks, and since it never
errs on the side of leniency there have been cases of execution
of true adherents of the Communist creed under suspicion of
being black sheep. On the other hand, the black sheep, being
imbued with those very qualities of guile, trickery, and unscru-
pulous deceit which make the Extraordinary Commission so
efficient a machine, generally manage to get off.

One of the most diabolic of the methods copied from Tsarist
days and employed by the Extraordinary Commission against
non-Bolsheviks is that known in Russia as *provocation*. Provocation
consisted formerly in the deliberate fomentation, by agents who
were known as *agents-provocateurs* of revolutionary sedition and
plots. Such movements would attract to themselves ardent revo-
lutionaries and when a conspiracy had matured and was about to
culminate in some act of terrorism it would be betrayed at the
last moment by the *agent-provocateur,* who frequently succeeded
in making himself the most trusted member of the revolutionary group. *Agents-provocateurs* were recruited from all classes, but
chiefly from the intelligentsia. Imitating Tsarism in this as in most
of its essentials, the Bolsheviks employ similar agents to foment
counter-revolutionary conspiracies and they reward munificently

a *provocateur* who yields to the insatiable *Tche-Ka* a plentiful crop of 'counter-revolutionary' heads.

As under the Tsar, every invention of exquisite villainy is practised to extract from captives, thus or otherwise seized, the secret of accomplices or sympathizers. Not without reason was Marsh haunted with fears that his wife, nerve-racked and doubt- less underfed if fed at all, might be subjected to treatment that would test her self-control to the extreme. She did not know where he was, but she knew all his friends and acquaintances, an exhaustive list of whom would be insistently demanded. She had already, according to the Policeman, given confused replies, which were bound to complicate her case. The inquisition would become ever more relentless, until at last—

On the day following my visit to Zorinsky I appeared punctually at eleven o'clock at the empty flat with 'No. 5' chalked on the back door. It was not far from Zorinsky's, but I approached it by a circuitous route, constantly looking round to assure myself I was not being followed. The filthy yard was as foul and noisome as ever, vying in stench with the gloomy stair- case, and I met no one. Maria, no longer suspicious, opened the door in answer to my three knocks. 'Peter Ivanitch is not here yet,' she said, 'but he should be in any minute.' So I sat down to read the Soviet newspapers.

Marsh's three thumps at the back door were not long in making themselves heard. Maria hurried along the passage, I heard the lock creak, the door stiffly tugged open, and then suddenly a little stifled cry from Maria. I rose quickly. Marsh burst, or rather tumbled, into the room with his head and face bound up in a big black shawl. As he laboriously unwound it I had a vision of Maria in the doorway, her fist in her mouth, staring at him speechless and terrified.

It was a strange Marsh that emerged from the folds of the black shawl. The invincible smile struggled to maintain itself, but his eyes were bleared and wandered aimlessly, and he shook with agitation despite his efforts to retain self-control.

'My wife—,' he stammered, half-coherently, dropping into a chair and fumbling feverishly for his handkerchief. 'She was subjected yesterday – seven hours' cross-examination – uninterruptedly – no food – not even allowed to sit down – until finally she swooned. She has said something – I don't know what. I am afraid—.' He rose and strode up and down, mumbling so that I could scarcely understand, but I caught the word 'indiscretion' – and understood all he wished to say.

After a few moments he calmed and sat down again. 'The Policeman came home at midnight,' he said, 'and told me all about it. I questioned and questioned again and am sure he is not lying. The Bolsheviks believe she was implicated in some conspiracy, so they made her write three autobiographies, and—' (he paused), 'they – are all different. Now – she is being compelled to explain discrepancies, but she can't remember anything and her mind seems to be giving. Meanwhile, the Bolsheviks are resolved to eradicate, once and for all, all "English machinations", as they call it, in Russia. They know I've shaved and changed my appearance and a special detachment of spies is on the hunt for me, with a big reward offered to the finder.'

He paused and swallowed at a gulp the glassful of tea Maria had placed beside him.

'Look here, old man,' he said, suddenly, laying his hands out flat on the table in front of him, 'I am going to ask you to help me out. The "Policeman" says it's worse for her that I should be here than if I go. So I'm going. Once they know I've fled, the Policeman says, they will cease plaguing her, and it may be easier to effect an escape. Tell me, will you take the job over for me?'

'My dear fellow,' I said, 'I had already resolved that I would attempt nothing else until we had safely got your wife out of prison. And the day she gets out I will escort her over the frontier myself. I shall have to go to Finland to report, anyway.'

He was going to thank me but I shut him up.

'When will you go?' I asked.

'Tomorrow. There are a number of things to be done. Have you got much money?'

'Enough for myself, but no reserve.'

'I will leave you all I have,' he said, 'and today I'll go and see a business friend of mine who may be able to get some more. He is a Jew, but is absolutely trustworthy.'

'By the way,' I asked, when this matter was decided, 'ever heard of a Captain Zorinsky?'

'Zorinsky? Zorinsky? No. Who is he?'

'A fellow who seems to know a lot about you,' I said. 'Says he is a friend of Melnikoff's, though I never heard Melnikoff mention him. Yesterday he was particularly anxious to know your present address.'

'You didn't tell him?' queried Marsh, nervously.

'What do you take me for?'

'You can tell him day after tomorrow,' he laughed.

Marsh went off to his business friend, saying he would premonish him of my possible visit, and stayed there all day. I remained at 'No. 5' and wrote up in minute handwriting on tracing paper a preliminary report on the general situation in Petrograd, which I intended to ask Marsh to take with him. To be prepared for all contingencies I gave the little scroll to Maria when it was finished and she hid it at the bottom of a pail of ashes.

Next morning Marsh turned up at 'No. 5' dressed in a huge sheepskin coat with a fur collar half engulfing his face. This was the disguise in which he was going to escape across the frontier. As passport he had procured the 'certificate of identification' of his coachman, who had come into Petrograd from the expropriated farm to see Maria. With his face purposely dirtied, and decorated with three days' growth of reddish beard, a driver's cap that covered his ears, and a big sack on his back to add a peasant touch to his get-up, Marsh looked – well, like nothing on earth, to use the colloquial expression! It was a get-up that defied description, yet in a crowd of peasants would not attract particular attention.

Confident that he was doing the right thing by quitting, Marsh had completely recovered his former good spirits and joked boisterously as he put a finishing touch here and there to his disguise. I gave him my report and folding it flat into a packet about two inches square he removed one of his top boots and hid it inside the sole of his sock. 'The population of hell will be increased by several new arrivals before the Bolsheviks find that,' he said, pulling on his boot again and slipping a heavy revolver inside his trousers.

Poor Maria was terribly distressed at Marsh's departure. So was the coachman, who could find no terms wherein to express his disgust and indignation at the conduct of the elder of the two stable-boys who had joined the Bolsheviks, assisted in sacking Marsh's country house and farm, and was now appointed Commissar in supreme control of the establishment. The coachman exhausted a luxuriant fund of expletives in describing how the stable boy now sprawled in Marsh's easy-chairs, spitting on the floor, how all the photographs had been smashed to pieces, and the drawing-room carpets littered with dirt, cigarette-ends, and rubbish. At all of which Marsh roared with laughter, much to the perplexity of the coachman and Maria.

With trembling hands Maria placed a rough meal on the table, while Marsh repeated to me final details of the route he was taking and by which I should follow with his wife. 'Fita,' he said, mentioning the name of the Finnish guide on whom he was relying, 'lives a mile from Grusino station. When you get out of the train walk in the other direction till everybody has dispersed, then turn back and go by the forest path straight to his cottage. He will tell you what to do.'

At last it was time to start. Marsh and I shook hands and wished each other good-luck, and I went out first, so as not to witness the pathetic parting from his humble friends. I heard him embrace them both, heard Maria's convulsive sobs – and

I hurried down the stone stairway and out into the street. I walked rapidly to the street-car terminal in the Mihailovsky Square, and wandered round it till Marsh appeared. We made no sign of recognition. He jumped on one of the cars, and I scrambled on to the next.

It was dark by the time we reached the distant Okhta railway station, a straggling wooden structure on the outskirts of the town. But standing on the wooden boards of the rough platform I easily discerned the massive figure, pushing and scrambling amid a horde of peasants toward the already over-crowded coaches. Might is right in Red Russia, as everywhere else. The Soviet Government has not yet nationalized muscle. I watched a huge bulk of sheepskin, with a dangling and bouncing gray sack, raise itself by some mysterious process of elevation above the heads and shoulders of the seething mass around and transplant itself on to the buffers. Thence it rose to the roof, and finally, assisted by one or two admiring individuals already ensconced within the coach, it lowered itself down the side and disappeared through the black aperture of what had once been a window. I hung around for half an hour or so, until a series of prolonged and piercing whistles from the antediluvian-looking locomotive announced that the driver had that day condescended to set his engine in motion. There was a jolt, a series of violent creaks, the loud ejaculations of passengers, a scramble of belated peasants to hook themselves on to protruding points in the vicinity of steps, buffers, footboards, etc., and the train with its load of harassed animality slowly rumbled forward out of the station.

I stood and watched it pass into the darkness and, as it vanished, the cold, the gloom, the universal dilapidation seemed to become intensified. I still stood, listening to the distant rumble of the train, until I found myself alone upon the platform. Then I turned, and as I slowly retraced my steps into town an aching sense of emptiness pervaded all around, and the future seemed nothing but impenetrable night.

Chapter III

The Green Shawl

I will pass briefly over the days that followed Marsh's flight. They were concentrated upon efforts to get news of Mrs Marsh and Melnikoff. There were frequent hold-ups in the street: at two points along the Nevsky Prospect all passengers were stopped to have their documents and any parcels they were carrying examined, but a cursory glance at my passport of the Extraordinary Commission sufficed to satisfy the militiamen's curiosity.

I studied all the soviet literature I had time to devour, attended public meetings and slept in turn at the homes of my new acquaintances, making it a rule, however, never to mention anywhere the secret of other night-haunts.

The meetings I attended were all Communist meetings, at each of which the same banal propagandist phraseology was untiringly reeled off. The vulgar violence of Bolshevist rhetoric and the triumphant inaccuracy of statement due to the prohibition of criticism soon became wearisome. In vain I sought meetings for discussion, or where the people's point of view would be expressed: freedom of speech granted by the revolution had come to mean freedom for Bolshevist speech only and prison for any other. Some of the meetings, however, were interesting, especially when a prominent leader such as Trotzky, Zinoviev or Lunacharsky spoke, for the unrivalled powers of speech of a few of the leading Bolsheviks, who possess in a marked degree 'the fatal gift of eloquence' had an almost irresistible attraction.

During these days also I cultivated the friendship of the ex-journalist whom, despite his timidity, I found to be a man of taste and culture. He had an extensive library in several languages, and spent his leisure hours writing (if I remember rightly) a treatise on philosophy, which, for some reason or other, he was convinced would be regarded as 'counter-revolutionary' and kept it locked up and hidden under a lot of books in a closet. I tried to persuade him of the contrary and urged him even to take his manuscript to the department of education, in the hope that some one of the less virulent type there might be impressed with the work and obtain for him concessions as regards leisure and rations.

When I visited him the day after Marsh's flight I found him, still wrapped in his green coat, running feverishly from stove to stove poking and coaxing the newly lit fires. He was chuckling with glee at the return of forgotten warmth and, in truly Russian style, had lit every stove in his flat and was wasting fuel as fast as he possibly could.

'What the devil is the use of that?' I said in disgust. 'Where the deuce do you think you will get your next lot of wood from? It doesn't *rain* wood in these regions, does it?'

But my sarcasm was lost on Dmitri Konstantinovitch, in whose system of economy, economy had no place. To his intense indignation I opened all the grates and, dragging out the half-burned logs and glowing cinders, concentrated them in one big blaze in the dining-room stove, which also heated his bedroom.

'That's just like an Englishman,' he said in unspeakable disgust as he shuffled round watching me at work. 'You understand,' I said, resolutely, 'this and the kitchen are the only stoves that are ever to be heated.'

Of course I found his larder empty and he had no prospect of food except the scanty and unappetizing dinner at four o'clock at the local communal eating-house two doors away. So, the weather being fine, I took him out to the little private dining room I had eaten at on the day of my arrival. Here I gave him the biggest meal that miniature establishment could provide, and intoxicated by the unaccustomed fumes of gruel, carrots and coffee he forgot – and forgave me – the stoves.

A day or two later the journalist was sufficiently well to return to work, and taking the spare key of his flat I let myself in whenever I liked. I took him severely to task in his household affairs, and as the result of our concerted labours we saved his untidy home from degenerating completely into a pigsty. Here I met some of the people mentioned by Marsh. The journalist was very loath to invite them, but in a week or so I had so firm a hold over him that by the mere hint of not returning any more I could reduce him to complete submission. If I disappeared for as much as three days he was overcome with anxiety.

Some people I met embarrassed me not a little by regarding me as a herald of the approaching Allies and an earnest of the early triumph of the militarist counter-revolution. Their attitude resembled at the other extreme that recently adopted by the Bolshevist Government toward impartial foreign labour delegates, who were embarrassingly proclaimed to be forerunners of the world-revolution.

One evening the journalist greeted me with looks of deep cunning and mystification. I could see he had something on his mind he was bursting to say. When at last we were seated, as usual huddled over the dining-room stove, he leaned over toward my chair, tapped me on the knee to draw my very particular attention, and began.

'Michael Mihailovitch,' he said in an undertone, as though the chairs and table might betray the secret, 'I have a wonderful idea!' He struck one side of his thin nose with his forefinger to indicate the wondrousness of his idea. 'Today I and some colleagues of former days,' he went on, his finger still applied to the side of his nose, 'determined to start a newspaper. Yes, yes, a secret newspaper – to prepare the way for the Allies!'

'And who is going to print it?' I asked, fully impressed with the wondrousness of his idea.

'The Bolshevist *Izvestia*,' he said, 'is printed on the presses of the *Novoye Vremya** but all the printer-men being strongly against the Bolsheviks, we will ask them to print a leaflet on the sly.'

'And who will pay for it?' I asked, amused by his simplicity.

'Well, here you can help, Michael Mihailovitch,' said the journalist, rather as though he were conferring an honour upon me. 'You would not refuse, would you? Last summer the English—'

'Well, apart from technique,' I interrupted, 'why are you so certain of the Allies?'

Dmitri Konstantinovitch stared at me.

'But you—' he began, then stopped abruptly.

There followed one of those pauses that are more eloquent than speech.

'I see,' I said at last. 'Listen, Dmitri Konstantinovitch, I will tell you a story. In the north of your vast country there is a town called Archangel. I was there in the summer and I was there again recently. When I was there in the summer the entire population was crying passionately for the Allies to intervene and save them from a Bolshevist hooligan clique, and when at last the city was occupied the path of the British General was strewn with flowers as he stepped ashore. But when I returned some weeks after the occupation, did I find jubilation and contentment, do you think? I am sorry to say I did not. I found strife, intrigue, and growing bitterness.

'A democratic government was nominally in power with the venerable revolutionist Tchaikovsky, protégé of the Allies, at its head. Well, one night a group of officers – Russian officers – summarily arrested this government established by the Allies, while the allied military leaders slyly shut one eye so as not to see what was going on. The hapless democratic ministers

---

*   A prominent pre-revolutionary journal. [Ed: *Novoye Vremya* was a liberal journal which published articles by, amongst others, Anton Chekov, but was despised by the Bolsheviks who shut it down the day after the revolution.]

were dragged out of their beds, whisked away by automobile to a waiting steam launch, and carried off to a remote island in the White Sea where they were unceremoniously deposited and left! Sounds like an exploit of Captain Kidd, doesn't it? Only two escaped, because they happened that evening to be dining with the American Ambassador, and he concealed them in his bedroom.

'Next morning the city was startled by a sensational announcement posted on the walls. "By order of the Russian Command," it ran, "the incompetent government has been deposed, and the supreme power in North Russia is henceforth vested exclusively in the hands of the military Commander of the occupying forces."

'There was a hell of a hubbub, I can tell you! For who was to untangle the knot? The allied military had connived at the kidnapping by Russian plotters of a Russian government established by order of the Allies! The diplomats and the military were already at logger-heads and now they were like fighting-cocks! Finally, after two days' wrangling, and when all the factories went on strike, it was decided that the whole proceeding had been most unseemly and undemocratic. "Diplomacy" triumphed, a cruiser was despatched to pick up the wretched ministers shivering on the remote White Sea island, and brought them back (scarcely a triumphal procession!) to Archangel, where they were restored to the tarnished dignity of their ministerial pedestals, and went on trying to pretend to be a government.'

The journalist gaped open-mouthed as I told him this story. 'And what is happening there now?' he asked after a pause. 'I am rather afraid to think of what is happening now,' I replied.

'And you mean,' he said, slowly, 'the Allies are not—'

'I do not know – they may come, and they may not.' I realized I was rudely tearing down a radiant castle the poor journalist had built in the air.

'But why – Michael Mihailovitch – are you—?'

'Why am I here?' I said, completing his unfinished question. 'Simply because I wanted to be.'

Dmitri Konstantinovitch gasped. 'You – wanted to here?'

'Yes,' I replied, smiling involuntarily at his incredulity. 'I wanted to be here and took the first chance that offered itself to come.' If I had told him that after mature consideration I had elected to spend eternity in Gehenna rather than in the felicity of celestial domains I should not have astonished the incredulous journalist more.

'By the way,' I said rather cruelly, as a possibility occurred to me, 'don't go and blurt that Archangel story everywhere, or you'll have to explain how you heard it.'

But he did not heed me. I had utterly demolished his castle of hope. I felt very sorry as I watched him. 'Maybe they will learn,' I added, wishing to say something kind, 'and not repeat mistakes elsewhere.'

Learn? As I looked into the journalist's tear-dimmed eyes, how heartily I wished they would!

‡

While the journalist's home until my arrival was only on the downward grade toward pigstydom, that of the Policeman had already long since arrived at the thirty-third degree. His rooms were in an abominable condition, and quite unnecessarily so. The sanitary arrangements in many houses were in a sad state of dilapidation, but people took urgent measures to maintain what cleanliness they could. Not so the Policeman, who lived in conditions too loathsome for words and took no steps to check the progressive accumulation of dust, dirt, and filth.

He kept a Chinese servant, who appeared to be permanently on strike, and whom he would alternately caressingly wheedle and tempestuously upbraid, so far as I could see with equal ineffect. In the nether regions of the house he occupied there lived, or frequently gathered, a bevy of Chinamen who loafed about the hall or peeped through gratings up the cellar stairways. There was also a mysterious lady, whom I never saw, but whom I would hear occasionally as I mounted the stairs, shrieking in a hysterical caterwaul, and apparently menacing the little Policeman with physical assault. Sometimes he would snarl back, and one such *scène d'amour* was terminated by a violent crash of crockery. But the affable female, whom I somehow figured as big and muscular with wild, floating hair, a sort of Medusa, had always vanished by the time I reached the top of the stairs, and the loud door-slam that coincided with her disappearance was followed by death-like silence. The little Policeman, whose bearing was always apologetic, would accost me as though nothing were amiss, while the insubordinate Chinese servant, if he condescended to open the front door, would stand at the foot of the staircase with an enigmatical sneering grin spread over his evil features. It was altogether an uncanny abode.

Marsh had prepared the way, and the Policeman received me with profuse demonstrations of regard. I was fortunately not obliged to accept his proffered hospitality often, but when I did, it was touching to note how he would put himself out in the effort to make me as comfortable as the revolting circumstances would permit. Despite his despicable character, his cringing deceitfulness, and mealy-mouthed flattery, he still possessed human feelings, showed at times a genuine desire to please not merely for the sake of gain, and was sincerely and passionately fond of his children, who lived in another house.

He was excessively vain and boastful. In the course of his career he had accumulated a collection of signed photographs of notables, and loved to demonstrate them, reiterating for the fiftieth time how Count Witte said this, Stolypin said that, and so-and-so said something else. I used to humour him, listening gravely, and he interpreted my endurance as ability to vener-ate the great ones of the earth, and an appreciation of his illustrious connections, and was mightily pleased. He was full of grandiose schemes for the downthrow of the Red regime, and the least sign of so much as patience with his suggestions excited his enthusiasm and inspired his genius for self-praise and loquacity.

'Your predecessors, if you will allow me to say so,' he launched forth on the occasion of my first visit, 'were pitifully incompetent. Even Mr Marsh, delightful man though he was, hardly knew his business. Now *you* Michael Ivanitch, I can see, are a man of understanding – a man of quite different stamp. I presented a scheme to Marsh, for instance,' and he bent over confidentially, 'for dividing Petrograd into ten sections, seizing each one in turn, and thus throwing the Bolsheviks out. It was sure of success, and yet Mr Marsh would not hear of it.'

'How were you going to do it?'

He seized a sheet of paper and began hastily making sketches to illustrate his wonderful scheme. The capital was all neatly divided up, the chiefs of each district were appointed to their respective posts, he had the whole police force at his beck and call and about half a dozen regiments.

'Give but the signal,' he cried, dramatically, 'and this city of Peter the Great is ours.'

'And the supreme commander?' I queried, 'who will be Governor of the liberated city?'

The sanguine little Policeman smiled a trifle confusedly. 'Oh, we will find a Governor,' he said, rather sheepishly, hesitant to utter the innermost hopes of his heart. 'Perhaps you, Michael Ivanitch—'

But this magnanimous offer was mere formal courtesy. It was plain that I was expected to content myself with the secondary role of kingmaker.

'Well, if all is so far ready,' I said, 'why don't you blow the trumpets and we will watch the walls of Jericho fall?'

The little man twirled his moustache, smirking apologetically. 'But, Michael Ivanitch,' he said, growing bold and bordering even on familiarity, 'er – funds, don't you know –

after all, nowadays, you know, you get nowhere without – er – money, *do* you? Of course, you *quite* understand, Michael Ivanitch, that I, personally—'

'How much did you tell Marsh it would cost?' I interrupted, very curious to see what he would say. He had not expected the question to be put in this way. Like a clock ticking I could hear his mind calculating the probability of Marsh's having told me the sum, and whether he might safely double it in view of my greater susceptibility.

'I think with 100,000 roubles we might pull it off,' he replied, tentatively, eyeing me cautiously to see how I took it. I nodded silently. 'Of course, we *might* do it for a little less,' he added as if by afterthought, 'but then there would be subsequent expenses.'

'Well, well,' I replied, indulgently, 'we will see. We'll talk about it again sometime.'

'There is no time like the present, Michael Ivanitch.'

'But there are other things to think of. We will speak of it again when—'

'When—?'

'When you have got Mrs Marsh out of prison.'

The little man appeared completely to shrivel up when thus dragged brusquely back into the world of crude reality. He flushed for a moment, it seemed to me, with anger, but pulled himself together at once and reassumed his original manner of demonstrative servility.

'At present we have business on hand, Alexei Fomitch,' I added, 'and I wish to talk first about that. How do matters stand?'

The Policeman said his agents were busily at work, studying the ground and the possibilities of Mrs Marsh's escape. The whole town, he stated, was being searched for Marsh, and the inability to unearth him had already given rise to the suspicion that he had fled. In a day or two the news would be confirmed by Bolshevist agents in Finland. He foresaw an alleviation of Mrs Marsh's lot owing to the probable cessation of cross-examinations. It only remained to see whether she would be transferred to another cell or prison, and then plans for escape might be laid.

'Fire ahead,' I said in conclusion. 'And when Mrs Marsh is free – we will perhaps discuss other matters.'

'There is no time like the present, Michael Ivanitch,' repeated the little Policeman, but his voice sounded forlorn.

‡

Meanwhile, what of Melnikoff?

Zorinsky was all excitement when I called him up.

'How is your brother?' I said over the phone. 'Was the accident serious? Is there any hope of recovery?'

'Yes, yes,' came the reply. 'The doctor says he fears he will be in hospital some time, but the chances are he will get over it.'

'Where has he been put?'

'He is now in a private sanatorium in Goróhovaya Street, but we hope he will be removed to some larger and more comfortable hospital.'

'The conditions, I hope, are good?'

'As good as we can arrange for under present-day circumstances. For the time being he is in a separate room and on limited diet. But can you not come round this evening, Pavel Ivanitch?'

'Thank you, I am afraid I have a meeting of our House Committee to attend, but I could come tomorrow.'

'Good. Come tomorrow. I have news of Leo, who is coming to Petrograd.'

'My regards to Elena Ivanovna.'

'Thanks. Goodbye.'

'Goodbye.'

The telephone was an inestimable boon, but one that had to be employed with extreme caution. From time to time at moments of panic the Government would completely stop the telephone service, causing immense inconvenience and exasperating the population whom they were trying to placate. But it was not in Bolshevist interests to suppress it entirely, the telephone being an effectual means of detecting 'counter-revolutionary' machinations. The lines were closely watched, a suspicious voice or phrase would lead to a line being 'tapped', the recorded conversations would be scrutinized for hints of persons or addresses, and then the Assyrian came down like a wolf on the fold to seize books, papers, and documents, and augment the number of occupants of *Goróhovayan* cells. So one either spoke in fluent metaphor or by prearranged verbal signals camouflaged behind talk of the weather or food. The 'news of Leo', for instance, I understood at once to mean news of Trotzky, or information regarding the Red army.

Zorinsky was enthusiastic when I called next day and stayed to dinner. 'We'll have Melnikoff out in no time,' he exclaimed. 'They are holding his case over for further evidence. He will be taken either to the Shpalernaya or Deriabinskaya prison, where we shall be allowed to send him food. Then we'll communicate by hiding notes in the food and let him know our plan of escape. Meanwhile, all's well with ourselves, so come and have a glass of vodka.'

I was overjoyed at this good news. The conditions at either of the two prisons he mentioned were much better than at *No. 2 Goróhovaya* and though transference to them meant delay in decision and consequent prolongation of imprisonment, the prison regime was generally regarded as more lenient.

'By the way,' said Zorinsky, 'it is lucky you have come today. A certain Colonel H. is coming in this evening. He works in the General Staff and has interesting news. Trotzky is planning to come up to Petrograd.'

Elena Ivanovna was in a bad mood because a lot of sugar that had been promised to her and her colleagues had failed to arrive and she had been unable to make cakes for two days.

'You must excuse the bad dinner tonight, Pavel Ivanitch,' she said. 'I had intended to have chocolate pudding for you, but as it is there will be no third course. Really, the way we are treated is outrageous.'

'Your health, Pavel Ivanitch,' said Zorinsky, undismayed by the prospect of no third course. 'Here we have something better even than chocolate pudding, haven't we?'

He talked on volubly in his usual strain, harping back again to pre-war days and the pleasures of regimental life. I asked him if he thought most of the officers were still monarchists.

'I don't know,' he said. 'I expect you'll find they are pretty evenly divided. Very few are socialists, but a lot think themselves republicans. Some, of course, are monarchists, and many are nothing at all. As for me,' he continued, 'when I joined my regiment I took the oath of allegiance to the Tsar.' (At the mention of the Tsar he stood upright and then sat down again, a gesture which astonished me, for it really seemed to be spontaneous and unfeigned.) 'But I consider myself absolved and free to serve whom I will from the moment the Tsar signed the deed of abdication. At present I serve nobody. I will not serve Trotzky, but I will work with him if he offers a career. That is, if the Allies do not come into Petrograd. By the way,' he added, checking himself abruptly and obviously desirous of knowing, 'do you think the Allies really will come – the English, for instance?'

'I have no idea.'

'Strange. Everyone here is sure of it. But that means nothing, of course. Listen in the queues or market places. Now Cronstadt has been taken, now the Allies are in Finland, and so on. Personally, I believe they will bungle everything. Nobody really understands Russia, not even we ourselves. Except, perhaps, Trotzky,' he added as an afterthought, 'or the Germans.'

'The Germans, you think?'

'Surely. Prussianism is what we want. You see these fat-faced commissars in leather jackets with three or four revolvers in their belts? Or the sailors with gold watch chains and rings, with their prostitutes promenading the Nevsky? Those rascals, I tell you, will be *working* inside of a year, working like hell, because if the Whites get here every commissar will be hanged, drawn and quartered. *Somebody* must work to keep things going. Mark my words, first the Bolsheviks will make their Communists work, they'll give them all sorts of privileges and power, and then they'll make the Communists make the others work. Forward the whip and knout! The good old times again! And if you don't like it, kindly step this way to *No. 2 Goróhovaya*! Ugh!' he shuddered. '*No. 2 Goróhovaya*! Here's to you, Pavel Ivanitch!'

Zorinsky drank heavily, but the liquor produced no visible effect on him.

'By the way,' he asked, abruptly, 'you haven't heard anything of Marsh, have you?'

'Oh, yes,' I said, 'he is in Finland.'

'*What*!' he cried, half-rising from the table. He was livid.

'In Finland,' I repeated, regarding him with astonishment. 'He got away the day before yesterday.'

'He got away – ha! ha! ha!' Zorinsky dropped back into his seat. His momentary expression changed as suddenly as it had appeared, and he burst into uproarious laughter. 'Do you *really* mean to say so? Ha! ha! My God, won't they be wild! Damned clever! Don't you know they've been turning the place upside down to find him? Ha, ha, ha! Now that really is good news, upon my soul!'

'Why should you be so glad about it?' I inquired. 'You seemed at first to—'

'I was astounded.' He spoke rapidly and a little excitedly. 'Don't you know Marsh was regarded as chief of allied organizations and a most dangerous man? But for some reason they were dead certain of catching him – dead certain. Haven't they got his wife, or his mother, or somebody, as hostage?'

'His wife.'

'It'll go badly with her,' he laughed cruelly.

It was my turn to be startled. 'What do you mean?' I said, striving to appear indifferent.

'They will shoot her.'

It was with difficulty that I maintained a tone of mere casual interest. 'Do you really think they will shoot her?' I said, incredulously.

'Sure to,' he replied, emphatically. 'What else do they take hostages for?'

For the rest of the evening I thought of nothing else but the possibility of Mrs Marsh being shot. The Policeman had said the direct opposite, basing his statement on what he said was inside information. On the other hand, why on earth should hostages be taken if they were to be liberated when the culprits had fled? I could elicit nothing more from Zorinsky except that in his opinion Mrs Marsh might be kept in prison a month or two, but in the long run would most undoubtedly be shot.

I listened but idly to the colonel, a pompous gentleman with a bushy white beard, who came in after dinner. Zorinsky told him he might speak freely in my presence and, sitting bolt upright, he conversed in a rather ponderous manner on the latest developments. He appeared to have a high opinion of Zorinsky. He confirmed the latter's statements regarding radical changes in the organization of the army, and said Trotzky was planning to establish a similar new regime in the Baltic Fleet. I was not nearly so attentive as I ought to have been, and had to ask the colonel to repeat it all to me at our next meeting.

‡

Maria was the only person I took into my confidence as to all my movements. Every morning I banged at the chalk-marked door. Maria let me in and I told her how things were going with Mrs Marsh. Of course, I always gave her optimistic reports. Then I would say, 'Tonight, Maria, I am staying at the journalist's – you know his address – tomorrow at Stepanovna's, Friday night at Zorinsky's, and Saturday, here. So if anything happens you will know where it probably occurred. If I disappear, wait a couple of days, and then get someone over the frontier – perhaps the coachman will go – and tell the British Consul.' Then I would give her my notes, written in minute handwriting on tracing paper, and she would hide them for me. Two more Englishmen left by Marsh's route a few days after his departure and Maria gave them another small packet to carry, saying it was a letter from herself to Marsh. So it was, only on the same sheet as she had scrawled a pencil note to Marsh I wrote a long message in invisible ink. I made the ink by – oh, it doesn't matter how.

Zorinsky's reports as to Melnikoff continued to be favourable. He hinted at a certain investigator who might have to be bought off, to which I gave eager assent. He gave me further information on political matters which proved to be quite accurate, and repellent though his bearing and appearance were, I began to feel less distrustful of him. It was about a week later, when I called him up, that he told me 'the doctors had decided his brother was sufficiently well to leave hospital'. Tingling with excitement and expectation I hurried round.

'The investigator is our man,' explained Zorinsky, 'and guarantees to let Melnikoff out within a month.'

'How will he do it?' I inquired. 'That rather depends. He may twist the evidence, but Melnikoff's is a bad case and there's not much evidence that isn't damaging. If that's too hard, he may swap Melnikoff's *dossier* for somebody else's and let the error be found out when it's too late. But he'll manage it all right.'

'And it must take a whole month?'

'Melnikoff will be freed about the middle of January. There's no doubt about it. And the investigator wants 60,000 roubles.'

'*Sixty thousand roubles*!' I gasped. I was appalled at this unexpected figure. Where should I get the money from? The rouble was still worth about 40 to the pound, so that this was some £1,500 or $6,000.

'Melnikoff's case is a hopeless one,' said Zorinsky, drily. 'No one can let *him* off and go scot free. The investigator wants to be guaranteed, for he will have to get over the frontier the same night, too. But I advise you to pay only half now, and the rest the day Melnikoff gets out. There will also be a few odd bribes to accomplices. Better allow 75,000 or 80,000 roubles all told.'

'I have very little money with me just now,' I said, 'but I will try to get you the first 30,000 in two or three days.'

'And by the way,' he added, 'I forgot to tell you last time you were here that I have seen Melnikoff's sister, who is in the direst straits. Elena Ivanovna and I have sent her a little food, but she also needs money. We have no money, for we scarcely use it nowadays, but perhaps you could spare a thousand or so now and again.'

'I will give you some for her when I bring the other.'

'Thank you. She will be grateful. And now, unpleasant business over, let's go and have a glass of vodka. Your health, Pavel Ivanitch.'

Rejoicing at the prospect of securing Melnikoff's release, and burdened at the same time with the problem of procuring this large sum of money, I rang up next day the business friend of whom Marsh had spoken, using a pre-arranged password. Marsh called this gentleman the 'Banker' though that was not his profession, because he had left his finances in his charge. When I visited him I found him to be a man of agreeable though nervous deportment, very devoted to Marsh. He was unable to supply me with all the money I required, and I decided I must somehow get the rest from Finland, perhaps when I took Mrs Marsh away.

The Banker had just returned from Moscow, whither he had been called with an invitation to accept a post in a new department created to check the ruin of industry. He was very sarcastic over the manner in which, he said, the 'government of horny hands' (as the Bolsheviks frequently designate themselves) was beginning 'to grovel before people who can read and write'.

'In public speeches,' said the Banker, 'they still have to call us "*bourzhu* (bourgeois) swine" for the sake of appearances, but in private, when the doors are closed, it is very different. They have even ceased "comrading": it is no longer "Comrade A." or "Comrade B." when they address us – that honour they reserve for themselves – but "Excuse me, Alexander Vladimirovitch", or "May I trouble you, Boris Konstantinovitch".' He laughed ironically. 'Quite "pogentlemensky",' he added, using a Russianized expression whose meaning is obvious.

'Did you accept the post?' I asked.

'I? No, sir!' he replied with emphasis. 'Do I want a dirty workman holding a revolver over me all day? That is the sort of "control" they intend to exercise.' (He did accept it, however, just a month later, when the offer was renewed with the promise of a tidy salary if he took it, and prison if he didn't.)

On the following day I brought the money to Zorinsky, and he said he would have it transferred to the investigator at once.

'By the way,' I said, 'I may be going to Finland for a few days. Do not be surprised if you do not hear from me for a week or so.'

'To Finland?' Zorinsky was very interested. 'Then perhaps you will not return?'

'I am certain to return,' I said, 'even if only on account of Melnikoff.'

'And of course you have other business here,' he said. 'By the way, how are you going?'

'I don't know yet; they say it is easy enough to walk over the frontier.'

'Not quite so easy,' he replied. 'Why not just walk across the bridge?'

'What bridge?'

'The frontier bridge at Bielo'ostrof.'

I thought he was mad. 'What on earth do you mean?' I asked.

'It can be fixed up all right – with a little care,' he went on.

'Five or six thousand roubles to the station commissar and he'll shut his eyes, another thousand or so to the bridge sentry and he'll look the other way, and over you go. Evening is the best time, when it's dark.'

I remembered I had heard speak of this method in Finland. Sometimes it worked, sometimes it didn't. It was the simplest thing in the world, but it wasn't sure. Commissars were erratic and not unfearful of burning their fingers. Furthermore, the Finns sometimes turned people back. Besides, Mrs Marsh would be with me – I hoped – and of that Zorinsky must know nothing.

'That is a splendid notion,' I exclaimed. 'I had never thought of that. I'll let you know before I start.'

Next day I told him I had decided not to go to Finland because I was thinking of going to Moscow.

‡

'Madame Marsh has not been moved from *No. 2 Goróhovaya*,' declared the little Policeman as I sat opposite him in his fetid den. 'Her case is in abeyance, and will doubtless remain so for some time. Since they learned of Marsh's flight they have left her alone. They may perhaps forget all about her. Now, I think, is the time to act.'

'What will they do to her if her case comes on again?'

'It is too early yet to conjecture.'

It was shortly before Christmas that the Policeman began to grow nervous and excited, and I could see that his emotion was real. His plan for Mrs Marsh's escape was developing, occupying his whole mind and causing him no small concern. Every day I brought him some little present, such as cigarettes, sugar, or butter, procured from Maria, so that he should have fewer household cares to worry over. At last I became almost as wrought up as he was himself, while Maria, whom I kept informed, was in a constant state of tremor resulting from her fever of anxiety.

December 18th dawned bleak and raw. The wind tore in angry gushes round the corners of the houses, snatching up the sandy snow, and flinging it viciously in the half-hidden faces of hurrying, harassed pedestrians. Toward noon the storm abated, and Maria and I set out together for a neighbouring market place. We were going to buy a woman's cloak, for that night I was to take Mrs Marsh across the frontier.

The corner of the Kuznetchny Pereulok and the Vladimirovsky Prospect has been a busy place for 'speculators' ever since private trading was prohibited. Even on this bitter winter day there were the usual lines of wretched people standing patiently, disposing of personal belongings or of food got by foraging in the country. Many of them were women of the educated class, selling off their last possessions in the effort to scrape together sufficient to buy meagre provisions for themselves or their families. Either they were unable to find occupation or were here in the intervals of work. Old clothing, odds and ends of every description, crockery, toys, nick-nacks, clocks, books, pictures, paper, pots, pans, pails, pipes, postcards – the entire paraphernalia of antiquarian and second-hand dealers' shops, could here be found turned out on to the pavements.

Maria and I passed the people selling sugar by the lump, their little stock of four or five lumps exposed on outstretched palms. We also passed the herrings, and the 'bread patties' of greenish colour. Passers-by would pick up a patty, smell it, and if they did not like it, would put it back and try the next. Maria was making for the old clothing, and as we pushed through the crowd we kept eyes and ears open for warning of a possible raid, for from time to time bands of guards would make a sudden dash at the 'speculators', arrest a few unlucky ones, and disperse the rest.

Maria soon found what she wanted – a warm cloak which had evidently seen better days. The tired eyes of the tall, refined lady from whom we bought it opened wide as I immediately paid the first price she asked.

'*Je vous remercie Madame*,' I said, and as Maria donned the cloak and we moved away the look of scorn on the lady's face passed into one of astonishment.

'Don't fail to have tea ready at five, Maria,' I said as we returned.

'Am I likely to fail, Ivan Ilitch?'

We sat and waited. The minutes were hours, the hours days. At three I said: 'I am going now, Maria.' Biting her fingers, Maria stood trembling as I left her and set out to walk across the town.

‡

The dingy interior of the headquarters of the Extraordinary Commission, with its bare stairs and passages, is an eerie place at all times of the year but never is its sombre, sorrow-laden gloom so intense as on a December afternoon when dusk is sinking into darkness. While Maria and I, unable to conceal our agitation, made our preparations, there sat in one of the inner chambers at *No. 2 Goróhovaya* a group of women, from thirty to forty in number. Their faces were undistinguishable in the growing darkness, sitting in groups on the wooden planks which took the place of bedsteads. The room was over-heated and nauseatingly stuffy, but the patient figures paid no heed, nor appeared to care whether it be hot or cold. A few chatted m undertones, but most of them sat motionless and silent, waiting, waiting, endlessly waiting.

The terror-hour had not yet come – it came only at seven each evening. The terror-hour was more terrible in the men's chambers, where the toll was greater, but it visited the women, too. Then, every victim knew that if the heavy door was opened and his name called, he passed out into eternity. For executions were carried out in the evening and the bodies removed at night.

At seven o'clock, all talk, all action ceased. Faces sat white and still, fixed on the heavy folding door. When it creaked every figure became a statue, a death-statue, stone-livid, breath-less, dead in life. A moment of ghastly, intolerable suspense, a silence that could be felt, and in the silence – a name. And when the name was spoken, every figure – but one – would imperceptibly relapse. Here and there a lip would twitch, here and there a smile would flicker. But no one would break the dead silence. One of their number was doomed.

The figure that bore the spoken name would rise, and move, move slowly with a wooden, unnatural gait, tottering along the narrow aisle between the plank couches. Some would look up and some would look down; some, fascinated, would watch the dead figure pass; and some would pray, or mutter, 'Tomorrow, maybe, I.' Or there would be a frantic shriek, a brutal strug-gle, and worse than death would fill the chamber, till where two were, one only would be left, heaving convulsively, insane, clutching the rough woodwork with bleeding nails.

But the silence was the silence of supreme compassion, the eyes that followed or the eyes that fell were alike those of brothers or sisters, for in death's hour vanish all differences and reigns the only true Communism – the Communism of Sympathy. Not there, in the Kremlin, nor there in the lying Soviets — but here in the terrible house of inquisition, in the Communist dungeons, is true Communism at last established!

But on this December afternoon the terror-hour was not yet. There were still three hours' respite, and the figures spoke low in groups or sat silently waiting, waiting, endlessly waiting.

Then suddenly a name was called. '*Lydia Marsh!*'

The hinges creaked, the guard appeared in the doorway, and the name was spoken loud and clearly. 'It is not the terror-hour yet,' thought every woman, glancing at the twilight through the high, dirt-stained windows.

A figure rose from a distant couch. 'What can it be?' 'Another interpellation?' 'An unusual hour!' Low voices sounded from the group. 'They've left me alone three days,' said the rising figure, wearily. 'I suppose now it begins all over again. Well, *à bientôt.*'

The figure disappeared in the doorway, and the women went on waiting – waiting for seven o'clock.

'Follow me,' said the guard. He moved along the corridor and turned down a side-passage. They passed others in the corridor, but no one heeded. The guard stopped. Looking up, the woman saw she was outside the women's lavatory. She waited. The guard pointed with his bayonet.

'In here?' queried the figure in surprise. The guard was silent. The woman pushed the door open and entered.

Lying in the corner were a dark green shawl and a shabby hat, with two slips of paper attached. One of them was a pass in an unknown name, stating that the holder had entered the building at four o'clock and must leave before seven. The other had scrawled on it the words: 'Walk straight into St. Izaac's Cathedral.'

Mechanically she destroyed the second slip, adjusted the shabby hat, and wrapping the shawl well round her neck and face passed out into the passage. She elbowed others in the corridor, but no one heeded her. At the foot of the main staircase she was asked for her pass. She showed it and was motioned on. At the main entrance she was again asked for her pass. She showed it and was passed out into the street. She looked up and down. The street was empty, and crossing the road hurriedly she disappeared round the corner.

Like dancing constellations the candles flickered and flared in front of the icons at the foot of the huge pillars of the vast cathedral. Halfway up the columns vanished in gloom. I had already burned two candles, and though I was concealed in the niche of a pillar, I knelt and stood alternately, partly from impatience, partly that my piety should be patent to any chance observer. But my eyes were fixed on the little wooden side-entrance. How interminable the minutes seemed. Quarter to five!

Then the green shawl appeared. It looked almost black in the dim darkness. It slipped through the doorway quickly, stood still a moment, and moved irresolutely forward. I walked up to the shrouded figure.

'Mrs Marsh?' I said quietly in English.

'Yes.'

'I am the person you are to meet. I hope you will soon see your husband.'

'Where is he?' she asked, anxiously.

'In Finland. You go there with me tonight.'

We left the cathedral and crossing the square took a cab and drove to the place called Five Corners. Here we walked a little and finding another cab drove near to 'No. 5', again walking the last hundred yards. I banged at the door three times.

How shall I describe the meeting with Maria! I left them weeping together and went into another room. Neither will I attempt to describe the parting, when an hour later Mrs Marsh stood ready for her journey, clad in the cloak we had purchased in the morning, and with a black shawl in place of the green one.

'There is no time to lose,' I said. 'We must be at the station at seven, and it is a long drive.'

The adieus were over at last, and Maria stood weeping at the door as we made our way down the dark stone stairs.

'I will call you Varvara,' I cautioned my companion. 'You call me Vania, and if by chance we are stopped, I am taking you to hospital.'

We drove slowly to the distant straggling Okhta station, where lately I had watched the huge figure of Marsh clamber on to the roof and disappear through the window. The little Policeman was on the platform, sincerely overjoyed at this happy ending to his design. I forgot his ways, his dirtiness, his messy quarters, and thanked him heartily, and as I thrust the packet of money Marsh had left for him into his hand, I felt that at this moment, at least, that was not what was uppermost in his thoughts.

'Come on, Varvara!' I shouted in Russian, rudely tugging

Mrs Marsh by the sleeve and dragging her along the platform. 'We shan't get places if you stand gaping like that! Come on, stupid!' I hauled her toward the train, and seeing an extra box-car being hitched on in front, rushed in its direction.

'Gently, gently, Vania!' cried my companion in genuine distress as I lifted her bodily and landed her on the dirty floor. '*Ne zieval*!' I cried. '*Sadyis*! *Na, beri mieshotchek*! Don't yawn! Get in! Here, take the bag!' and while I clambered up, I handed her the packet of sandwiches made by Maria for the journey. 'If anything happens,' I whispered in English when we were safely ensconced, 'we are "speculators" – looking for milk; that's what nearly everybody here is doing.'

The compact seething mass of beings struggling to squirm into the car resembled a swarm of hiving bees, and in a few moments the place was packed like a sardine-box. In vain late arrivals endeavoured, headforemost, to burrow a path inward. In vain some dozens of individuals pleaded to the inmates to squeeze 'just a little tighter' and make room 'for just one more'. Somehow the doors were slid to, and we sat in the pitch darkness and waited.

Though the car must have held nearly a hundred people, once we were encased conversation ceased completely; scarcely any one spoke, and if they did it was in undertones. Until the train started, the silence, but for audible breathing, was uncanny. Only a boy, sitting next to my companion, coughed during the whole journey – coughed rackingly and incessantly, nearly driving me mad. After a while a candle was produced, and round the flickering light at one end of the car some Finns began singing folk-songs. A few people tumbled out at wayside stations, and four hours later when we arrived at Grusino, the car was only three quarters full.

It was nearly midnight. Animality surged from the train and dispersed rapidly into the woods in all directions. I took my companion, as Marsh had directed, along a secluded path in the wrong direction. A few minutes later we turned, and crossing the rails a little above the platform, took the forest track that led to Fita's house.

Fita was a Finn, the son of a peasant who had been shot by the Bolsheviks for 'speculation'. While Fita was always rewarded for his services as guide, his father's death was a potent incentive to him to do whatever lay in his power to help those who were fleeing from his parent's murderers. Eventually he was discovered in this occupation, and suffered the same fate as his father, being shot 'for conspiring against the proletarian dictatorship'. He was only sixteen years of age, very simple and shy, but courageous and enterprising.

We had an hour to wait at Fita's cottage, and while Mrs Marsh lay down to rest I took the boy aside to speak about the journey and question him as to four other people, obviously fugitives like ourselves, whom we found in his house.

'Which route are we going by,' I asked, 'north or west?'

'North,' he answered. 'It is much longer, but when the weather is good it is not difficult walking and is the safest.'

'You have the best sledge for me?'

'Yes, and the best horse.'

'These other people, who are they?'

'I don't know. The man is an officer. He came inquiring in these parts three days ago and the peasants directed him to me. I promised to help him.'

Besides the Russian officer, clad in rough working clothes, there was a lady who spoke French, and two pretty girls of about 15 and 17 years of age. The girls were dressed rather *à la turcque*, in brown woollen jerkins and trousers of the same material. They showed no trace of nervousness, and both looked as though they were thoroughly enjoying a jolly adventure. They spoke to the officer in Russian and to the lady in French, and I took it that she was a governess and he an escort.

We drove out from Fita's cottage at one o'clock. The land through which the Russian frontier passes west of Lake Ladoga is forest and morass, with few habitations. In winter the morass freezes and is covered with deep snow. The next stage of our journey ended at a remote hut five miles from the frontier on the Russian side, the occupant of which, likewise a Finnish peasant, was to conduct us on foot through the woods to the first Finnish village, ten miles beyond. The night was a glorious one. The day's storm had completely abated. Huge white clouds floated slowly across the full moon, and the air was still. The fifteen-mile sleigh-drive from Fita's cottage to the peasant's hut, over hill and dale, by sideways and occasionally straight across the marshes when outposts had to be avoided, was one of the most beautiful I have ever experienced – even in Russia.

In a large open clearance of the forest stood three or four rude huts, with tumbledown outhouses, black, silent, and fairy-picturesque, throwing blue shadows on the dazzling snow. The driver knocked at one of the doors. After much waiting it was opened, and we were admitted by an old peasant and his wife, obviously torn from their slumbers.

We were joined a quarter of an hour later by the other party, exchanging, however, no civilities or signs of recognition. When the peasant had dressed we set out.

Deserting the track-roadway almost immediately, we launched into the deep snow across the open ground, making directly for the forest. Progress was retarded by the soft snow-drifts into which our feet sank as high as the knees, and for the sake of the ladies we had to make frequent halts. Winding in and out of the forest, avoiding tracks, and skirting open spaces, it seemed an interminable time before we arrived anywhere near the actual frontier line.

Mrs Marsh and the French lady patched up a chatting acquaintance, and during one of our halts, while the girls were lying outstretched on the snow, I asked her if the French lady had told her who our companions were. But the French lady, it appeared, would not say, until we had actually crossed the frontier.

I was astonished at the manner in which Mrs Marsh

stood the strain of our night adventure. She had been
in prison nearly a month, living on the scanty and atrocious
prison food, subjected to long, nerve-racking, and searching
cross-examinations, yet she bore up better than any of the
other females in our party, and after rest-halts was always the
first to be ready to restart. There were ditches to cross and
narrow, rickety bridges to be traversed. Once our guide, laden
with parcels, suddenly vanished, sinking completely into an
invisible dyke which had filled with snowdrift. He scrambled
up the other side all wet from the water into which he had
plunged through the thin ice. The snow was so soft that we
could find no foothold to jump, and it looked as if there were
no means of crossing except as our poor guide had done, until
the idea occurred to me that by sprawling on my stomach the
snowdrift might not collapse. So, planting my feet as deeply
as I could, I threw myself across, digging with my hands into
the other side till I got a grip, and thus forming a bridge. Mrs
Marsh walked tentatively across my back, the drift still held, the
others followed. I wriggled over on my stomach, and we all got
over dry.

At last we arrived at a dyke about eight or ten feet broad,
filled with water and only partially frozen over. A square white-
and-black post on its bank showed that we were at the frontier.
'The outposts are a mile away on either hand,' whispered our
peasant-guide. 'We must get across as quickly as possible.'

The dyke lay across a clearance in the forest. We walked
along it, looking wistfully at the other bank ten feet away, and
searching for the bridge our guide said should be somewhere
here. All at once a black figure emerged from the trees a
hundred yards behind us. We stood stock-still, expecting others
to appear, and ready, if attacked, to jump into the dyke and
reach the other bank at all costs. Our guide was the most terrified of the party, but the black figure turned out only to be a
peasant acquaintance of his from another village, who told us
there was a bridge at the other end of the clearance.

The 'bridge' we found to be a rickety plank, ice-covered and slippery, that threatened to give way as each one of us stepped on to it. One by one we crossed it, expecting it every moment to collapse, and stood in a little group on the farther side.

'This is Finland,' observed our guide, laconically, 'that is the last you will see of *Sovdepia*.' He used an ironical popular term for Soviet Russia constructed from the first syllables of the words Soviets of Deputies.

The moment they set foot on Finnish soil the two girls crossed themselves devoutly and fell on their knees. Then we moved up to a fallen tree-trunk some distance away and sat down to eat sandwiches.

'It's all right for you,' the peasant went on, suddenly beginning to talk. 'You're out of it, but I've got to go back.' He had scarcely said a word the whole time, but once out of Russia, even though '*Sovdepia*' was but a few yards distant, he felt he could say what he liked. And he did. But most of the party paid but little attention to his complaints against the hated '*Kommuna*'. That was now all behind.

It was easy work from thence onward. There was another long walk through deep snow, but we could lie down as often as we pleased without fear of discovery by Red patrols. We should only have to report to the nearest Finnish authorities and ask for an escort until we were identified. We all talked freely now – no longer in nervous whispers – and everyone had some joke to tell that made everybody else laugh. At one of our halts Mrs Marsh whispered in my ear, 'They are the daughters of the Grand Duke Paul Alexandrovitch, the Tsar's uncle, who was imprisoned the other day.'

The girls were his daughters by morganatic marriage. I thought little of them at the time, except that they were both very pretty and very tastefully dressed in their sporting costumes. But I was reminded of them a few weeks later when I was back in Petrograd. Without trial, their father was shot one night in the fortress of St. Peter and St. Paul, and his body, together with other near relatives of the murdered Tsar, was thrown into a common and unmarked grave.

The incident did not impress me as it did some, for in the revolutionary tornado those of high estate pass like chaff before the wind. I could not but feel more for the hundreds less known and less fortunate who were unable to flee and escape the cruel scythe of revolution. Still, I was glad the young girls I had travelled with were no longer in the place called *Sovdepia*. How, I wondered, would they learn of the grim tragedy of the gloomy fortress? Who would tell them? To whom would fall the bitter lot to say: 'Your father was shot for bearing the name he bore – shot, not in fair fight, but like a dog, by a gang of Letts and Chinese hirelings, and his body lies none knows where'? And I was glad it was not I.

Chapter IV

Meshes

'**W**hy, yes, Maria!' I exclaimed, 'the way Mrs Marsh bore up was just wonderful to see! Twelve miles in deep snow, heavy marching through thickets and scrub, over ditches and dykes, stumps and pit-falls, with never a word of complaint, just like a picnic! You'd never have dreamt she was just out of prison.'

'Yes, of course,' said Maria, proudly, 'that would be just like her. And where is she now, Ivan Ilitch?'

'On the way to England, I guess.'

I was back again in Red Petrograd after a brief stay in Finland. That little country was supposed to be the headquarters of the Russian counter-revolution, which meant that everyone who had a plan to overthrow the Bolsheviks (and there were almost as many plans as there were patriots) conspired with as much noise as possible to push it through to the detriment of everybody else's. So tongues wagged fast and viciously, and any old cock-and-bull story about anybody else was readily believed, circulated, and shouted abroad. You got it published if you could, and if you couldn't (the papers, after all, had to set some limits), then you printed it yourself in the form of a libellous pamphlet. I felt a good deal safer in Petrograd, where I was thrown entirely on my own resources, than in Helsingfors, where the appearance of a stranger in a café or restaurant in almost anybody's company was sufficient to set the puppets of a rival faction in commotion, like an ant nest when a stone is dropped on it.

So I hid, stayed at a room in a private house, bought my own food or frequented insignificant restaurants, and was glad when I was given some money for expenses and could return to my friends Maria, Stepanovna, the Journalist, and others in Petrograd. 'How did you get back here, Ivan Ilitch?' 'Same old way, Maria. Black night. Frozen river. Deep snow. Everything around – bushes, trees, meadows – still and gray-blue in the starlight. Finnish patrols kept guard as before – lent me a white sheet, too, to wrap myself up in. Sort of cloak of invisibility, like in the fairy tales. So while the Finns watched through the bushes, I shuffled across the river, looking like Caesar's ghost.'

Maria was fascinated. 'And did nobody see you?' 'Nobody, Maria. To make a good story I should have knocked at the door of the Red patrol and announced myself as the spirit of His Late Imperial Majesty, returned to wreak vengeance, shouldn't I? But I didn't. Instead of that I threw away the sheet and took a ticket to Petrograd. Very prosaic, wasn't it? I'll have some more tea, please.'

I found a new atmosphere developing in the city which is proudly entitled the 'Metropolis of the World Revolution'. Simultaneously with the increasing shortage of food and fuel and the growing embitterment of the masses, new tendencies were observable on the part of the ruling Communist Party. Roughly, these tendencies might be classed as political or administrative, social, and militarist.

Politically the Communist Party was being driven in view of popular discontent to tighten its control by every means on all branches of administrative function in the country. Thus the people's cooperative societies and trade unions were gradually being deprived of their liberties and independence and the 'boss' system under Communist bosses was being introduced. At the same time elections had to be strictly 'controlled',' that is, manipulated in such a way that only Communists got elected.

As an off-set to this, it was evident the Communists were beginning to realize that political 'soundness' (that is, public confession of the Communist creed) was a bad substitute for administrative ability. The premium on ignorance was being replaced by a premium on intelligence and training, and bourgeois 'specialists' of every calling, subject to rigid Communist control, were being encouraged to resume their avocations or accept posts with remunerative pay under the Soviet Government. Only two conditions were required, namely, that the individual renounce all claim to former property and all participation in politics. These overtures were made particularly to members of the liberal professions, doctors, nurses, matrons, teachers, actors, and artists, but also to industrial and commercial experts, and even landlords who were trained agriculturalists. Thus was established a compromise with the bourgeoisie.

No people in the world are so capable of heroic and self-sacrificing labour for purely altruistic motives as a certain type of Russian. I remember in the summer of 1918, when the persecution of the intelligentsia was at its height, drawing attention in an official report to the remarkable fact of the large number of educated Russians who had heroically stuck to their posts and were struggling in the face of adversity to save at least something from the general wreck. Such individuals might be found at times even within the ranks of 'the party', but they cared little for the silly politics of Bolshevism and nothing whatever for the world revolution. Credit is due to the Communists at least to this extent, that they realized ultimately the value of such humane service, and, when they discovered it, encouraged it, especially if the credit for it accrued to themselves. The work done by heroic individuals of this type served largely to counterbalance the psychological effect of ever-increasing political and industrial slavery, and it has therefore been denounced as 'treacherous' by some counter-revolutionary émigrés, and especially by those in whose eyes the alleviation of the bitter lot of the Russian people was a minor detail compared with the task of restoring themselves to the seat of power.

The third growing tendency, the militarist, was the most interesting, and, incidentally, to me the most embarrassing. The stimulus to build a mighty Red army for world-revolutionary purposes was accentuated by the pressing need of mobilizing

forces to beat off the counter-revolutionary, or 'White', armies
gathering on the outskirts of Russia, particularly in the south
and east. The call for volunteers was a complete failure from
the start, except in so far as people joined the Red army
with the object of getting bigger rations until being sent to the
front, and then deserting at the first opportunity. So mobilization orders increased in frequency and stringency and until I
got some settled occupation I had to invent expedients to keep
my passport papers up to date.

My friends the Finnish patrols had furnished me with
a renewed document better worded than the last and with a
later date, so I left the old one in Finland and now keep it as
a treasured relic. As a precautionary measure I changed my
name to Joseph Krylenko. But the time was coming when even
those employees of the Extraordinary Commission who were
not indispensable might be subject to mobilization. The Tsarist
police agents, of course, and Chinese and other foreign hirelings, who eavesdropped and spied in the factories and public
places, were indispensable, but the staff of clerical employees,
one of whom I purported to be, might be cut down. So I had
somehow to get a document showing I was exempt from military service.

It was Zorinsky who helped me out. I called him up the day
after my return, eager to have news of Melnikoff. He asked me
to come round to dinner and I deliberated with myself whether,
having told him I expected to go to Moscow, I should let him
know I had been to Finland. I decided to avoid the subject and
say nothing at all.

Zorinsky greeted me warmly. So did his wife. As we seated
ourselves at the dinner table I noticed there was still no lack
of comestibles, though Elena Ivanovna of course complained.

'Your health, Pavel Ivanitch,' exclaimed Zorinsky as usual,
'glad to see you back. How are things over there?'

'Over where?' I queried.

'Why, in Finland, of course.'

So he knew already! It was a good thing for me that I had devoted a deal of thought to the enigmatical personality of my companion. I could not make him out. Personally, I disliked him intensely, yet he had already been of considerable service and in any case I needed his assistance to effect Melnikoff's release. On one occasion he had mentioned, in passing, that he knew Melnikoff's friend Ivan Sergeievitch, so it had been my intention to question the latter on the subject while in Finland, but he was away and I had seen no one else to ask. The upshot of my deliberations was that I resolved to cultivate Zorinsky's acquaintance for my own ends, but until I knew him better never to betray any true feelings of surprise, fear, or satisfaction.

Disconcerted, therefore, as I was by his knowledge of my movements, I managed to divert my undeniable confusion into an expression of disgust.

'Rotten,' I replied with a good deal of emphasis, and, incidentally, of truth. 'Absolutely rotten. If people here think Finland is going to do anything against the Bolsheviks they are mistaken. I never saw such a mess-up of factions and feuds in my life.'

'But is there plenty to eat there?' put in Elena Ivanovna, this being the sole subject that interested her.

'Oh, yes, there is plenty to eat,' and to her delight and envy I detailed a comprehensive list of delicacies unobtainable in Russia even by the theatrical world.

'It is a pity you did not let me put you across the bridge at Bielo'ostrof,' observed Zorinsky, referring to his offer to assist me in getting across the frontier.'

'Oh, it was all right,' I said. 'I had to leave at a moment's notice. It was a long and difficult walk, but not unpleasant.'

'I could have put you across quite simply,' he said, '—both of you.'

'Who "both of us"?'

'Why, you and Mrs Marsh, of course.'

Phew! So he knew that, too!

'You seem to know a lot of things,' I remarked, as casually as I could.

'It is my hobby,' he replied, with his crooked, cynical smile. 'You are to be congratulated, I must say, on Mrs Marsh's escape. It was, I believe, very neatly executed. You didn't do it yourself, I suppose?'

'No,' I said, 'and, to tell the truth, I have no idea how it was done.' I was prepared to swear by all the gods that I knew nothing of the affair.

'Nor have they any idea at *No. 2 Goróhovaya*,' he said. 'At least, so I am told.' He appeared not to attach importance to the matter. 'By the way,' he continued a moment later, 'I want to warn you against a fellow I have heard Marsh was in touch with. Alexei – Alexei – what's his name? – Alexei Fomitch something-or-other – I've forgotten the surname.'

The Policeman!

'Ever met him?'

'Never heard of him,' I said, indifferently.

'Look out if you do,' said Zorinsky, 'he is a German spy.'

'Any idea where he lives?' I inquired, in the same tone.

'No, he is registered under a pseudonym, of course. But he doesn't interest me. I chanced to hear of him the other day and thought I would caution you.'

Was it mere coincidence that Zorinsky mentioned the Policeman? I resolved to venture a query.

'Any connection between Mrs Marsh and this – er – German spy?' I asked, casually.

'Not that I know of.' For a moment a transitory flash appeared in his eyes. 'You really think Mrs Marsh was ignorant of how she escaped?' he added.

'I am positive. She hadn't the faintest notion.'

Zorinsky was thoughtful. We changed the subject, but after a while he approached it again.

'It is impertinent of me to ask questions,' he said, courteously, 'but I cannot help being abstractly interested in your chivalrous rescue of Mrs Marsh. I scarcely expect you to answer, but I should, indeed, be interested to know how you learned she was free.'

'Why, very simply,' I replied. 'I met her quite by chance at a friend's house and offered to escort her across the frontier.'

Zorinsky relapsed, and the subject was not mentioned again. Though it was clear he had somehow established a connection in his mind between the Policeman's name and that of Mrs Marsh, my relief was intense to find him now on the wrong tack and apparently indifferent to the subject.

As on the occasion of my first visit to this interesting personage, I became so engrossed in subjects he introduced that I completely forgot Melnikoff, although the latter had been uppermost in my thoughts since I successfully landed Mrs Marsh in Finland. Nor did the subject recur to mind until Zorinsky himself broached it.

'Well, I have lots of news for you,' he said as we moved into the drawing room for coffee. 'In the first place, Vera Alexandrovna's café is rounded up and she's under lock and key.'

He imparted this information in an indifferent tone.

'Are you not sorry for Vera Alexandrovna?' I said.

'Sorry? Why should one be? She was a nice girl, but foolish to keep a place like that, with all those stupid old fogeys babbling aloud like chatterboxes. It was bound to be found out.'

I recalled that this was exactly what I had thought about the place myself.

'What induced *you* to frequent it?' I asked.

'Oh, just for company,' he replied. 'Sometimes one found someone to talk to. Lucky I was not there. The Bolsheviks got quite a haul, I am told, something like twenty people. I just happened to miss, and should have walked right into the trap next day had I not chanced to find out just in time.'

My misgivings, then, regarding Vera's secret café had been correct, and I was thankful I had fought shy of the place after my one visit. But I felt very sorry for poor Vera Alexandrovna.

I was still thinking of her when Zorinsky thrust a big blue sheet of oil paper into my hands.

'What do you think of that?' he asked.

The paper was a pen-sketch of the Finnish Gulf, but for some time I could make neither head nor tail of the geometrical designs which covered it. Only when I read in the corner the words *Fortress of Cronstadt, Distribution of Mines*, did I realize what the map really was.

'Plan of the minefields around Cronstadt and in the Finnish Gulf,' explained Zorinsky. The mines lay in inner and outer fields and the course was shown which a vessel would have to take to pass through safely. The plan proved subsequently to be quite correct.

'How did you get hold of it?' I asked, interested and amused.

'Does it matter?' he said. 'There is generally a way to do these things. That is the original. If you would like to make a copy of it, you must do so tonight. It must be returned to its locked drawer in the Admiralty not later than half-past nine tomorrow morning.'

A few days later I secured through my regular admiralty connections whom I met at the Journalist's confirmation of this distribution of mines. They could not procure me the map, but they gave a list of the latitudes and longitudes, which tallied precisely with those shown on Zorinsky's plan.

While I was still examining the scheme of minefields my companion produced two further papers and asked me to glance at them. I found them to be official certificates of exemption from military service on the ground of heart trouble, filled up with details, date of examination (two days previously), signatures of the officiating doctor, who was known to me by name, the doctor's assistant, and the proxy of the controlling commissar. One was filled out in the name of Zorinsky. The other was complete – except for the name of the holder! A close examination and comparison of the signatures convinced me they were genuine. This was exactly the certificate I so much needed to avoid mobilization and I began to think Zorinsky a genius – an evil genius, perhaps, but still a genius!

'One for each of us,' he observed, laconically. 'The doctor is a good friend of mine. I needed one for myself, so I thought I might as well get one for you, too. At the end of the day the doctor told the commissar's assistant he had promised to examine two individuals delayed by business half an hour later. There was no need for the official to wait, he said; if he did not mind putting his signature to the empty paper, he assured him it would be all right. He knew exactly what was the trouble with the two fellows; they were genuine cases, but their names had slipped his memory. Of course, the commissar's assistant might wait if he chose, but he assured him it was unnecessary. So the commissar's assistant signed the papers and departed. Shortly after, the doctor's assistant did the same. The doctor waited three quarters of an hour for his two cases. They did not arrive, and here are the exemption certificates. Will you fill in your name at once?'

What? *My name*! I suddenly recollected that I had never told Zorinsky what surname I was living under, nor shown him my papers, nor initiated him into any kind of personal confidence whatsoever. Nor had my reticence been accidental. At every house I frequented I was known by a different Christian name and patronymic (the Russian mode of address), and I felt intensely reluctant to disclose my assumed surname or show the passport in my possession.

The situation was one of great delicacy, however. Could I decently refuse to inscribe my name in Zorinsky's presence after the various favours he had shown me and the assistance he was lending me – especially by procuring me the very exemption certificate I so badly needed? Clearly it would be an offence. On the other hand, I could not invent another name and thus lose the document, since it would always have to be shown together with a regular passport. To gain time for reflection I picked up the certificate to examine it again.

The longer I thought the clearer I realized that, genuine though the certificate undoubtedly was, the plot had been laid deliberately to make me disclose the name under which I was living! Had it been the Journalist, or even the Policeman, I should not have hesitated, certainly not have winced as I did now. But it was Zorinsky, the clever, cynical, and mysterious Zorinsky, for whom I suddenly conceived, as I cast a sidelong glance at him, a most intense and overpowering repugnance. Zorinsky caught my sidelong glance. He was lolling in a rocking chair, with a bland expression on his malformed face as he swung forward and backward, intent on his nails. He looked up, and as our eyes met for the merest instant I saw he had not failed to note my hesitation.

I dropped into the desk chair and seized a pen.

'Certainly,' I said, 'I will inscribe my name at once. This is, indeed, a godsend.'

Zorinsky rose and stood at my side. 'You must imitate the writing,' he said. 'I am sorry I am not a draftsman to assist you.'

I substituted a pencil for the pen and began to draw my name in outline, copying letters from the hand-writing on the certificate. I rapidly detected the essentials of the handwriting, and Zorinsky applauded admiringly as I traced the words – *Joseph Krylenko*. When they were done I finished them off in ink and laid down the pen, very satisfied.

'Occupation?' queried my companion, as quietly as if he were asking the hour.

Occupation! A revolver-shot at my ear could not have startled me more than this simple but completely unexpected query! The two blank lines I took to be left for the name only, but, looking closer, I saw that the second was, indeed, intended for the holder's business or occupation. The word *zaniatia* (occupation) was not printed in full, but abbreviated – *zan.*, while these three letters were concealed by the scrawling handwriting of the line below, denoting the age 'thirty', written out in full.

I managed somehow not to jump out of my seat. 'Is it essential?' I asked. 'I have no occupation.'

'Then you must invent one,' he replied. 'You must have some sort of passport with you. What do you show the guards in the street? Copy whatever you have from that.'

Cornered! I had put my foot in it nicely. Zorinsky was inquisitive for some reason or other to learn how I was living and under what name, and had succeeded effectually in discovering part at least of what he wanted to know. There was nothing for it. I reluctantly drew my passport of the Extraordinary Commission from my pocket in order that I might copy the exact wording.

'May I see?' asked my companion, picking up the paper. I scrutinized his face as he slowly perused it. An amused smile flickered round his crooked mouth, one end of which jutted up into his cheek. 'A very nice passport, indeed,' he said, finally, looking with peculiar care at the signatures. 'It will be a long time before you land in the cells of *No. 2 Goróhovaya* if you continue like this.'

He turned the paper over. Fortunately the regulation had not yet been published rendering all 'documents of identification' invalid unless stamped by one's house committee, showing the full address. So there was nothing on the back.

'You are a pupil of Melnikoff, that is clear,' he said, laying the paper down on the desk. 'By the way, I have something to tell you about Melnikoff. But finish your writing first.'

I soon inscribed my occupation of clerk in an office of the Extraordinary Commission, adding also 'six' to the age to conform with my other papers. As I traced the letters I tried to sum up the situation. Melnikoff, I hoped, would now soon be free, but misgivings began to arise regarding my own position, which I had a disquieting suspicion had in some way become jeopardized as a result of the disclosures I had had to make that evening to Zorinsky.

When I had finished I folded the exemption certificate and put it with my passport in my pocket.

'Well, what is the news of Melnikoff?' I said.

Zorinsky was engrossed in *Pravda*, the official press organ of the Communist Party. 'I beg your pardon? Oh, yes – Melnikoff. I have no doubt he will be released, but the investigator wants the whole 60,000 roubles first.'

'That is strange,' I observed, surprised. 'You told me he would only want the second half *after* Melnikoff's release.'

'True. But I suppose now he fears he won't have time to get it, since he also will have to quit.'

'And meanwhile what guarantee have I – have we – that the investigator will fulfil his pledge?'

Zorinsky looked indifferently over the top of his newspaper.

'Guarantee? None,' he replied, in his usual laconic manner.

'Then why the devil should I throw away another 80,000 roubles on the off-chance—'

'You needn't if you don't want to,' he put in, in the same tone.

'Are you not interested in the subject?' I said, secretly indignant at his manner.

'Of course I am. But what is the use of getting on one's hind legs about it? The investigator wants his money in advance. Without it he will certainly risk nothing. With it, he may, and there's an end of it. If I were you I would pay up, if you want Melnikoff let out. What is the good of losing your first 80,000 for nothing? You won't get that back, anyway.'

I thought for a moment. It seemed to me highly improbable that a rascal investigator, having got his money, would deliberately elect to put his neck in a noose to save someone he didn't care two pins about. Was there no other means of effecting the escape? I thought of the Policeman. But with inquiries being made along one line, inquiries along a second would doubtless be detected by the first, with all sorts of undesirable complications and discoveries. An idea occurred to me.

'Can we not threaten the life of the investigator if he plays false?' I suggested.

Zorinsky considered. 'You mean hire someone to shoot

him? That would cost a lot of money and we should be in the hands of our hired assassin as much as we are now in those of our investigator, while if he were shot we should lose the last chance of saving Melnikoff. Besides, the day after we threaten the investigator's life he will decamp with the first thirty thousand in his pocket. Pay up, Pavel Ivanitch, pay up and take the chance – that's my advice.'

Zorinsky picked up his paper and went on reading.

What should I do? Faint though the chance seemed I resolved to take it, as it was the only one. I told Zorinsky I would bring him the money on the morrow.

'All right,' he said, adding thoughtfully, as he laid aside the newspaper, 'by the way, I think you were perhaps right about threatening the investigator's life. Yes. It is not a bad idea. He need not know we know we are really powerless. We will tell him he is being tracked and cannot escape us. I will see what can be done about it. You are right, after all, Pavel Ivanitch.'

Satisfied at having made this suggestion, I set about to copy the map of the minefields and then retired for the night.

Not to sleep, however. For hours I paced up and down the soft carpet, recalling every word of the evening's conversation, and trying to invent a means of making myself again independent of Zorinsky.

Would Melnikoff be released? The prospects seemed suddenly to have diminished. Meanwhile, Zorinsky knew my name, and might, for all I knew, out of sheer curiosity, be designing to discover my haunts and acquaintances. I recalled poignantly how I had been cornered that evening and forced to show him my passport.

With this train of thought I took my newly procured exemption certificate from my pocket and examined it again. Yes, it certainly was a treasure. 'Incurable heart-trouble' – that meant permanent exemption. With this and my passport, I considered, I might with comparative safety even register myself and take regular rooms somewhere on the outskirts of the town.

However, I resolved I would not do that as long as I could conveniently live in the centre of the city, moving about from house to house.

The only thing I did not like about my new 'document' was its patent newness. I have never yet seen anybody keep tidy 'documents' in Russia, the normal condition of a passport being the verge of dissolution. There was no need to reduce my certificate to that state at once, since it was only two days old, but I decided that I would at least fold and crumple it as much as my passport, which was only five days old. I took the paper and, folding it tightly in four, pressed the creases firmly between finger and thumb. Then, laying it on the table, I squeezed the folds under my thumb-nail, drawing the paper backward and forward. Finally, the creases looking no longer new, I began to ruffle the edges.

And then a miracle occurred!

You know, of course, the conundrum: 'Why is paper money preferable to coin?' – the answer being, 'Because when you put it in your pocket you double it, and when you take it out you find it in creases.' Well, that is what literally did occur with my exemption certificate! While holding it in my hands and ruffling the edges, the paper all at once appeared to move of itself, and, rather like protozoa propagating its species, most suddenly and unexpectedly divided, revealing to my astonished eyes not one exemption certificate – *but two*!

Two of the printed sheets had by some means become so closely stuck together that it was only when the edges were ruffled that they fell apart, and neither the doctor nor Zorinsky had noted it. Here was the means of eluding Zorinsky by filling in another paper! How shall I describe my joy at the unlooked-for discovery! The nervous reaction was so intense that, much to my own amusement, I found tears streaming down my cheeks. I laughed and felt like the Count of Monte Cristo unearthing his treasure – until, sobering down a little, I recollected that the blank form was quite useless until I had another passport to back it up.

That night I thrashed out my position thoroughly and determined on a line of action. Zorinsky, I reflected, was a creature whom in ordinary life I should have been inclined to shun like a pest. I record here only those incidents and conversations which bear on my story, but when not discussing 'business' he lavished a good deal of gratuitous information about his private life, particularly of regimental days, which was revolting. But in the abnormal circumstances in which I lived, to 'cut' with anybody with whom I had once formed a close association was very difficult, and in Zorinsky's case doubly so. Suppose he saw me in the street afterward, or heard of me through any of his numerous connections? Pursuing his 'hobby' of *contre-espionage* he would surely not fail to follow the movements of a star of the first magnitude like myself. There was no course open but to remain on good terms and profit to the full by the information I obtained from him and the people I occasionally met at his house – information which proved to be invariably correct. But he must learn nothing of my other movements, and in this respect I felt the newly discovered blank exemption form would surely be of service. I had only to procure another passport from somewhere or other.

What was Zorinsky's real attitude toward Melnikoff, I wondered? How well had they known each other? If only I had some means of checking – but I knew none of Melnikoff's connections in Russia. He had lived at a hospital. He had spoken of a doctor friend. I had already twice seen the woman at the lodge to which he had directed me. I thought hard for a moment.

Yes, good idea! On the morrow I would resort once more to Melnikoff's hospital on The Islands, question the woman again, and, if possible, seek an interview with the doctor. Perhaps he could shed light on the matter. Thus deciding, I threw myself dressed on the bed and fell asleep.

Chapter V

Melnikoff

Some three weeks later, on a cold Sunday morning in January, I sat in the Doctor's study at his small flat in one of the big houses at the end of the Kamenostrovsky Prospect. The news had just arrived that the German Communist leaders, Karl Liebknecht and Rosa Luxembourg, had been killed in Berlin, the former in attempted flight, the latter mobbed by an incensed crowd. Nobody in Russia had any idea who these two people were, but their deaths caused consternation in the Communist camp, for they had been relied upon to pull off a Red revolution in Germany and thus accelerate the wave of Bolshevism westward across Europe.

Little known as Liebknecht and Luxembourg had been outside Germany until the time of their death, in the hierarchy of Bolshevist saints they were placed second only to Karl Marx and Engels, the Moses and Aaron of the Communist Party. Russians are noted for their veneration of icons, representing to them the memory of saintly lives, but their religious devotion is equalled by that of the Bolsheviks. Though he does not cross himself, the true Bolshevik bows down in spirit to the images of Marx and kindred revolutionists with an obsequiousness unexcelled by devotees of the church. The difference in the two creeds lies in this: that whereas the orthodox Christian venerates saintly lives according to their degree of unworldliness, individual goodness, and spiritual sanctity, the Bolsheviks revere their saints for the vehemence with which they promoted the class war, fomented discontent, and preached world-wide revolution.

To what extent humanity suffered as the result of the decease of the two German Communists, I am unable to judge, but their loss was regarded by the revolutionary leaders as a catastrophe of the first magnitude. The official press had heavy headlines about it, and those who read the papers asked one another who the two individuals could have been. Having studied the revolutionary movement to some extent, I was better able to appreciate the mortification of the ruling party, and was therefore interested in the great public demonstration announced for that day in honour of the dead.

My new friend the Doctor was both puzzled and amused by my attitude.

'I can understand your being here as an intelligence officer,' he said. 'After all, your Government has to have someone to keep them informed, though it must be unpleasant for you. But why you should take it into your head to go rushing round to all the silly meetings and demonstrations the way you do is beyond me. And the stuff you read! You have only been here three or four times, but you have left a train of papers and pamphlets enough to open a propaganda department.'

The Doctor, who I learned from the woman at the lodge was Melnikoff's uncle, was a splendid fellow. As a matter of fact, he had sided wholeheartedly with the revolution in March, 1917, and held very radical views, but he thought more than spoke about them. His nephew, Melnikoff, on the contrary, together with a considerable group of officers, had opposed the revolution from the outset, but the Doctor had not quarrelled with them, realizing one cardinal truth the Bolsheviks appear to fail to grasp, namely, that the criterion whereby men must ultimately be judged is not politics, but character.

The Doctor had a young and very intelligent friend named Shura, who had been a bosom friend of Melnikoff's. Shura was a law student. He resembled the Doctor in his radical sympathies but differed from both him and Melnikoff in that he was given to philosophizing and probing deeply beneath the surface of things. Many were the discussions we had together, when, some weeks later, I came to know Shura well.

'Communist speeches,' he used to say, 'often sound like a tale told by an idiot, full of sound and fury signifying nothing. But behind the interminable jargon there lie both an impulse and an ideal. The ideal is a proletarian millennium, but the impulse is not love of the worker, but hatred of the bourgeois. The Bolshevik believes if a perfect proletarian state be forcibly established by destroying the bourgeoisie, the perfect proletarian citizen will automatically result! There will be no crime, no prisons, no need of government. But by persecuting liberals and denying freedom of thought the Bolsheviks are driving independent thinkers into the camp of that very section of society whose provocative conduct caused Bolshevism! That is why I will fight to oust the Bolsheviks,' said Shura, 'they are impedimenta in the path of the revolution.'

It had been a strange interview when I first called on the Doctor and announced myself as a friend of Melnikoff's. He sat bolt upright, smiling affably, and obviously ready for every conceivable contingency. The last thing in the world he was prepared to do was to believe me. I told him all I could about his nephew and he evidently thought I was very clever to know so much. He was polite but categorical. No, sir, he knew nothing whatsoever of his nephew's movements, it was good of me to interest myself in his welfare, but he himself had ceased to be interested. I might possibly be an Englishman, as I said, but he had never heard his nephew mention an Englishman. He had no knowledge nor any desire for information as to his nephew's past, present, or future, and if his nephew had engaged in counter-revolutionary activities it was his own fault. I could not but admire the placidity and suavity with which he said all this, and cursed the disguise which made me look so unlike what I wanted the Doctor to see.

'Do you speak English?' I said at last, getting exasperated.

I detected a twinge – ever so slight. 'A little,' he replied.

'Then, damn it all, man,' I exclaimed in English, rising and striking my chest with my fist – rather melodramatically, it must have seemed – 'why the devil can't you see I am an Englishman and not a *provocateur*? Melnikoff must have told you something about me. Except for me he wouldn't have come back here. Didn't he tell you how we stayed together at Viborg, how he helped dress me, how he drank all my whisky, how—'

The Doctor all at once half rose from his seat. The urbane, fixed smile that had not left his lips since the beginning of the interview suddenly burst into a half-laugh.

'Was it you who gave him the whisky?' he broke in, in Russian.

'Of course it was,' I replied. 'I—'

'That settles it,' he said, excitedly. 'Sit down, I'll be back in a moment.' He left the room and walked quickly to the front door. Half suspecting treachery, I peered out into the hall and feeling for the small revolver I carried, looked round to see if there were any way of escape in an emergency. The Doctor opened the front door, stepped on to the landing, looked carefully up and down the stairs, and, returning, closed all the other doors in the hall before re-entering the cabinet. He walked over to where I stood and looked me straight in the face.

'Why on earth didn't you come before?' he exclaimed, speaking in a low voice.

‡

We rapidly became friends. Melnikoff's disappearance had been a complete mystery to him, a mystery which he had no means of solving. He had never heard of Zorinsky, but names meant nothing. He thought it strange that so high a price should be demanded for Melnikoff, and thought I had been unwise to give it all in advance under any circumstances; but he was none the less overjoyed to hear of the prospects of his release.

After every visit to Zorinsky I called on the Doctor to tell him the latest news. On this particular morning I had told him how the evening before, in a manner which I disliked intensely, Zorinsky had shelved the subject, giving evasive answers. We

had passed the middle of January already, yet apparently there
was no information whatever as to Melnikoff's case.

'There is another thing, too, that disquiets me. Doctor,'
I added. 'Zorinsky shows undue curiosity as to where I go
when I am not at his house. He happens to know the passport on which I am living, and examination of papers being
so frequent, I wish I could get another one. Have you any idea
what Melnikoff would do in such circumstances?'

The Doctor paced up and down the room.

'Would you mind telling me the name?' he asked.

I showed him all my documents, including the exemption
certificate, explaining how I had received them.

'Well, well, your Mr Zorinsky certainly is a useful friend to
have, I must say,' he observed, looking at the certificate, and
wagging his head knowingly. 'By the way, does he cost you
much, if one may ask?'

'He himself? Nothing at all, or very little. Besides the sixty
thousand for Melnikoff,' I calculated, 'I have given him a
few thousand for odd expenses connected with the case; I insist
on paying for meals; I gave his wife an expensive bouquet at
New Year with which she was very pleased; then I have given
him money for the relief of Melnikoff's sister, and—'

'For Melnikoff's sister?' ejaculated the Doctor. 'But he
hasn't got one!'

Vot tibie ná! No sister – then where did the money go? I
suddenly remembered Zorinsky had once asked if I could give
him English money. I told the Doctor.

'Look out, my friend, look out,' he said. 'Your friend is
certainly a clever and a useful man. But I'm afraid you will have
to go on paying for Melnikoff's non-existent sister. It would
not do for him to know you had found out. As for your passport, I will ask Shura. By the way,' he added, 'it is twelve o'clock.
Will you not be late for your precious demonstration?'

I hurried to leave. 'I will let you know how things go,' I said.
'I will be back in two or three days.'

The morning was a frosty one with a bitter wind. No street cars ran on Sundays and I walked into town to the Palace Square, the great space in front of the Winter Palace, famous for another January Sunday – 'Bloody Sunday' – thirteen years before. Much had been made in the press of the present occasion, and it appeared to be taken for granted that the proletariat would surge to bear testimony to their grief for the fallen German Communists. But round the base of a red-bedizened tribune in the centre of the square there clustered a mere handful of people and two rows of soldiers, stamping to keep their feet warm. The crowd consisted of the sturdy Communist veterans who organized the demonstration, and on-lookers who always join any throng to see whatever is going on.

As usual the proceedings started late, and the small but patient crowd was beginning to dwindle before the chief speakers arrived. A group of commonplace-looking individuals, standing on the tribune, lounged and smoked cigarettes, apparently not knowing exactly what to do with themselves. I pushed myself forward to be as near the speakers as possible.

To my surprise I noticed Dmitri, Stepanovna's nephew, amongst the soldiers who stood blowing on their hands and looking miserable. I moved a few steps away, so that he might not see me. I was afraid he would make some sign of recognition which might lead to questions by his comrades, and I had no idea who they might be. But I was greatly amused at seeing him at a demonstration of this sort.

At length an automobile dashed up, and amid faint cheers and to the accompaniment of bugles, Zinoviev, president of the Petrograd Soviet, alighted and mounted the tribune. Zinoviev, whose real name is Apfelbaum, is a very important person in Bolshevist Russia. He is considered one of the greatest orators of the Communist party, and now occupies the proud position of president of the Third International, the institution that is to effect the world revolution.

It is to his oratorical skill rather than any administrative ability that Zinoviev owes his prominence. His rhetoric is of a peculiar order. He is unrivalled in his appeal to the ignorant mob, but, judging by his speeches, logic is unknown to him, and on no thinking audience could he produce any impression beyond that of wonderment at his uncommon command of language, ready though cheap witticisms, and inexhaustible fund of florid and vulgar invective. Zinoviev is, in fact, the consummate gutter-demagogue. He is a coward, shirked office in November, 1917, fearing the instability of the Bolshevist *coup*, has since been chief advocate of all the insaner aspects of Bolshevism, and is always the first to lose his head and fly into a panic when danger clouds appear on any horizon.

Removing his hat Zinoviev approached the rail, and stood there in his rich fur coat until someone down below gave a signal to cheer. Then he began to speak in the following strain:

'Comrades! Wherefore are we gathered here today? What mean this tribune and this concourse of people? Is it to celebrate a triumph of world-revolution, to hail another conquest over the vicious ogre of Capitalism? Alas, no! Today we mourn the two greatest heroes of our age, murdered deliberately, brutally, and in cold blood by blackguard capitalist agents. The German Government, consisting of the social-traitor Scheidemann and other supposed Socialists, the scum and dregs of humanity, have sold themselves like Judas Iscariot for thirty shekels of silver to the German bourgeoisie, and at the command of the capitalists ordered their paid hirelings foully to murder the two chosen representatives of the German workers and peasants...' and so on.

I never listened to Zinoviev without recalling a meeting in the summer of 1917 when he was the chief speaker. He had just returned to Russia with a group of other Bolshevist leaders (very few of whom were present during the revolution) and held incendiary meetings in out-of-the-way places. He was thin and slim and looked the typical Jewish student of any Russian university. But after a year's fattening on the Russian proletariat he had swelled not only politically but physically, and his full, handsome features and flowing bushy hair spoke of anything but privation.

Contrary to custom, Zinoviev's speech was short. It must have been cold, speaking in the chilly wind, and in any case there were not many people to talk to.

The next speaker was more novel – Herr Otto Pertz, president of the German Soviet of Petrograd. Why a German Soviet continued to live and move and have its being in Petrograd, or what its functions were, nobody seemed to know. The comings and goings of *unsere deutsche Genossen* appeared to be above criticism and were always a mystery. Herr Otto Pertz was tall, clean shaven, Germanly tidy, and could not speak Russian.

'*Genossen*! *heute feiern wir*—' he began, and proceeded to laud the memory of the fallen heroes and to foretell the coming social revolution in Germany. The dastardly tyrants of Berlin, insolently styling themselves Socialists, would shortly be overthrown. *Kapitalismus, Imperialismus*, in fact everything but *Kommunismus* would be demolished. He had information that within a week or two *Spartacus* (the German Bolshevist group), with all Germany behind it, would successfully seize power in Berlin and join in a triumphant and indissoluble alliance with the Russian Socialist Federative Soviet Republic.

As Otto Pertz commenced his oration a neatly dressed little lady of about fifty, who stood at my side near the foot of the tribune, looked up eagerly at the speaker. Her eyes shone brightly and her breath came quickly. Seeing I had noticed her she said timidly, '*Spricht er nicht gut? Sagen Sie doch, spricht er nicht gut?*'

To which I of course replied, '*Sehr gut*,' and she relapsed bashfully into admiration of Otto, murmuring now and again, '*Ach! es ist doch wahr, nicht?*' with which sentiment also I would agree.

The crowd listened patiently, as the Russian crowd always listens, whoever speaks, and on whatever subject. The soldiers shivered and wondered what the speaker was talking about. His speech was not translated.

But when Otto Pertz ceased there was a commotion in the throng. For some moments I was at a loss as to what was in progress, until at last a passage was made and, borne on valiant Communist shoulders, a guy was produced, the special attraction of the day. The effigy, made of pasteboard, represented a ferocious-looking German with Kaiser-like moustachios, clothed in evening dress, and bearing across its chest in large letters on cardboard the name of the German Socialist,

SCHEIDEMANN.

At the same time an improvised gallows was thrust over the balustrade of the tribune. Amid curses, jeers, and execrations, the moustachioed effigy was raised aloft. Eager hands attached the dangling loop and there it hung, most abjectly, most melancholy, encased in evening dress and black trousers with hollow extremities flapping in the breeze.

The crowd awoke and tittered and even the soldiers smiled. Dmitri, I could see, was laughing outright. This was after all worth coming to see. Kerosene was poured on the dangling Scheidemann and he was set alight. There were laughter, howls, and fanfares. Zinoviev, in tragic pose, with uplifted arm and pointed finger, cried hoarsely, 'Thus perish traitors!' The bugles blew. The people, roused with delight, cheered lustily. Only the wretched Scheidemann was indifferent to the interest he was arousing, as with stony glare on his cardboard face he soared aloft amid sparks and ashes into eternity.

Crowd psychology, I mused as I walked away, has been an important factor on all public occasions since the revolution, but appreciated to the full only by the Bolsheviks. Everyone who was in Russia in 1917 and who attended political meetings when free speech became a possibility remembers how a speaker would get up and speak, loudly applauded by the whole audience; then another would rise and say the precise opposite, rewarded with equally vociferous approbation; followed again by a third who said something totally at variance with the first two, and how the enthusiasm would increase proportionately to the bewilderment as to who was actually right. The crowds were just like little children. Totally unaccustomed to free speech, they appeared to imagine that anybody who spoke must *ipso facto* be right. But just when the people, after the Bolshevist *coup d'état*, were beginning to demand reason in public utterance and deeds for promises, down came a super-Tsarist Bolshevist censorship like a huge candle-snuffer and clapping itself on the flame of public criticism, snuffed it out altogether.

Public demonstrations, however, were made an important item in the curriculum of the Bolshevist administration, and soon became as compulsory as military service. I record the above one not because of its intrinsic interest (it really had very little), but because it was, I believe, one of the last occasions on which it was left to the public to make the demonstration a success or not, and regiments were merely 'invited'.

I made my way to Stepanovna's in the hope of meeting Dmitri. He came in toward the close of the afternoon, and I asked him if he had enjoyed the demonstration.

'Too cold,' he replied, 'they ought to have had it on a warmer day.'

'Did you come voluntarily?'

'Why, yes.' He pulled out of the spacious pocket of his tunic a parcel wrapped up in newspaper, and unwrapping it, disclosed a pound of bread. 'We were told we should get this if we came. It has just been doled out.'

Stepanovna's eyes opened wide. Deeply interested, she asked when the next demonstration was going to be.

'Why didn't more soldiers come, then?' I asked.

'Not enough bread, I suppose,' said Dmitri. 'We have been getting it irregularly of late. But we have a new commissar who is a good fellow. They say in the regiment he gets everything for us first. He talks to us decently, too. I am beginning to like him. Perhaps he is not one like the rest.'

'By the way, Dmitri,' I said, 'do you happen to know who those people were for whom we demonstrated today?'

From the depths of his crumb-filled pocket Dmitri extracted a crumpled and soiled pamphlet. Holding it to the light he slowly read out the title: '*Who were Karl Liebknecht and Rosa Luxembourg?*'

'We were each given one yesterday,' he explained, 'after an agitator had made a long speech to us. Nobody listened to the agitator – some Jew or other – but the commissar gave me this. I read little nowadays, but I think I will read it when I have time.'

'And the speakers and the guy?' I queried.

'I didn't notice the speakers. One of them spoke not in our way – German, someone said. But the guy! That was funny! My, Stepanovna, you ought to have seen it! How it floated up into the air! You would have cracked your sides laughing. Who was it supposed to represent, by the way?'

I explained how the revolution in Germany had resulted in the downfall of the Kaiser and the formation of a radical cabinet with a Socialist – Scheidemann – at its head. Scheidemann was the guy today, I said, for reasons which I presumed he would find stated in '*Who were Karl Liebknecht and Rosa Luxembourg?*'

'But if the Kaiser is out, why do our Bolsheviks burn – what's his name?'

'Ah, but, Dmitri,' I put in, 'if you had understood the German speaker today, you would have heard him tell how there is shortly to be another revolution in Germany like that which happened here in November, 1917, and they will set up a soviet government like Lenin's.'

As our conversation proceeded, Stepanovna and Varia stopped their work to listen, their interest grew apace, and at last they hung on to every word as if it were of profound significance. When I repeated the substance of Otto Pertz's predictions, all three of my companions were listening spellbound and with mouths agape. There was a long pause, which at length Stepanovna broke.

'Is it really possible,' she exclaimed, slowly, and apparently in utter bewilderment, 'that the Germans – are – such – fools?'

‡

'Evasive, Doctor, very evasive,' I said, as we sat over tea and a few dry crust-biscuits the Doctor had procured from somewhere. 'Yesterday evening he gave me some interesting information about industrial developments, alteration of railway administration, and changes in the Red fleet; but the moment Melnikoff is mentioned then it is, "Oh, Melnikoff? in a day or two I think we may know definitely", or "My informant is out of town", and so on.'

'Perhaps there is a hitch, somewhere,' suggested the Doctor. 'I suppose there is nothing to do but wait. By the way, you wanted a passport, didn't you? How will that suit you?'

I have forgotten the precise wording of the paper he handed me, for I had to destroy it later, but it was an ordinary certificate of identification, in the name of Alexander Vasilievitch Markovitch, aged 33, clerical assistant at the head Postal-Telegraph Office. There was no photograph attached, but in view of the strict requirements regarding passports, which included their frequent renewal (except in certain cases no passports might be made out for more than two months), and the difficulty of getting photographs, the latter were dropping out of general use.

'Shura procured it,' the Doctor explained. 'A friend of his, by name Markov, arrived recently from Moscow to work at the Telegraph Office. A week later he heard his wife was seriously ill and got special permission to return. A week in Petrograd was enough for him anyway, for living is much better in Moscow, so he doesn't intend to come back. Shura asked him for his passport and after Markov had got his railroad pass and paper showing he was authorized to return to Moscow, he gave it him. If they ask for it in Moscow, he will say he has lost it. He would have to have a new one anyway, since a Petrograd one is useless there. My typewriter at the hospital has the same type as this, so we altered the date a little, added "itch" to the name – and there you are, if you wish, a ready-made postal official.'

'What about clothing?' I said. 'I don't look much like a postal official.'

'There is something more important than that. What about military service?'

From my pocket I produced a new pamphlet on the soviet system. Opening a pocket of the uncut leaves at a certain page, I drew forth my blank exemption certificate and exhibited it to the Doctor.

'What are you, a prestidigitator?' he asked admiringly. 'Or is this another gift from your friend Z.?'

'The certificates were born twins,' I said. 'Zorinsky was accoucheur to the first, I to the second.'

In an hour I had filled in the blank exemption form with all particulars relating to Alexander Vasilievitch Markovitch. Tracing the signatures carefully, and inserting a recent date, I managed to produce a document indistinguishable as regards authenticity from the original, and thus was possessed of two sets of documents, one in the name of Krylenko for the benefit of Zorinsky, the other in that of Markovitch for presentation in the streets and possible registration.

Considering once more the question of uniform I recalled that at my own rooms where I had lived for years I had left a variety of clothing when last in Petrograd six or eight months previously. The question was: how could I gain admittance to my rooms, disguised as I was and with an assumed name? Furthermore, a telephone call having elicited no response, I had no idea whether the housekeeper whom I had left was still there, nor whether the apartment had been raided, locked up, or occupied by workmen. All these things I was curious to know, quite apart from obtaining clothing.

I enlisted the services of Varia as scout. Varia was the

first person to whom I confided my English name, and doing it with due solemnity, and with severe cautionings that not even Stepanovna should be told, I could see that the girl was impressed with my confidence in her. Armed with a brief note to my housekeeper purporting to be written by a fictitious friend of mine, and warned to turn back unless everything were precisely as I described, Varia set out on a voyage of discovery.

She returned to impart the information that the front door of the house being locked she had entered by the yard, had encountered nobody on the backstairs, and that in answer to persistent ringing a woman, whom I recognized by the description as my housekeeper, had opened the kitchen door on a short chain, and, peering suspiciously through the chink, had at first vehemently denied any acquaintance with any English people at all. On perusing the note from my non-existent friend, however, she admitted that an Englishman of my name had formerly lived there, but she had the strictest injunctions from him to admit nobody to the flat.

Pursuing my instructions, Varia informed the housekeeper that my friend, Mr Markovitch, had just arrived from Moscow. He was busy today, she said, and had sent her round to enquire after my affairs, but would call himself at an early opportunity.

The one article of clothing which I frequently changed and of which I had a diverse stock was headgear. It is surprising how headdress can impart character (or the lack of it) to one's appearance. Donning my most bourgeois fur-cap, polishing my leather breeches and brushing my jacket, I proceeded on the following day to my former home, entering by the yard as Varia had done and ringing at the back door. The house appeared deserted, for I saw no one in the yard, nor heard any sounds of life. When, in reply to persistent ringing, the door was opened on the chain, I saw my housekeeper peering through the chink just as Varia had described. My first impulse was to laugh, it seemed so ridiculous to be standing on one's own back stairs, pretending to be someone else, and begging admittance to one's own rooms by the back door.

I hadn't time to laugh, however. The moment my house-keeper saw the apparition on the stairway she closed the door again promptly and rebolted it, and it was only after a great deal of additional knocking and ringing that at last the door was once again timidly opened just a tiny bit.

Greeting the woman courteously, I announced myself as Mr Markovitch, close personal friend and school companion of the Englishman who formerly had occupied these rooms. My friend, I said, was now in England and regretted the impossibility of returning to Russia under present conditions. I had recently received a letter from him, I declared, brought somehow across the frontier, in which, sending his greetings to Martha Timofeievna (the housekeeper), he had requested me at the earliest opportunity to visit his home and report on its condition. To reduce Martha Timofeievna's suspicions, I assured her that before the war I had been a frequent visitor to this flat, and gave numerous data which left no doubt what-soever in her mind that I was at least well acquainted with the arrangement of the rooms, and with the furniture and pictures that had formerly been in them. I added, of course, that on the last occasion when I had seen my friend, he had spoken of his new housekeeper in terms of the highest praise, and assured me again in his letter that I should find her good-mannered, hospitable, and obliging.

The upshot was that, though Martha Timofeievna was at first categorical in her refusal to admit anyone to the flat, she ultimately agreed to do so if I could show her the actual letter written by 'Monsieur Dukes', requesting permission for his friend to be admitted.

I told her I would bring it to her that very afternoon, and, highly satisfied with the result of the interview, I retired at once to the nearest convenient place, which happened to be the Journalist's, to write it.

'Dear Sasha,' I wrote in Russian, using the familiar name for Alexander (my Christian name according to my new papers), 'I can scarcely hope you will ever receive this, yet on the chance that you may—etc.,' – and I proceeded to give a good deal of imaginary family news. Toward the end I said, 'By the way, when you are in Petrograd, please go to my flat and see Martha Timofeievna—etc.,' and I gave instructions as to what 'Sasha' was to do, and permission to take anything he needed. 'I write in Russian,' I concluded, 'so that in case of necessity you may show this letter to M. T. She is a good woman and will do everything for you. Give her my hearty greetings and tell her I hope to return at the first opportunity. Write if ever you can. Goodbye. Yours ever, Pavlusha.'

I put the letter in an envelope, addressed it to 'Sasha Markovitch', sealed it up, tore it open again, crumpled it, and put it in my pocket.

The same afternoon I presented myself once more at my back door. Martha Timofeievna's suspicions had evidently already been considerably allayed, for she smiled amiably even before perusing the letter I put into her hand, and at once admitted me as far as the kitchen. Here she laboriously read the letter through (being from the Baltic provinces she spoke Russian badly and read with difficulty), and, paying numerous compliments to the author, who she hoped would soon return because she didn't know what she was going to do about the flat or how long she would be able to keep on living there, she led me into the familiar rooms.

Everything was in a state of confusion. Many of the pictures were torn down, furniture was smashed, and in the middle of the floor of the dining room lay a heap of junky consisting of books, papers, pictures, furniture, and torn clothing. In broken Russian Martha Timofeievna told me how first there had been a search, and when she had said that an Englishman had lived there the Reds had prodded and torn everything with their bayonets. Then a family of working people had taken possession,

fortunately, however, not expelling her from her room. But the
flat had not been to their liking and, deserting it soon after,
they took a good many things with them and left everything
else upside down.

Between them, the Reds and the uninvited occupants had
left very little that could be of use to me. I found no boots or
overclothing, but amongst the litter I discovered some under-
clothing of which I was glad. I also found an old student hat,
which was exactly what I wanted for my postal uniform. I put it
in my pocket and, tying the other things in a parcel, said I would
send Varia for them next day.

While I was disentangling with my housekeeper's aid the
heap of stuff on the floor I came upon my own photograph
taken two or three years before. For the first time I fully and
clearly realized how complete was my present disguise, how
absolutely different I now appeared in a beard, long hair, and
glasses. I passed the photo to Martha Timofeievna.

'That is a good likeness,' I said. 'He hasn't altered one bit.'

'Yes,' she replied. 'Was he not a nice man? It is dreadful
that he had to go away. I wonder where he is now and what he
is doing?'

'I wonder,' I repeated, diving again into the muck on the
floor. To save my life I could not have looked at Martha
Timofeievna at that moment and kept a straight face.

Failing to obtain an overcoat from the remnant of my
belongings, I searched the markets and from a destitute gentleman of aristocratic mien procured a shabby black coat with
a worn velvet collar. In this and my student hat I was the
'complete postal official'. I adopted this costume for daytime
purposes, but before every visit to Zorinsky I went to 'No. 5',
where I kept what few belongings I possessed, and changed,
visiting Zorinsky only in the attire in which he was accustomed
to see me.

As the end of January approached my suspicion that
Zorinsky would not secure Melnikoff's release grew. Once or

twice he had not even mentioned the subject, talking energetically in his usual vivacious manner about other things. He was as entertaining as ever, and invariably imparted interesting political news, but if I broached the subject of Melnikoff he shelved it at once.

So I resolved, in spite of risks, to see if I could obtain through the Policeman information as to Melnikoff's case. I had not seen the Policeman since I had returned from Finland, so I told him I had been delayed in that country and had only just come back. Without telling him who Melnikoff was, I imparted to him the data regarding the latter's arrest, and what I had learned 'through accidental channels' as to his imprisonment. I did not let him know my concern, lest he should be inclined purposely to give a favourable report, but charged him to be strict and accurate in his investigation, and, in the event of failing to learn anything, not to fear to admit it.

About a week later, when I 'phoned to him, he said 'he had received an interesting letter on family matters'. It was with trepidation that I hurried to his house, struggling to conceal my eager anticipation as I mounted the stairs, followed by the gaze of the leering Chinaman.

The little Policeman held a thin strip of paper in his hand.

'Dmitri Dmitrievitch Melnikoff,' he read. 'Real name Nicholas Nicholaievitch N—?'

'Yes,' I said.

'He was shot between the 15th and 20th of January,' said the Policeman.

Chapter VI

Stepanovna

Meanwhile, as time progressed, I made new acquaintances at whose houses I occasionally put up for a night. Over most of them I pass in silence. I accepted their hospitality as a Russian emigrant who was being searched for by the Bolsheviks, a circumstance which in itself was a recommendation. But if I felt I could trust people I did not hesitate to reveal my nationality, my reception then being more cordial still. I often reflected with satisfaction that my mode of living resembled that of many revolutionists, not only during the reign of Tsarism, but also under the present regime. People of every shade of opinion from Monarchist to Socialist-Revolutionary dodged and evaded the police agents of the Extraordinary Commission, endeavouring either to flee from the country or to settle down unobserved under new names in new positions.

One of my incidental hosts whom I particularly remember, a friend of the Journalist and a school inspector by profession, was full of enterprise and enthusiasm for a scheme he propounded for including gardening and such things in the regular school curriculum of his circuit. His plans were still regarded with some mistrust by those in power, for his political prejudices were known, but he none the less had hope that the Communists would allow him to introduce his innovations, which I believe he eventually did successfully.

The Journalist was promoted to the position of *dieloproizvoditel* of his department, a post giving him a negligible rise of salary, but in which practically all official papers passed through his hands. At his own initiative he used to abstract papers he thought would be of interest to me, restoring them before their absence could be discovered. Some of the things he showed me were illuminating, others useless. But good, bad, or indifferent, he always produced them with a sly look and with his finger at the side of his nose, as if the information they contained must be of the utmost consequence.

I persuaded him to sell off some of his books as a subsidiary means of subsistence, and we called a Jew in, who haggled long and hard. The Journalist was loath to do this, but I refused ever to give him more than the cost of his fuel, over which also I exerted a control of Bolshevist severity. He had no conception whatever of relative values, and attached though he was to me I thought I sometimes detected in his eye a look which said with unspeakable contempt: 'You miserly Englishman!'

I was unfortunate in losing Maria as a regular companion and friend. She returned to Marsh's country farm in the hope of saving at least something from destruction, and visited town but rarely. In her place there came to live at the empty flat 'No. 5' the younger of the two stable boys, a dull but decent youth who had not joined the looters. This boy did his best no doubt to keep things in order, but tidiness and cleanliness were not his peculiar weaknesses. He could not understand why glasses or spoons should be washed, or why even in an untenanted flat tables and chairs should occasionally be dusted. Once, the tea he had made me tasting unusually acrid, I went into the kitchen to investigate the tea-pot. On removing the lid I found it to be half full of dead beetles.

Stepanovna continued to be a good friend. Dmitri's regiment was removed to a town in the interior, and Dmitri, reluctant though he was to leave the capital, docilely followed, influenced largely by the new regimental commissar who had succeeded in making himself popular – a somewhat rare achievement amongst commissars. Even Stepanovna admitted this unusual circumstance, allowing that the commissar was a *poriadotchny tcheloviek* i.e., a decent person, 'although he was a Communist', and she thus acquiesced in Dmitri's departure.

It was in Stepanovna's company that I first witnessed the extraordinary spectacle of an armed raid by the Bolshevist authorities on a public market. Running across her in the busy Siennaya Square one morning I found she had been purchasing meat, which was a rare luxury. She had an old black shawl over her head and carried a basket on her arm.

'Where did you get the meat?' I asked. 'I will buy some too.'

'Don't,' she said, urgently. 'In the crowd they are whispering that there is going to be a raid.'

'What sort of a raid?'

'On the meat, I suppose. Yesterday and today the peasants have been bringing it in and I have got a little. I don't want to lose it. They say the Reds are coming.'

Free-trading being clearly opposed to the principles of Communism, it was officially forbidden and denounced as 'speculation'. But no amount of restriction could suppress it, and the peasants brought food in to the hungry townspeople despite all obstacles and sold it at their own prices. The only remedy the authorities had for this 'capitalist evil' was armed force, and even that was ineffective.

The meat was being sold by the peasants in a big glass-covered shed. One of these sheds was burned down in 1919, and the only object that remained intact was an icon in the corner. Thousands came to see the icon that had been 'miraculously' preserved, but it was hastily taken away by the authorities. The icon had apparently been overlooked, for it was the practice of the Bolsheviks to remove all religious symbols from public places.

I moved toward the building to make my purchase, but Stepanovna tugged me by the arm.

'Don't be mad,' she exclaimed. 'Don't you realize, if there is a raid they will arrest everybody?'

She pulled me down to speak in my ear.

'And what about your... I am sure ... your papers ... are...'

'Of course they are,' I laughed. 'But you don't expect a clown of a Red guard to see the difference, do you?'

I made up my mind to get rid of Stepanovna and come back later for some meat, but all at once a commotion arose in the crowd over the way and people began running out of the shed. Round the corner, from the side of the Ekaterina Canal, appeared a band of soldiers in sheepskin caps and brown-gray tunics, with fixed bayonets. The exits from the building were quickly blocked. Fugitives fled in all directions, the women shrieking and hugging their baskets and bundles and looking back as they ran to see if they were pursued.

Stepanovna and I stood on a doorstep at the corner of the Zabalkansky Prospect, where we could see well, and whence, if need be, we could also make good our escape.

The market place was transformed in the twinkling of an eye. A moment before it had been bristling with life and the crowded street-cars had stopped to let their passengers scramble laboriously out. But now the whole square was suddenly as still as death, and, but for a few onlookers who watched the scene from a distance, the roadway was deserted.

From fifty to sixty soldiers filed slowly into the shed and a few others, with rifles ready, hurried now and again round the outside of the building. A fiendish din arose with the entry of the soldiers. The shrieking, howling, hooing, cursing, and moaning sounded as if hell itself had been let loose! It was an uncanny contrast – the silent square, and the ghastly noise within the shed!

Stepanovna muttered something, but the only word I caught was 'devils'. Sacks and bundles were being dragged out by the guards and hoisted on to trucks and lorries. At one door people were let out one by one after examination of their clothes and papers. The women were set at liberty, but the men, except the old and quite young boys, were marched off to the nearest Commissariat.

'What does it all mean?' I exclaimed, as we moved off along the Zabalkansky Prospect.

'Mean, Ivan Pavlovitch? Don't you see? "Let's grab!" "Down with free trading!" "Away with speculators!" That is what they say. "Speculation" they call it. I am a "speculator" too,' she chuckled. 'Do you think I ever got any work from the labour bureau, where I have been registered these three months? Or Varia, either, though we both want jobs. The money Ivan Sergeievitch left us is running out, but we must live somehow, mustn't we?'

Stepanovna lowered her voice.

'So we have sold a sideboard ... Yes,' she chuckled, 'we sold it to some people downstairs. "Speculators", too, I expect. They came up early in the morning and took it away quietly, and our house committee never heard anything about it!'

Stepanovna laughed outright. She thought it a huge joke.

For all your furniture, you see, was supposed to be registered and belonged not to yourself but to the community. Superfluous furniture was to be confiscated in favour of the working man, but generally went to decorate the rooms of members of the committee or groups of Communists in whose charge the houses were placed. Sailor Communists seemed to make the largest demands. 'Good morning,' they would say on entering your home. 'Allow us please to look around and see how much furniture you have.' Some things, they would tell you, were required by the house committee. Or a new 'worker' had taken rooms downstairs. He was a 'party man', that is, he belonged to the Communist party and was therefore entitled to preference, and he required a bed, a couch, and some easy chairs.

It was useless to argue, as some people did and got themselves into trouble by telling the 'comrades' what they thought of them. The wise and thoughtful submitted, remembering that while many of these men were out just to pocket as much as they could, there were others who really believed they were thus distributing property in the interests of equality and fraternity.

But the wily and clever would exclaim; 'My dear comrades, I am delighted! Your comrade is a "party man"? That is most interesting, for I am intending to sign on myself. Only yesterday I put some furniture by for you. As for this couch you ask for, it is really indispensable, but in another room there is a settee you can have. And that picture, of course, I would willingly give you, only I assure you it is an heirloom. Besides, it is a very bad painting, an artist told me so last week. Would you not rather have this one, which he said was really good?'

And you showed them any rotten old thing, preferably something *big*. Then you would offer them tea and apologize for giving them nothing but crusts with it. You explained you wished to be an 'idealist' Communist, and your scruples would not permit you to purchase delicacies from 'speculators'.

Your visitors were not likely to linger long over your crusts, but if you succeeded in impressing them with your devotion to the Soviet regime they would be less inclined to molest a promising candidate for comradeship.

But Stepanovna possessed no such subtlety. She was, on the contrary, unreasonably outspoken and I wondered that she did not get into difficulties.

Stepanovna and Varia often used to go to the opera, and when they came home they would discuss intelligently and with enthusiasm the merits and demerits of respective singers.

'I did not like the man who sang Lensky tonight,' one of them would say. 'He baa-ed like a sheep and his acting was poor.'

Or, 'So-and-so's voice is really almost as good as Shaliapin's except in the lowest notes, but of course Shaliapin's acting is much more powerful.'

'Stepanovna,' I once said, 'used you to go to the opera before the revolution?'

'Why yes,' she replied, 'we used to go to the *Narodny Dom*.'
The *Narodny Dom* was a big theatre built for the people by the
Tsar.

'But to the state theatres, the Marinsky opera or ballet?'

'No, that was difficult.'

'Well, then, why do you abuse the Bolsheviks who make it
easy for you to go to what used to be the Imperial Theatres and
see the very best plays and actors?'

Stepanovna was stooping over the samovar. She raised
herself and looked at me, considering my question.

'Hmm, yes,' she admitted, 'I enjoy it, it is true. But who is
the theatre full of? Only school children and our "comrades"
Communists. The school children ought to be doing home-
lessons and our 'comrades' ought to be hanging on the gallows.
Varia and I can enjoy the theatre because we just have enough
money to buy food in the markets. But go and ask those who
stand in queues all day and all night for half a pound of bread
or a dozen logs of firewood! How much do they enjoy the
cheap theatres? I wonder, ah?'

So I said no more. Stepanovna had very decided notions of
things. If she had been an Englishwoman before the war she
would have been a militant suffragist.

It was at the beginning of February that I saw Stepanovna
for the last time. My acquaintance with her ceased abruptly as
with other people under similar circumstances. Varia, it transpired, got into trouble through trying to communicate with
Ivan Sergeievitch in Finland.

Before going to Stepanovna's flat I always 'phoned and
asked, 'Is your father any better?' – which meant, May I come
and stay the night? To which she or Varia would reply, 'Quite
well, thank you, and he would like you to go and see him when
you have time.'

On the last occasion when I called up, Stepanovna did not at
once answer. Then in a voice full of indecision she stammered,
'I don't know – I think – I will ask – please wait a moment.' I

waited and could hear she had not left the telephone. At last she continued tremblingly, 'No, he is no better, he is very bad indeed – dying.' There was a pause. 'I am going to see him,' she went on, stammering all the time, 'at eleven o'clock tomorrow morning, do – do you understand?'

'Yes,' I said, 'I will go too and wait for you.'

Wondering if we had understood each other, I stationed myself at the corner of the street a little before eleven, and watched from a distance the entrance to Stepanovna's house. One glance, when she came out, satisfied her I was there. Walking off in the other direction, she followed Kazanskaya Street, only once looking round to make sure I was behind, and, reaching the Kazan Cathedral, entered it. I found her in a dark corner to the right.

'Varia is arrested,' she said, in great distress. 'You must come to our flat no more, Ivan Pavlovitch. A messenger came from Viborg the day before yesterday and asked Varia, if she could, to get out to Finland. They went together to the Finland Station and got on the train. There they met another man who was to help them get over the frontier. He was arrested on the train and the other two with him.'

'Is there any serious charge?' I asked. 'Simply running away is no grave offence.'

'They say the two men will be shot,' she replied. 'But Varia only had some things she was taking to Ivan Sergeievitch's wife.'

I tried to reassure her, saying I would endeavour to discover how Varia's case stood, and would find some means of communication.

'I am expecting a search,' she went on, 'but of course I have made preparations. Maybe we shall meet again someday, Ivan Pavlovitch. I hope so.'

I felt very sorry for poor Stepanovna in her trouble. She was a fine type of woman in her way, though her views on things were often crude. But it must be remembered that she was only a peasant. As I was crossing the threshold of the cathedral, something moved me to turn back for a moment, and I saw Stepanovna shuffle up to the altar and fall on her knees. Then I came away.

I was resolved to get the Policeman on the job at once to find out the circumstances of Varia's case, which I felt sure could not be serious. But I was not destined to make this investigation. I never saw either Varia or Stepanovna again, nor was it possible for me to discover what ultimately became of them. Tossed hither and thither by the caprice of circumstance, I found myself shortly after suddenly placed in a novel and unexpected situation, of which and its results, if the reader have patience to read a little further, he will learn.

Chapter VII

Finland

Stáraya Derévnya, which means 'the Old Village', is a remote suburb of Petrograd, situated at the mouth of the most northerly branch of the River Neva, overlooking the Gulf of Finland. It is a poor and shabby locality, consisting of second-rate summer villas and a few small timber-yards and logmen's huts. In winter when the gulf is frozen it is the bleakest of bleak places, swept by winds carrying the snow in blizzard-like clouds across the dreary desert of ice. You cannot tell then where land ends and sea begins, for the flats, the shores, the marshes, and the sea lie hidden under a common blanket of soft and sand-like snowdrifts. In olden times I loved to don my skis and glide gently from the world into that vast expanse of frozen water, and there, miles out, lie down and listen to the silence.

A few days after I had parted from Stepanovna in the Kazan Cathedral, I sat in one of the smallest and remotest huts of Stáraya Derévnya. It was eleven o'clock of a dark and windless night. Except for the champing of a horse outside, the silence was broken only by the grunting and snoring of a Finnish contrabandist lying at full length on the dirty couch. Once, when the horse neighed, the Finn rose hurriedly with a curse. Lifting the latch cautiously, he stole out and led the animal round to the seaward side of the cottage, where it would be less audible from the road. Having recently smuggled a sleigh-load of batter into the city, he was now returning to Finland – with me.

It was after midnight when we drove out, and, conditions being good, the drive over the sea to a point well along the Finnish coast, a distance of some forty-odd miles, was to take us between four and five hours. The sledge was of the type

known as *drovny* a wooden one, broad and low, filled with hay.
The *drovny* used mostly for farm haulage, is my favourite kind
of sledge, and nestling comfortably at full length under the hay
I thought of long night-drives in the interior in days gone by,
when someone used to ride ahead on horseback with a torch to
keep away the wolves.

In a moment we were out, flying at breakneck speed across
the clear ice, windswept after recent storms. The half inch of
frozen snow just gave grip to the horse's hoofs. Twice, suddenly
bumping into snow ridges, we capsized completely. When we
got going again the runners sang just like a saw-mill. The driver
noticed this too, and was alive to the danger of being heard
from shore a couple of miles away; but his sturdy pony, exhila-
rated by the keen frosty air, was hard to restrain.

Some miles out of Petrograd there lies on an island in
the Finnish Gulf the famous fortress of Cronstadt, one of the
most impregnable in the world. Searchlights from the fortress
played from time to time across the belt of ice, separating the
fortress from the northern shore. The passage through this
narrow belt was the crucial point in our journey. Once past
Cronstadt we should be in Finnish waters and safe.

To avoid danger from the searchlights, the Finn drove
within a mile of the mainland, the runners hissing and singing
like saws. As we entered the narrows a dazzling beam of light
swept the horizon from the fortress, catching us momentar-
ily in its track; but we were sufficiently near the shore not to
appear as a black speck adrift on the ice.

Too near, perhaps? The dark line of the woods seemed but
a stone's throw away! You could almost see the individual trees.
Hell! what a noise our sledge-runners made!

'Can't you keep the horse back a bit, man?'

'Yes, but this is the spot we've *got* to drive past quickly!'

We were crossing the line of Lissy Nos, a jutting point on
the coast marking the narrowest part of the strait. Again a
beam of light shot out from the fortress, and the wooden pier

and huts of Lissy Nos were lit as by a flash of lightning. But we had passed the point already. It was rapidly receding into the darkness as we regained the open sea.

Sitting upright on the heap of hay, I kept my eyes riveted on the receding promontory. We were nearly a mile away now, and you could no longer distinguish objects clearly. But my eyes were still riveted on the rocky promontory.

Were those rocks – moving? I tried to pierce the darkness, my eyes rooted to the black point!

Rocks? Trees? Or – or –

I sprang to my feet and shook the Finn by the shoulders with all my force.

'Damn it, man! Drive like hell – we're being pursued!'

Riding out from Lissy Nos were a group of horsemen, five or six in number. My driver gave a moan, lashed his horse, the sleigh leaped forward, and the chase began in earnest.

'Ten thousand marks if we escape!' I yelled in the Finn's ear.

For a time we kept a good lead but in the darkness it was impossible to see whether we were gaining or losing. My driver was making low moaning cries, he appeared to be pulling hard on the reins, and the sleigh jerked so that I could scarcely stand.

Then I saw that the pursuers were gaining – and gaining rapidly! The moving dots grew into figures galloping at full speed. Suddenly there was a flash and a crack, then another, and another. They were firing with carbines, against which a pistol was useless. I threatened the driver with my revolver if he did not pull ahead, but dropped like a stone into the hay as a bullet whizzed close to my ear.

At that moment the sledge suddenly swung round. The driver had clearly had difficulty with his reins, which appeared to get caught in the shaft, and before I realized what was happening the horse fell, the sledge whirled round and came to a sudden stop.

At such moments one has to think rapidly. What would the pursuing Red guards go for first? A fugitive? Not if there was possible loot. And what more likely than that the sledge contained loot?

Eel-like, I slithered over the side and made in the direction of the shore. Progress was difficult for there were big patches of ice, coal-black in colour, which were completely windswept and as slippery as glass. Stumbling along, I drew from my pocket a packet wrapped in dark brown paper, containing maps and documents which were sufficient, if discovered, to assure my being shot without further ado, and held it ready to hurl away across the ice.

If seized, I would plead smuggling. It seemed impossible that I should escape! Looking backward I saw the group round the sledge. The Reds, dismounted, were examining the driver; in a moment they would renew the pursuit, and running over the ice I should be spotted at once.

Then an idea occurred. The ice, where completely wind-swept, formed great patches as black as ink. My clothes were dark. I ran into the middle of a big black patch and looked at my boots. I could not see them!

To get to the shore was impossible anyway, so this was the only chance. Jerking the packet a few yards from me where I might easily find it, I dropped flat on the black ice and lay motionless, praying that I should be invisible.

It was not long before I heard the sound of hoofs and voices approaching. The search for me had begun. But the riders avoided the slippery windswept places as studiously as I had done in running, and – thank heaven! – just there much of the ice was windswept. As they rode round and about, I felt that someone was bound to ride just over me! Yet they didn't, after all.

It seemed hours and days of night and darkness before the riders retreated to the sledge and rode off with it, returning whence they had come. But time is measured not by degrees of hope or despair, but by fleeting seconds and minutes, and by my luminous watch I detected that it was only half past one. Prosaic half past one!

Was the sombre expanse of frozen sea really deserted? Cronstadt loomed dimly on the horizon, the dark line of woods lay behind me, and all was still as death – except for the sea below, groaning and gurgling as if the great ice-burden were too heavy to bear.

Slowly and imperceptibly I rose, first on all fours, then kneeling, and finally standing upright. The riders and the sledge were gone, and I was alone. Only the stars twinkled, as much as to say: 'It's all over! 'Twas a narrow squeak, wasn't it? But a miss is as good as a mile!'

It must have been a weird, bedraggled figure that stumbled, seven or eight hours later, up the steep bank of the Finnish shore. That long walk across the ice was one of the hardest I ever had to make, slipping and falling at almost every step until I got used to the surface. On reaching light, snow-covered regions, however, I walked rapidly and made good progress. Once while I was resting I heard footsteps approaching straight in my direction. Crawling into the middle of another black patch, I repeated the manoeuvre of an hour or two earlier, and lay still. A man, walking hurriedly toward Cronstadt from the direction of Finland, passed within half a dozen paces without seeing me.

Shortly after daylight, utterly exhausted, I clambered up the steep shore into the woods. Until I saw a Finnish sign-board I was still uncertain as to whether I had passed the frontier in the night or not. But convincing myself that I had, though doubtful of my precise whereabouts, I sought a quiet spot behind a shed, threw myself on to the soft snow and fell into a doze.

It was here that I was discovered by a couple of Finnish patrols, who promptly arrested me and marched me off to the nearest coastguard station. No amount of protestation availed to convince them I was not a Bolshevist spy. The assertion that I was an Englishman only seemed to intensify their suspicions, for my appearance completely belied the statement. Seizing all my money and papers, they locked me up in a cell, but removed me during the day to the office of the Commandant at Terijoki, some miles distant.

The Commandant, whom I had seen on the occasion of my last visit to Finland, would, I expected, release me at once. But I found a condition of things totally different from that obtaining six weeks earlier. A new commandant had been appointed, who was unpersuaded even by a telephone conversation conducted in his presence with the British representatives at the Finnish capital. The most he would do was to give me a temporary pass saying I was a Russian travelling to Helsingfors: with the result that I was re-arrested on the train and again held in detention at the head police office in the capital until energetic representations by the British Chargé d'Affaires secured my release, with profuse apologies from the Finnish authorities for the not unnatural misunderstanding.

The reader will, I hope, have become sufficiently interested in my story to inquire what were the circumstances which led to my taking this sudden journey to Finland. They were various. Were I writing a tale of fiction, and could allow free rein to whatsoever imagination I possess, I might be tempted at this point to draw my story to a startling climax by revealing Zorinsky in the light of a grossly misunderstood and unappreciated friend and saviour, while Stepanovna, the Journalist, or the Doctor would unexpectedly turn out to be treacherous wolves in sheep's clothing, plotting diabolically to ensnare me in the toils of the Extraordinary Commission. As it is, however, fettered by the necessity of recording dull and often obvious events as they occurred, it will be no surprise to the reader to learn that the wolf, in a pretty bad imitation of sheep's clothing (good enough, however, to deceive me), turned out actually to be Zorinsky.

It was the day after I had parted from Stepanovna that the Doctor told me that Melnikoff's friend Shura, through sources at his disposal, had been investigating the personality of this interesting character, and had established it as an indisputable fact that Zorinsky was in close touch with people known to be in the employ of *No. 2 Goróhovaya*. This information, though unconfirmed and in itself proving nothing (was not the Policeman also in close touch with people in the employ of *No. 2 Goróhovaya?*) yet following on the news of Melnikoff's death and Zorinsky's general duplicity, resolved me to seek the first opportunity to revisit Finland and consult Ivan Sergeievitch.

There were other motives, also. I had communicated across the frontier by means of couriers, one of whom was found me by the Doctor, and another by one of the persons who play no part in my story, but whom I met at the Journalist's. One of these couriers was an N. C. O. of the old army, a student of law, and a personal friend of the Doctor: the other a Russian officer whose known counter-revolutionary proclivities precluded the possibility of his obtaining any post in Soviet Russia at this time. Both crossed the frontier secretly and without mishap, but only one returned, bearing a cipher message which was all but indecipherable. Sending him off again, but getting no reply, I was in ignorance as to whether he had arrived or not, and, left without news, it was becoming imperative that I repeat my visit to the Finnish capital.

Furthermore, with passage of time I felt my position, in spite of friends, becoming not more secure but rapidly less so. What might suddenly arise out of my connections with Zorinsky, for instance, no one could foresee, and I determined that the best thing would be to disappear completely for a short period and, returning, to start all over afresh.

I learned of the ice-route to Finland from my courier, who came back that way, and who returned to Finland the following night on the same sledge. Discreet inquiries at the logman's hut produced the information that the courier's smuggler, granted that he had safely reached Finland, was not due back for some time, but another one had arrived and would take anyone who was willing to pay. The sum demanded, two thousand marks, when converted into foreign exchange was about twenty pounds. But the Finn thinks of a mark as a shilling.

As ill-luck would have it, I found on arrival in Finland that Ivan Sergeievitch was in the Baltic States and no one knew when he would return. But I saw his wife, who had sent the indiscreet message to Petrograd leading to Varia's arrest. She was mortified when I broke this news to her, but was unable to throw any light on Zorinsky. I also met several other Russian officers, none, however, who had known Melnikoff, and I thus got no further information.

The Doctor, of course, had denounced Zorinsky as a *provocateur*, but there was as yet little evidence for the charge. Zorinsky might be an extortionist without being a *provocateur*. Wild charges are brought against anybody and everybody connected with *Sovdepia* on the slightest suspicion, and I myself have been charged, on the one hand, by the Bolsheviks with being a rabid monarchist, and, on the other, by reactionaries with being a 'subtle' Bolshevik. However, my aversion to Zorinsky had become so intense that I resolved that under no pretext or condition would I have anything more to do with him.

My time in Helsingfors was occupied mostly with endeavours to obtain official assurances that any couriers I dispatched from Russia would not be seized or shot by the Finns, and that reasonable assistance should be given them in crossing the frontier in either direction. The Finnish Foreign and War Offices were willing enough to cooperate, but appeared to have but little sway over their own frontier authorities. The last word belonged to the new Commandant at Terijoki, a man of German origin, who defied the Government whenever instructions ran counter to his open German sympathies. Being in league with German Intelligence organizations in Russia, he was naturally disinclined to do anything that would assist the Allies, and it was only when his insubordination passed all limits and he was at last dismissed by the Finnish Government, that facilities could be granted which made the operation of a secret courier service across the frontier in any degree feasible.

The story of intrigue and counter-intrigue amongst Finns, Germans, Russians, Bolsheviks, and the Allies at this time, both in the Finnish capital and along the Russian frontier, would be a fascinating one in itself, but that is not my province. On the occasion of my brief visits to Finland my prime object was not to become involved, and this was the main reason why, depressing though the prospect of returning to Petrograd was under existing circumstances, I nevertheless cut short my stay in Finland and prepared to return the moment I learned positively that the German frontier commandant was to be removed.

Earnestly as I had striven to remain *incognito* my unavoidable participation in the negotiations for arranging a courier-service had drawn me into unfortunate prominence. The German Commandant, still at his post, appeared to regard me as his very particular foe, and learning of my intention to return to Russia by sea he issued orders that the strictest watch should be kept on the coast and any sledge or persons issuing on to the ice be fired upon. Thus, although I had a Government permit to cross the frontier, the smuggler who was to carry me positively refused to venture on the journey, while all patrols had orders to afford me no facilities whatsoever.

But I evaded the Commandant, and very simply. At the other extremity of the Russo-Finnish frontier, close to Lake Ladoga, there is a small village named Rautta, lying four or five miles from the frontier line. This place had formerly also been a rallying point for smugglers and refugees, but in view of its remoteness and the difficulties of forest travel it was very inaccessible in mid-winter from the Russian side. At the Commandant's headquarters it was never suspected that I would attempt to start from this remote spot. But protesting, much to the Commandant's delight, that I would return and compel him to submit to Government orders, I travelled by a very circuitous route to the village of Rautta, where I was completely unknown, and where I relied on finding some peasant or other who would conduct me to the border.

Once arriving at the frontier I was content to be left to my
own resources.

Luck was with me. It was in the later stages of the tedious
journey that I was accosted in the train by a young Finnish
lieutenant bound for the same place. Russians being in ill-
favour in Finland, I always travelled as an Englishman in that
country, whatever I may have looked like. At this time I did
not look so bad, attired in an old green overcoat I had bought
at Helsingfors. Noticing that I was reading an English paper,
the lieutenant addressed me in English with some trifling
request, and we fell into conversation. I was able to do him
a slight service through a note I gave him to an acquaintance
in Helsingfors, and when I further presented him with all my
newspapers and a couple of English books for which I had
no further use, he was more than delighted. Finding him so
well-disposed I asked him what he was going to do at Rautta,
to which he replied that he was about to take up his duties as
chief of the garrison of the village, numbering some fifteen or
twenty men. At this I whipped out my Finnish Government
permit without further ado and appealed to the lieutenant to
afford me, as the document said, 'every assistance in crossing
the Russian frontier'.

He was not a little nonplussed at this unexpected request.
But realizing that a pass such as mine could only have been
issued by the Finnish Ministry of War on business of first-class
importance he agreed to do what he could. I soon saw that
he was much concerned to do his utmost. Within a couple of
hours after our arrival at Rautta I was assured not only of a safe
conduct by night to the frontier, but also of a guide, who was
instructed to take me to a certain Russian village about twenty
miles beyond.

Nothing could be more truly proletarian than Finnish
administration in regions where neither German nor *ancien-
régime* Russian influence has penetrated. It is the fundamentally
democratic character of the Finnish people that has enabled

them since the time of which I speak to master in large measure
their would-be foreign counsellors and controllers and build up
a model constitution. The elder of the village of Rautta, who
was directed by my friend the lieutenant to show me hospitality
and procure me a guide, was a rough peasant, literate and intelligent, living with his wife in a single large room in which I was
entertained. His assistants were men of the same type, while
the guide was a young fellow of about twenty, a native of the
village, who had had a good elementary education at Viborg.
In the hands of people of this sort I always felt myself secure.
Their crude common sense – the strongest defence against
nonsensical Red propaganda – made them as a class trustier
friends than a spoilt intelligentsia or the scheming intrigants of
the militarist caste.

My guide produced half a dozen pairs of skis, all of which
were too short, as I require a nine- or ten-foot ski, but I took
the longest pair. About eleven o'clock our skis were strapped
to a *drovny* sledge, and with a kindly send-off by the elder and
his wife, we drove rapidly to a lonely hut, the last habitation on
the Finnish side of the frontier. The proprietor was roused and
regaled us with tea, while a scout, who chanced to come in a
few moments after our arrival, advised my guide as to the latest
known movements of Red patrols. Our peasant host possessed
no candles or oil in this solitary abode, and we sat in the flickering light of long burning twigs, specially cut to preserve their
shaky flare as long as possible.

About midnight we mounted the skis and set out on our
journey, striking off the track straight into the forest. My
companion was lightly clad, but I retained my overcoat, which
I should need badly later, while round my waist I tied a little
parcel containing a pair of shoes I had bought for Maria
in Helsingfors.

By the roundabout way we were going it would be some
twenty-five miles to the village that was our destination. For
four years I had not run on skis, and though ski-running is like

swimming in that once you learn you never forget, yet you can get out of practice. Moreover, the skis I had were too short, and any ski-runner will tell you it is no joke to run on short skis a zigzag route across uneven forest ground – and in the dark!

We started in an easterly direction, moving parallel to the border-line. I soon more or less adapted my steps to the narrow seven-foot ski and managed to keep the guide's moderate pace. We stopped frequently to listen for suspicious sounds, but all that greeted our ears was the mystic and beautiful winter silence of a snow-laden northern forest. The temperature was twenty degrees below zero, with not a breath of wind, and the pines and firs bearing their luxuriant white burdens looked as if a magic fairy-wand had lulled them into perpetual sleep. Some people might have 'seen things' in this dark forest domain, but peering into the dim recesses of the woods I felt all sound and motion discordant, and loved our halts just to listen, listen, listen. My guide was taciturn; if we spoke it was in whispers. We moved noiselessly but for the gentle swish of our skis, which scarcely broke the stillness, and the stars that danced above the tree-tops smiled down upon us approvingly.

After travelling a little over an hour the Finn suddenly halted, raising his hand. For some minutes we stood motionless. Then, leaving his skis, he walked cautiously back to me and pointing at a group of low bushes a hundred yards away, visible through a narrow aisle in the forest, he whispered: 'You see those farthest shrubs? They are in Russia. We are about to cross the line, so follow me closely.'

Moving into the thickets, we advanced slowly under their cover until we were within a few yards of the spot indicated. I then saw that before us there lay, crosswise through the forest, a narrow clearance some ten yards wide, resembling a long avenue. This was the Russian borderline, and we stood at the extreme edge of the Finnish forest. My guide motioned to me to sidle up alongside him.

'It is to those bushes we must cross,' he whispered so low

as to be scarcely audible. 'The undergrowth everywhere else is impassable. We will watch the shrubbery a moment. The question is: is there any one behind it? Look hard.'

Weird phenomenon! – but a moment ago it seemed that motion in the forest was inconceivable. Yet now, with nerves tense from anticipation, all the trees and all the bushes seemed to stir and glide. But oh! so slyly, so noiselessly, so imperceptibly! Every shrub knew just when you were looking at it, and as long as you stared straight, it kept still; but the instant you shifted your gaze, a bough swung – ever so little! – a trunk swayed, a bush shrank, a thicket shivered; it was as if behind everything were something, agitating, toying, to taunt you with deceits!

But it was not really so. The forest was still with a death-like stillness. The dark trees like sentinels stood marshalled in sombre array on either side of the avenue. Around us, above, and below, all was silence – the mystic, beautiful winter silence of the sleeping northern forest.

Like a fish, my companion darted suddenly from our hiding place, bending low, and in two strides had crossed the open space and vanished in the shrubbery. I followed, stealing one rapid glance up and down as I crossed the line, to see nothing but two dark walls of trees on either hand separated by the gray carpet of snow. Another stride, and I, too, was in Russia, buried in the thick shrubbery.

I found my guide sitting in the snow, adjusting his ski-straps.

'If we come upon nobody in the next quarter-mile,' he whispered, 'we are all right till daybreak.'

'But our ski-tracks?' I queried; 'may they not be followed?'

'Nobody will follow the way we are going.'

The next quarter-mile lay along a rough track skirting the Russian side of the frontier. Progress was difficult because the undergrowth was thick and we had to stoop beneath overhanging branches. Every twenty paces or so we stopped to listen – but only to the silence.

At last we came out on the borders of what seemed like a great lake. My companion explained that it was a morass and that we should ski straight across it, due south, making the best speed we might. Travelling now was like finding a level path after hard rocky climbing. My guide sailed away at so round a pace that although I used his tracks I could not keep up. By the time I had crossed the open morass he had already long disappeared in the woods. I noticed that although he had said no one would follow us, he did not like the open places.

Again we plunged into the forest. The ground here began to undulate and progress in and out amongst the short firs was wearisome. I began to get so tired that I longed to stretch myself out at full length on the snow. But we had to make our village by day-break and my guide would not rest.

It was after we had crossed another great morass and had been picking our way through pathless forest for about four hours, that I saw by the frequency with which my companion halted to consider the direction, and the hesitation with which he chose our path, that he had lost his way. When I asked him he frankly admitted it, making no effort also to conceal his anxiety. There was nothing to do, however, but to keep straight ahead, due south by the pole star.

The first streaks of dawn stole gently over the sky. Coming out on to an open track, my guide thought he recognized it, and we followed it in spite of the danger of running into an early patrol. In a few moments we struck off along a side track in an easterly direction. We should soon reach our destination now, said the Finn – about a mile more.

I moved so slowly that my companion repeatedly got long distances ahead. We travelled a mile, but still no sign of village or open country. At length the Finn disappeared completely, and I struggled forward along his tracks.

The gray dawn spread and brightened, and it was quite light, though the sun had not yet risen, when at last I drew near the outskirts of the forest. Sitting on the bank of a small running stream sat my guide, reproaching me when I joined him for my tardiness. Across a large meadow outside the forest he pointed to a group of cottages on the side of a hill to the right.

'The Reds live there,' he said. 'They will be out about eight o'clock. We have come over a mile too far inland from Lake Ladoga: but follow my tracks and we shall soon be there.'

He rose and mounted his skis. I wondered how he proposed to cross the stream. Taking a short run, he prodded his sticks deftly into the near bank as he quitted it, and lifting himself with all his force over the brook, glided easily on to the snow on the far side. Moving rapidly across the meadow, he disappeared in the distant bushes.

But in springing he dislodged a considerable portion of the bank of snow, thus widening the intervening space. I was bigger and weightier than he, and more heavily clad, and my endeavour to imitate his performance on short skis met with a disastrous end. Failing to clear the brook, my skis, instead of sliding on to the opposite snow, plunged into the bank, and I found myself sprawling in the water! It was a marvel that neither ski broke. I picked them up and throwing them on to the level, prepared to scramble out of the stream.

The ten minutes that ensued were amongst the silliest in sensation and most helpless I ever experienced. Nothing would seem easier than to clamber up a bank not so high as one's shoulder. But every grab did nothing but bring down an avalanche of snow on top of me! There was no foothold, and it was only when I had torn the deep snow right away that I was able to drag myself out with the aid of neighbouring bushes.

Safely on shore I looked myself over despondently. From the waist downward I was one solid mass of ice. The flags of ice on my old green overcoat flapped heavily against the ice-pillars encasing my top-boots. With considerable labour and difficult I scraped soles and skis sufficiently to make it possible to stand on them, and once again crawled slowly forward.

I do not know how I managed to traverse the remaining three miles to the village whither my guide had preceded me. It should have been the hardest bit of all, for I was in the last stages of fatigue. Yet it does not seem to have been so now. I think, to tell the truth, I completely gave up the game, convinced my black figure creeping up the white hillside must inevitably attract attention, and I mechanically trudged forward till I should hear a shot or a cry to halt. Or, perhaps, even in this plight, and careless of what befell me, I was fascinated by the glory of a wondrous winter sunrise! I remember how the sun peeped venturously over the horizon, throwing a magic rose-coloured mantle upon the hills. First the summits were touched, the pink flush crept gently down the slopes, turning the shadows palest blue, and when at last the sun climbed triumphant into the heaven, the whole world laughed. And with it, I!

The cottages of the Reds were left far behind. I had crossed more than one hill and valley, and passed more than one peasant who eyed me oddly, before I found myself at the bottom of the hill on whose crest was perched the village I was seeking! I knew my journey was over at last, because my guide's tracks ceased at the top. He had dismounted to walk along the rough roadway. But which cottage had he entered?

I resolved to beg admission to one of the huts on the outskirts of the village. They were all alike, low wooden and mud buildings with protruding porch, two tiny square windows in the half where the family lived, but none in the other half, which formed the barn or cattle-shed. The peasants are kindly folk, I mused, or used to be, and there are few Bolsheviks amongst them. So I approached the nearest cottage, propped up my skis against the wall, timidly knocked at the door, and entered.

Chapter VIII

A Village 'Bourgeois-Capitalist'

The room in which I found myself was a spacious one. On the right stood a big white stove, always the most prominent object in a Russian peasant dwelling, occupying nearly a quarter of the room. Beyond the stove in the far corner was a bedstead on which an old woman lay. The floor was strewn with several rough straw mattresses. Two strapping boys, a little lass of ten, and two girls of eighteen or nineteen had just dressed, and one of the latter was doing her hair in front of a piece of broken mirror.

In the other far corner stood a rectangular wooden table, with an oil lamp hanging over it. The little glass closet of icons behind the table, in what is called 'beautiful corner' because it shelters the holy pictures, showed the inmates to be Russians, though the district is inhabited largely by men of Finnish race. To the left of the door stood an empty wooden bedstead, with heaped-up bedcovers and sheepskin coats as if someone had lately risen from it. All these things, picturesque, though customary, I took in at a glance. But I was interested to notice an old harmonium, an unusual decoration in a village hut, the musical accomplishments of the peasant generally being limited to the concertina, the guitar, the balalaika, and the voice, in all of which, however, he is adept.

'Good morning,' I said, apologetically. I turned to the icons and bowing, made the sign of the Cross. 'May I sit down just for a little moment? I am very tired.'

Everyone was silent, doubtless very suspicious. The little girl stared at me with wide-open eyes. I seated myself opposite the big white stove, wondering what I should do next.

In a few minutes there entered a rough peasant of about fifty-five, with long hair streaked with gray, and haggard, glistening eyes. There was a look of austerity in his wrinkled face, though at the same time it was not unkind, but he rarely smiled. He nodded a curt good morning and set about his ablutions, paying no further heed to me. The old woman mentioned that I had come in to rest.

I explained. 'I set out from the nearest station early this morning with a companion,' I said, 'to ski here. We are looking for milk. But we lost our way in the woods. I tumbled into a stream. My companion is somewhere in the village and I will go and look for him later. But I would like to rest a little first for I am very tired.'

The old peasant listened but did not seem interested. He filled his mouth with water from a jug, bent over an empty bucket, and letting the water trickle out of his mouth into the cup of his hands, scrubbed his face and neck. I suppose it was warmer this way. When he had finished I asked if I might have some milk to drink, and at a sign from the old man one of the boys fetched me some in a big tin mug.

'It is hard to get milk nowadays,' grunted the old peasant, surlily, and went on with his work.

The boys slipped on their sheepskin coats and left the cottage, while the girls removed the mattresses and set the samovar. I rejoiced when I saw the old woman preparing to light the stove. My legs gradually thawed, forming pools of water on the floor, and one of the boys, when he came in, helped me pull my boots off. But this was a painful process, for both my feet were partially frozen.

At last the samovar was boiling and I was invited to table to have a mug of tea. It was not real tea and tasted nothing like it, though the packet was labelled 'Tea'. Black bread and salt herrings made up the meal. I did not touch the herrings.

'We have not much bread,' said the old man, significantly, as he put a small piece in front of me.

While we were at table my companion of night adventure came in, after having searched for me all through the village. I wished to warn him to be prudent in speech and repeat the same tale as I had told, but he merely motioned reassuringly with his hand. 'You need fear nothing here,' he said, smiling.

It appeared that he knew my old *muzhik* well. Taking him aside, he whispered something in his ear. What was he saying? The old man turned and looked at me intensely with an interest he had not shown before. His eyes glistened brightly, as if with unexpected satisfaction. He returned to where I sat.

'Would you like some more milk?' he asked, kindly, and fetched it for me himself.

I asked who played the harmonium. With amusing modesty the old man let his eyes fall and said nothing. But the little girl, pointing her finger at the peasant, put in quickly that '*Diedushka* [grandpa] did.'

'I like music,' I said. 'Will you please play something afterwards?'

Ah? Why was everything different all at once – suspicions evaporated, fears dissipated? I felt the change intuitively. The Finn had somehow aroused the crude old man's interest in me (had he told him who I was?), but by my passing question I had touched his tenderest spot – music!

So Uncle Egor (as I called him), producing an old and much be-fingered volume of German hymn tunes which he had picked up in a market at Petrograd, seated himself nervously and with touching modesty at the old harmonium. His thick, horny fingers, with black fingernails, stumbled clumsily over the keys, playing only the top notes coupled in octaves with one finger of his left hand. He blew the pedals as if he were beating time, and while he played his face twitched and his breath caught. You could see that in music he forgot everything else. The rotten old harmonium was the possession he prized above all else in the world – in fact, for him it was not of this world. Crude old peasant as he was, he was a true Russian.

'Would you like me to play you something?' I asked when he had finished.

Uncle Egor rose awkwardly from the harmonium, smiling confusedly when I complimented him on his achievement. I sat down and played him some of his hymns and a few other simple tunes. When I variegated the harmonies, he followed, fascinated. He leaned over the instrument, his eyes rooted on mine. All the rough harshness had gone from his face and the shadow of a faint smile flickered round his lips. I saw in his eyes a great depth of blue.

'Sit down again, my little son,' he said to me several times later, 'and play me more.'

At midday I lay down on Uncle Egor's bed and fell fast asleep. At three o'clock they roused me for dinner, consisting of a large bowl of sour cabbage soup, which we all ate with brown polished wooden spoons, dipping in turn into the bowl. Uncle Egor went to a corner of the room, produced from a sack a huge loaf, and cutting off a big square chunk, placed it before me.

'Eat as much bread as you like, my son,' he said.

He told me all his woes – how he was branded as a village 'fist, bourgeois, and capitalist', because he had possessed three horses and five cows; how four cows and two horses had been 'requisitioned'; and how half his land had been taken by the Committee of the Village Poor to start a Commune on.

Committees of the Village Poor were bodies from which were excluded all such as by enterprise, industry, and thrift, had raised themselves to positions of independence. Staffed by the lowest elements of stupid, illiterate, and idle peasants, beggars and tramps, these committees, endowed with supreme power, were authorized to seize the property of the prosperous and divide it amongst themselves, a portion going to the Government.

The class of 'middle' peasants, that is, those who were half way to prosperity, incited by agitators, sided at first with the poor in despoiling the rich, until it was their turn to be despoiled, when they not unnaturally became enemies of the Bolshevist system. The imposition of a war tax, however, finally alienated the sympathies of the entire peasantry, for the enriched 'poor' would not pay because they were technically poor, while the impoverished 'rich' could not pay because they had nothing left. This was the end of Communism throughout nine tenths of the Russian provinces, and it occurred when the Bolsheviks had ruled for only a year.

'Uncle Egor,' I said, 'you say your district still has a Committee of the Poor. I thought the committees were abolished. There was a decree about it last December.'

'What matters it what they write?' he exclaimed bitterly. 'Our "comrades" – whatever they want to do, they do. They held a Soviet election not long ago and the voters were ordered to put in the Soviet all the men from the Poor Committee. Now they say the village must start what they call a "Commune", where the lazy will profit by the labour of the industrious. They say they will take my last cow for the Commune. But they will not let *me* join, even if I wanted to, because I am a "fist". Ugh!'

'When they held the election,' I asked, 'did you vote?'

Uncle Egor laughed. 'I? How should they let me vote? I have worked all my life to make myself independent. I once had nothing, but I worked till I had this little farm, which I thought would be my own. Vasia here is my helper. But the Soviet says I am a "fist" and so I have no vote!'

'Who works in the Commune?' I asked.

'Who knows?' he replied. 'They are not from these parts. They thought the poor peasants would join them, because the poor peasants were promised our grain. But the Committee kept the grain for themselves, so the poor peasants got nothing and are very angry. Ah, my little son,' he cried, bitterly, 'do you know what Russia wants? Russia, my son, wants a Master – a Master who will restore order, and not that things should be as they are now, with every scoundrel pretending to be master. That is what Russia wants!'

A 'master' – now one of the most dangerous words to use in Russia, because it is the most natural!

'Do you mean – a "Tsar"?' I queried, hesitatingly. But Uncle Egor merely shrugged his shoulders. He had said his say.

That night I slept on the rickety wooden bedstead side by side with Uncle Egor and covered with the same coverlets and quilts. There were long whisperings between him and my Finnish guide before we retired, for early in the morning we were going on to Petrograd, and arrangements had to be made to drive to the nearest station by such devious routes as not to be stopped on the way. I was nearly asleep when Uncle Egor clambered in by my side.

It was long before dawn when we rose and prepared to set out. Uncle Egor, one of his daughters, the Finn, and I made up the party. To evade patrols we drove by side ways and across fields. Uncle Egor was taking his daughter to try to smuggle a can of milk into the city. What he himself was going to do I don't know. He wouldn't tell me.

We arrived at the station at four in the morning, and here I parted from my Finnish guide who was returning with the sledge. He positively refused to take any reward for the service he had rendered me.

Our train, the only train of the day, was due to start at six, and the station and platform were as busy as a hive. While the young woman got tickets we tried to find places. Every coach appeared to be packed, and the platform was teeming with peasants with sacks on their backs and milk cans concealed in bundles in their hands. Failing to get into a box-car or third-class coach, where with the crush it would have been warmer, we tried the only second-class car on the train, which we found was not yet full up. Eventually there were fourteen people in the compartment intended for six

At length the train rumbled off. Wedged in tight between Uncle Egor and his daughter, I sat and shivered. The train was searched by Red guards on the journey, and it was found that quite half the supposed cans of 'milk' carried by the peasants were packed to the brim with matches! There was no end of a tumult as the guards came round. Some people jumped out of the windows and fled. Others hid under the train till the compartment had been searched and were then hauled in again through the windows by willing hands from inside.

The Bolshevist Government, you see, had laid a special embargo on matches, as on many things of public use, with the result that they were almost unobtainable. So that when you did get them from 'sackmen', as the people were called who smuggled provisions into the city in bags and sacks, instead of paying one copeck per box, which was what they used to cost, you paid just one thousand times as much – ten roubles, and felt glad at that. The design, of course, was to share such necessities equally amongst the populace, but the soviet departments were so incompetent and corrupt and so strangled by bureaucratic administration, that nothing, or very little, ever got distributed, and the persecuted 'sackmen' were hailed as benefactors.

At one moment during the journey one of the other peasants bent over to Uncle Egor, and, glancing at me, asked him in an undertone, 'if his companion had come from "over there"' – which meant over the frontier; in reply to which Uncle Egor gave him a tremendous kick, which explained everything, and no more was said.

I had one nasty moment when the train was searched. Despite mishaps I still clung to the little parcel of shoes for Maria. As they were tied round my waist I did not lose them even when I tumbled into the stream. Some people got up when the searchers came, but having no milk can or sack I moved into the corner and sat on the parcel. When the soldier told me to shift along to let him see what was in the corner I sat the shoes along with me, so that both places looked empty. It was lucky he did not make me get up, for new shoes could only have come from 'over there'.

At nine we reached the straggling buildings of the Okhta

Station, the scene of my flight with Mrs Marsh in December, and there I saw a most extraordinary spectacle – the attempted prevention of sackmen from entering the city.

As we stood pushing in the corridor waiting for the crowd in front of us to get out, I heard Uncle Egor and his daughter conversing rapidly in low tones.

'I'll make a dash for it,' whispered his daughter.

'Good,' he replied in the same tone. 'We'll meet at Nadya's.'

The moment we stepped on to the platform Uncle Egor's daughter vanished under the railroad coach and that was the last I ever saw of her. At each end of the platform stood a string of armed guards, waiting for the onslaught of passengers, who flew in all directions as they surged from the train. How shall I describe the scene of unutterable pandemonium that ensued! The soldiers dashed at the fleeing crowds, brutally seized single individuals, generally women, who were least able to defend themselves, and tore the sacks off their backs and out of their arms. Shrill cries, shrieks, and howls rent the air. Between the coaches and on the outskirts of the station you could see lucky ones who had escaped, gesticulating frantically to unlucky ones who were still dodging guards. 'This way! This way!' they yelled wildly, 'Sophia! Marusia! Akulina! Varvara! Quick! Haste!'

In futile efforts to subdue the mob the soldiers discharged their rifles into the air, only increasing the panic and intensifying the tumult. Curses and execrations were hurled at them by the seething mass of fugitives. One woman I saw, frothing at the mouth, with blood streaming down her cheek, her frenzied eyes protruding from their sockets, clutching ferociously with her nails at the face of a huge sailor who held her pinned down on the platform, while his comrades detached her sack.

How I got out of the fray I do not know, but I found myself carried along with the running stream of sackmen over the Okhta Bridge and toward the Suvorov Prospect. Only here, a mile from the station, did they settle into a hurried walk, gradually dispersing down side streets to dispose of their precious goods to eager clients.

Completely bewildered, I limped along, my frost-bitten feet giving me considerable pain. I wondered in my mind if people at home had any idea at what a cost the population of Petrograd secured the first necessities of life in the teeth of the 'communist' rulers. Still musing, I came out on the Znamenskaya Square in front of the Nicholas Station, the scene of many wild occurrences in the days of the Great Revolution.

You could still see the hole in the station roof whence in those days a machine gun manned by Protopopoff's police had fired down on the crowds below. I had watched the scene from that little alcove just over there near the corner of the Nevsky. While I was watching, the people had discovered another policeman on the roof of the house just opposite. They threw him over the parapet. He fell on the pavement with a heavy thud, and lay there motionless. Everything, I remembered, had suddenly seemed very quiet as I looked across the road at his dead body, though the monotonous song of the machine gun still sounded from the station roof.

But next day a new song was sung in the hearts of the people, a song of Hope and a song of Freedom. Justice shall now reign, said the people! For it was said, 'The Tsarist ways, and the Tsarist police are no more!'

Today, two years later, it was just such a glorious winter morning as in those days of March, 1917. The sun laughed to scorn the silly ways of men. But the song of Hope was dead, and the people's faces bore the imprint of starvation, distress, and terror – terror of those very same Tsarist police! For these others, who did not make the Revolution, but who were encouraged by Russia's enemies to return to Russia to poison it – these others copied the Tsarist ways, and, restoring the Tsarist police, made them their own. The men and women who made the Revolution, they said, were the enemies of the Revolution! So they put them back in prison, and hung other flags up. Here, stretched across the Nevsky Prospect, on this winter morning there still fluttered in the breeze the tattered shreds of their washed-out red flags, besmirched with the catchwords with which the Russian workers and the Russian peasants had been duped. There still stood unremoved in the middle of the square the shabby, dilapidated, four-months-old remains of the tribunes and stages which had been erected to celebrate the anniversary of the Bolshevist revolution. The inscriptions everywhere spoke not of the 'bourgeois prejudices' of Liberty and Justice, but of the Dictatorship of the Proletariat (sometimes hypocritically called the 'brotherhood of workers'), of class war, of the sword, of blood, hatred, and world-wide revolution.

Looking up from my bitter reverie I saw Uncle Egor, from whom I had got separated in the scramble at the railway station. I wanted to thank and recompense him for the food and shelter he had given me.

'Uncle Egor,' I asked him, 'how much do I owe you?'

But Uncle Egor shook his head. He would take no recompense.

'Nothing, my little son,' he replied, 'nothing. And come back again when you like.' He looked round, and lowering his voice, added cautiously, 'And if ever you need ... to run away ... or hide ... or anything like that ... you know, little son, who will help you.'

Chapter IX

Metamorphosis

I never saw Uncle Egor again. I sometimes wonder what has become of him. I suppose he is still there, and he is the winner! The Russian peasant is the ultimate master of the Russian Revolution, as the Bolsheviks are learning to their pain. Once I did set out, several months later, to invoke his help in escaping pursuit, but had to turn back. Uncle Egor lived in a very inaccessible spot, the railway line that had to be traversed was later included in the war zone, travelling became difficult, and sometimes the trains were stopped altogether.

There was a cogent reason, however, why I hesitated to return to Uncle Egor except in an emergency. He might not have recognized me – and that brings me back to my story.

Traversing the city on this cold February morning, I sensed an atmosphere of peculiar unrest and subdued alarm. Small groups of guards – Lettish and Chinese, for the most part – hurrying hither and thither, were evidence of special activity on the part of the Extraordinary Commission. I procured the soviet newspapers, but they, of course, gave no indication that anything was amiss. It was only later that I learned that during the last few days numerous arrests of supposed counter-revolutionists had been made, and that simultaneously measures were being taken to prevent an anticipated outbreak of workers' strikes.

By usual devious routes I arrived in the locality of my empty flat 'No. 5'. This, I was confident, was the safest place for me to return to first. From here I would telephone to the Journalist, the Doctor, and one or two other people, and find out if all was fair and square in their houses. If no one had 'been taken ill', or 'gone to hospital', or been inflicted with 'unexpected visits from country relatives', I would look them up and find out how the land lay and if anything particular had happened during my absence.

The prevailing atmosphere of disquietude made me approach the flat with especial caution. The street was all but deserted, the yard was as foul and noisome as ever, and the only individual I encountered as I crossed it, holding my breath, was a hideous wretch, shaking with disease, digging presumably for food in the stinking heaps of rubbish piled in the corner. His jaws munched mechanically, and he looked up with a guilty look, like a dog discovered in some overt misdeed. From the window as I mounted the stairs I threw him some money without waiting to see how he took it.

Arriving at 'No. 5', I listened intently at the back door. There was no sound within. I was about to knock, when I recalled the poor devil I had seen in the yard. An idea occurred – I would give him another forty roubles and tell *him* to come up and knock. Meanwhile, I would listen at the bottom of the stairs, and if I heard unfamiliar voices at the door I would have time to make off. They would never arrest that miserable outcast anyway. But the fellow was no longer in the yard, and I repented that I had thrown him money and interrupted his repast. Misplaced generosity! I remounted the stairs and applied my ear to the door.

Thump – thump – thump! Nothing being audible, I knocked boldly, hastily re-applying my ear to the keyhole to await the result.

For a moment there was silence. Impatient, I thumped the door a second time, louder. Then I heard shuffling footsteps moving along the passage. Without waiting, I darted down the steps to the landing below. Whoever came to the door, I hurriedly considered, would be certain, when they found no one outside, to look out over the iron banisters. If it were a stranger, I would say I had mistaken the door, and bolt.

The key squeaked in the rusty lock and the door was stiffly pushed open. Shoeless feet approached the banisters, and a face peered over. Through the bars from the bottom I saw it was the dull and unintelligent face of the boy, Grisha, who had replaced Maria.

'Grisha,' I called, as I mounted the stairs, to prepare him for my return, 'is that you?'

Grisha's expressionless features barely broke into a smile. 'Are you alone at home?' I asked when I reached him.

'Alone.'

Grisha followed me into the flat, locking the back door behind him. The air was musty with three weeks' unimpeded accumulation of dust.

'Where is Maria? See! I have brought her a lovely pair of brand-new shoes. And for you a slab of chocolate. There!'

Grisha took the chocolate, muttering thanks, and breaking off a morsel slowly conveyed it to his mouth.

'Well? Nothing new, Grisha? Is the world still going round?'

Grisha stared and, preparatory to speech, laboriously transferred the contents of his mouth into his cheek. At last he got it there, and, gulping, gave vent somewhat inarticulately to the following unexpected query:

'Are you *Kr-Kr-Kry-len-ko*?'

Krylenko! How the deuce should this youngster know my name of Krylenko – or Afirenko, or Markovitch, or any other? He knew me only as 'Ivan Ilitch', a former friend of his master.

But Grisha appeared to take it for granted. Without waiting he proceeded:

'They came again for you this morning.'

'Who?'

'A man with two soldiers.'

'Asking for "Krylenko"?'

'Yes.'

'And what did you say?'

'What you told me, Ivan Ilitch. That you will be away a long time and perhaps not come back at all.'

'By what wonderful means, I should like to know, have you discovered a connection between me and anyone called Krylenko?'

'They described you.'

'What did they say? Tell me precisely.'

Grisha shifted awkwardly from foot to foot. His sluggish brain exerted itself to remember.

'Tall – sort of, they said, black beard ... long hair ... one front tooth missing ... speaks not quite our way ... walks quickly.'

Was Grisha making this up? Surely he had not sufficient ingenuity! I questioned him minutely as to when the unwelcome visitors had first come and made him repeat every word they had said and his replies. I saw then, that it was true. I was known, and they were awaiting my return.

'Today was the second time,' said Grisha. 'First they came a few days ago. They looked round and opened the cupboards, but when they found them all empty, they went away. "*Uyehal* – departed," said one to the others. "There's nothing here, so it's useless to leave anyone. When will he return?" he asks me. "There's no knowing," I tell him. "Maybe you'll never come back," I said. Early this morning when they came I told them the same.'

A moment's consideration convinced me that there was only one line of action. I must quit the flat like lightning. The next step must be decided in the street.

'Grisha,' I said, 'you have acquitted yourself well. If ever anyone asks for me again, tell them I have left the city for good, and shall never return. Does Maria know?'

'Maria is still at the farm. I have not seen her for two weeks.'

'Well, tell her the same – because it's true. Goodbye.'

Arriving in the street, I began to think. Had I not better have told Grisha simply to say nobody had come back at all? But Grisha was sure to bungle the moment he was cross-questioned and then they would think him an accomplice. It was too late, anyway. I must now think of how to change my appearance completely and with the minimum of delay. The nearest place to go to was the Journalist's. If he could not help me I would lie low there till nightfall and then go to the Doctor's.

Limping along painfully, half covering my face with my scarf as if I had a toothache, I approached the Journalist's home. He lived on the first floor, thank heaven, so there would be only one flight of stairs to ascend.

From the opposite side of the street I scrutinized the exterior of the house. Through the glass door I could see nobody in the hall and there was nothing to indicate that anything was amiss. So I crossed the road and entered.

The floor-tiling in the hall was loose and had long needed repair, but I tiptoed over it gently and without noise. Then, with one foot on the bottom stair, I stopped dead. What was that disturbance on the first landing just over my head? I listened intently.

Whispering.

There must be two or three people on the first landing, conferring in low tones, and from the direction of the voices it was clear they were just outside the Journalist's door. I caught the word 'pick-lock', and somebody passed some keys, one of which seemed to be inserted in the lock.

Thieves, possibly. But robbery was becoming rare in these days when the bourgeoisie had scarcely anything more to be relieved of, and anyway why should the Journalist's flat particularly be selected and the theft perpetrated in broad daylight? It was far more likely that the dwelling was to be subjected to a sudden search, and that the raiders wished to surprise the occupant or occupants without giving them time to secrete anything. In any case, thieves or searchers, this was no place for me. I turned and tiptoed hurriedly out of the hall.

And very foolish it was of me to hurry, too! For I should have remembered the flooring was out of repair. The loose tiles rattled beneath my feet like pebbles, the noise was heard above, and down the stairs there charged a heavy pair of boots. Outside was better than in, anyway, so I did not stop, but just as I was slipping into the street I was held up from behind by a big burly workman, dressed in a leather jacket covered with belts of cartridges, who held a revolver at my head.

It is a debatable point, which tactic is more effective in a tight corner – to laugh defiantly with brazen audacity, or to assume a crazy look of utter imbecility. Practised to an extreme, either will pull you through almost any scrape, granted your adversary displays a particle of doubt or hesitancy. From my present bedraggled and exhausted appearance to one of vacant stupidity was but a step, so when the cartridge-bedecked individual challenged me with his revolver and demanded to know my business, I met his gaze with terrified blinking eyes, shaking limbs, slobbering lips, and halting speech.

'Stand!' he bawled, 'what do you want here?' His voice was raucous and threatening.

I looked up innocently over his head at the lintel of the door.

'Is – is this No. 29?' I stammered, with my features contorted into an insane grin. 'It is – I – I mistook it for No. 39, wh-which I want. Thank you.'

Mumbling and leering idiotically, I limped off like a cripple. Every second I expected to hear him shout an order to halt. But he merely glared, and I remembered I had seen just such a glare before, on the face of that other man whom I encountered in Marsh's house the day of my first arrival in Petrograd. As I stumbled along, looking up with blinking eyes at all the shop- and door-lintels as I passed them, I saw out of the corner of my eye that the cartridge-covered individual had lowered his revolver to his side. Then he turned and re-entered the house.

‡

'The blades are pretty blunt, I am afraid,' observed the Doctor, as he produced his Gillette razor and placed it on the table before me. 'They still mow me all right, but I've got a soft chin. The man who smuggles a box-full of razor-blades into this country will make his fortune. Here's the brush, and soap – my last piece.'

It was late in the afternoon of the same day. I sat in the Doctor's study before a mirror, preparing to perform an excruciating surgical operation, namely, the removal with a blunt safety-razor of the shaggy hirsute appendage that for nearly six months had decorated my cheeks, chin, and nether lip.

The Doctor, as you see, was still at liberty. It was with some trepidation that I had approached his house on this day when everything seemed to be going wrong. But we had agreed upon a sign by which I might know, every time I called, whether it were safe to enter. A large box was placed in the window in such a position as to be visible from the street. Its absence would be a danger-signal. The Doctor had suggested this device as much for his own sake as mine: he had no desire that I should come stumbling in if he were engaged in an altercation with a delegation from *No. 2 Goróhovaya*, and there was no house in the city that was immune from these unwelcome visitors. But the box was in the window, so I was in the flat.

Before operating with the razor I reduced my beard as far as possible with the scissors. Even this altered my appearance to a remarkable degree. Then I brought soap-brush and blade into play – but the less said of the ensuing painful hour the better! The Doctor then assumed the role of hair-dresser. He cut off my flowing locks, and, though it was hardly necessary, dyed my hair coal-black with some German dye-stuff he had got.

Except for one detail, my transformation was now complete. Cutting open the lapel of the jacket I was discarding, I extracted a tiny paper packet, and unwrapping it, took out the contents – my missing tooth, carefully preserved for this very emergency. A little wadding served effectually as a plug. I inserted it in the gaping aperture in my top row of teeth, and what had so recently been a diabolic leer became a smile as seemly (I hope) as that of any other normal individual.

The clean-shaven, short-haired, tidy but indigent-looking person in eye-glasses, who made his way down the Doctor's staircase next morning attired in the Doctor's old clothes, resembled the shaggy-haired, limping maniac of the previous day about as nearly as he did the cook who preceded him down the stairs. The cook was going to engage the house-porter's attention if the latter presented himself, in order that he might not notice the exit of a person who had never entered. So when the cook disappeared into the porter's cave-like abode just inside the front door, covering with her back the little glass window through which he or his wife always peered, and began greeting the pair with enthusiastic heartiness, I slipped unnoticed into the street.

In the dilapidated but capacious boots the Doctor found for me I was able to walk slowly without limping. But I used a walking-stick, and this added curiously to my new appearance, which I think may be described as that of an ailing, underfed 'intellectual' of student type. It is a fact that during these days, when in view of my lameness I could not move rapidly, I passed unmolested and untouched out of more than one scuffle when raiders rounded up 'speculators', and crossed the bridges without so much as being asked for my papers.

It took me several days to get thoroughly accustomed to my new exterior. I found myself constantly glancing into mirrors and shop-windows in the street, smiling with amusement at my own reflection. In the course of ensuing weeks and months I encountered several people with whom I had formerly had connections, and though some of them looked me in the face I was never recognized.

It was about a week later, when walking along the river quay, that I espied to my surprise on the other side of the road Melnikoff's friend of Viborg days whom I had hoped to find in Finland – Ivan Sergeievitch. He was well disguised as a soldier, with worn-out boots and shabby cap. I followed him in uncertainty, passing and repassing him two or three times to make sure. But a scar on his cheek left no further doubt. So, waiting until he was close to the gate of the garden on the west side of the Winter Palace, the wall of which with the imperial monograms was being removed, I stepped up behind him.

'Ivan Sergeievitch,' I said in a low voice.

He stopped dead, not looking round.

'It is all right,' I continued, 'step into the garden, you will recognize me in a minute.'

He followed me cautiously at some paces distance and we sat down on a bench amongst the bushes. In this little garden former emperors and empresses had promenaded when occupying the Winter Palace. In the olden days before the revolution I often used to wonder what was hidden behind the massive wall and railings with imperial monograms that surrounded it. But it was only a plain little enclosure with winding paths, bushes, and a small fountain.

'My God!' exclaimed Ivan Sergeievitch, in astonishment, when I had convinced him of my *bona fide* identity. 'Is it possible? No one would recognize you! It is you I have been looking for.'

'Me?'

'Yes. Do you not know that Zorinsky is in Finland?'

Zorinsky again! Though it was only a week, it seemed ages since I had last crossed the frontier, and the Zorinsky episode already belonged to the distant past – when I was somebody and something else. I was surprised how little interest the mention of his name excited in me. I was already entirely engrossed in a new political situation that had arisen.

'Is he?' I replied. 'I went to Finland myself recently, partly to see you about that very fellow. I saw your wife. But nobody seems to know anything about him, and I have ceased to care.'

'You have no notion what a close shave you have had, Pavel Pavlovitch. I will tell you what I know. When I heard from my wife that Varia was arrested and that you were in touch with Zorinsky, I returned to Finland and, although I am condemned by the Bolsheviks to be shot, set out at once for Petrograd. You see, Zorinsky –'

And Ivan Sergeievitch unfolded to me a tale that was strange indeed. I have forgotten some details of it but it was roughly as follows:

Zorinsky, under another name, had been an officer in the old army. He distinguished himself for reckless bravery at the front and drunkenness in the rear. During the war he had had some financial losses, became implicated in attempted embezzlement, and later was caught cheating at cards. He was invited to resign from his regiment, but was reinstated after an interval in view of his military services. He again distinguished himself in battle, but was finally excluded from the regiment shortly before the revolution, this time on the ground of misconduct. During 1917 he was known to have failed in some grandiose deals of a speculative and doubtful character. He then disappeared for a time, but in the summer of 1918 was found living in Petrograd under various names, ostensibly hiding from the Bolsheviks. Although his business deals were usually unsuccessful, he appeared always to be in affluent circumstances. It was this fact, and a certain strangeness of manner, that led Ivan Sergeievitch to regard him with strong suspicion. He had him watched, and established beyond all doubt that he was endeavouring to gain admission to various counter-revolutionary organizations on behalf of the Bolsheviks.

Shortly afterward, Ivan Sergeievitch was arrested under circumstances that showed that only Zorinsky could have betrayed him. But he escaped on the very night that he was to be shot by breaking from his guards and throwing himself over the parapet of the Neva into the river. In Finland, whither he fled, he met and formed a close friendship with Melnikoff , who, after the Yaroslavl affair and his own escape, had assisted in the establishment of a system of communication with Petrograd, occasionally revisiting the city himself.

'Of course I told Melnikoff of Zorinsky,' said Ivan Sergeievitch, 'though I could not know that Zorinsky would track him. But he got the better of us both.'

'Then why,' I asked, 'did Melnikoff associate with him?'

'He never saw him, so far as I know.'

'What!' I exclaimed. 'But Zorinsky said he knew him well and always called him "an old friend"!'

'Zorinsky may have *seen* Melnikoff, but he never *spoke* to him, that I know of. Melnikoff was a friend of a certain Vera Alexandrovna X., who kept a secret café – you knew it? Ah, if I had known Melnikoff had told you of it I should have warned you. From other people who escaped from Petrograd I learned that Zorinsky frequented the café too. He was merely lying in wait for Melnikoff.'

'You mean he deliberately betrayed him?'

'It is evident. Put two and two together. Melnikoff was a known and much-feared counter-revolutionary. Zorinsky was in the service of the Extraordinary Commission and was well paid, no doubt. He also betrayed Vera Alexandrovna and her café, probably receiving so much per head. I heard of that from other people.'

'Then why did he not betray me too?' I asked incredulously.

'You gave him money, I suppose?'

I told Ivan Sergeievitch the whole story, how I had met Zorinsky, his offer to release Melnikoff, the sixty thousand roubles and other payments 'for odd expenses' amounting to about a hundred thousand in all. I also told him of the valuable and accurate information Zorinsky had provided me with.

'That is just what he would do,' said Ivan Sergeievitch. 'He worked for both sides. A hundred thousand, I suppose, is all he thought he could get out of you, so now he has gone to Finland. Something must have happened to you here, for he wanted to prevent your returning to Russia and pose as your saviour. Is it not true that something has happened?'

I told him of the discovery of the Journalist's flat and 'No. 5', but, unless I had been tracked unnoticed, there was no especial reason to believe Zorinsky could have discovered either of these. The betrayal of the name 'Krylenko' was of course easily traceable to him, but whence had he known the addresses?

And then I remembered that I had never telephoned to

Zorinsky from anywhere except from 'No. 5' and the Journalist's, for those were the only places where I could speak without being overheard. I suggested the coincidence to Ivan Sergeievitch.

'Aha!' he cried, obviously regarding the evidence as conclusive. 'Of course he enquired for your telephone numbers directly you had spoken! But he would not betray you as long as you continued to pay him. Besides, he doubtless hoped eventually to unearth a big organization. As for your betrayal, any time would do, and the reward was always certain. It might be another hundred thousand for your haunts. And then, you see, in Finland he would warn you against returning and get some more out of you for this further great service. He was furious to find you had just left.'

From the windows of the Winter Palace prying eyes were looking down into the garden. Two figures sitting so long on a cold day in the bushes would begin to be suspicious. We rose and walked out on to the quay.

Seating ourselves on one of the stone benches set in the parapet of the river, Ivan Sergeievitch told me many things that were of the greatest value. An entirely new set of associations grew out of this conversation. He also said that Varia had just been released from prison and that he was going to take her with him across the frontier that night. He had been unable to find Stepanovna, but supposed she was staying with friends. I agreed if ever I heard of her to let him know.

'Will Zorinsky come back to Russia, do you think?' I asked.

'I have no idea,' was the reply; and he added, again staring at my transformed physiognomy and laughing, 'but you certainly have no cause to fear his recognizing you now!'

Such was the strange story of Zorinsky as I learned it from Ivan Sergeievitch. I never heard it corroborated except by the Doctor, who didn't know Zorinsky, but I had no reason to doubt it. It certainly tallied with my own experiences. And he was only one of several. As Ivan Sergeievitch observed: 'There are not a few Zorinskys, I fear, and they are the ruin and shame of our class.'

Twice, later, I was reminded acutely of this singular personage, who, as it transpired, did return to Russia. The first time was when I learned through acquaintances of Ivan Sergeievitch that Zorinsky believed me to be back in Petrograd, and had related to somebody in tones of admiration that he himself had seen me driving down the Nevsky Prospect in a carriage and pair in the company of one of the chief Bolshevist Commissars!

The second time was months later, when I espied him standing in a doorway, smartly dressed in a blue 'French' and knee-breeches, about to mount a motorcycle. I was on the point of descending from a street car when our eyes met. I stopped and pushed my way back into the crowd of passengers. Being in the uniform of a Red soldier I feared his recognition of me not by my exterior, but by another peculiar circumstance. Under the influence of sudden emotion a sort of telepathic communication sometimes takes place without the medium of words and even regardless of distance. It has several times happened to me. Rightly or wrongly I suspected it now. I pushed my way through the car to the front platform and looking back over the heads of the passengers, imagined (maybe it was mere imagination) I saw Zorinsky's eyes also peering over the passengers' heads toward me.

I did not wait to make sure. The incident occurred in the Zagorodny Prospect. Passing the Tsarskoselsky station I jumped off the car while it was still in motion, stooped beneath its side till it passed, and boarded another in the opposite direction. At the station I jumped off, entered the building and sat amongst the massed herds of peasants and 'speculators' till dusk.

Eventually I heard that Zorinsky had been shot by the Bolsheviks. If so, it was an ironic and fitting close to his career. Perhaps they discovered him again serving two or more masters. But the news impressed me but little, for I had ceased to care whether Zorinsky was shot or not.

PART II

Chapter X

The Sphinx

$\mathbf{A}$ detailed narrative of my experiences during the following six months would surpass the dimensions to which I must limit this book. Some of them I hope to make the subject of a future story. For I met other 'Stepanovnas', 'Marias' and 'Journalists', in whom I came to trust as implicitly as in the old and who were a very present help in time of trouble. I also inevitably met with scoundrels, but though *No. 2 Goróhovaya* again got close upon my track – even closer than through Zorinsky – and one or two squeaks were very narrow indeed, still I have survived to tell the tale.

This is partly because the precautions I took to avoid detection became habitual. Only on one occasion was I obliged to destroy documents of value, while of the couriers who, at grave risk, carried communications back and forth from Finland, only two failed to arrive and I presume were caught and shot. But the messages they bore (as indeed any notes I ever made) were composed in such a manner that they could not possibly be traced to any individual or address.

I wrote mostly at night, in minute handwriting on tracing-paper, with a small caoutchouc bag about four inches in length, weighted with lead, ready at my side. In case of alarm all my papers could be slipped into this bag and within thirty seconds be transferred to the bottom of a tub of washing or the cistern of the water-closet. In efforts to discover arms or incriminating documents, I have seen pictures, carpets, and book shelves removed and everything turned topsy-turvy by diligent searchers, but it never occurred to anybody to search through a pail of washing or thrust his hand into the water-closet cistern.

Through the agency of friends I secured a post as

draftsman at a small factory on the outskirts of the city. A relative of one of the officials of this place, whose signature was attached to my papers and who is well known to the Bolsheviks, called on me recently in New York. I showed him some notes I had made on the subject, but he protested that, camouflaged though my references were, they might still be traced to individuals concerned, most of whom, with their families, are still in Russia. I therefore suppressed them. For similar reasons I am still reticent in details concerning the regiment of the Red army to which I was finally attached.

Learning through military channels at my disposal that men of my age and industrial status were shortly to be mobilized and despatched to the eastern front, where the advance of Kolchak was growing to be a serious menace, I forestalled the mobilization order by about a week and applied for admission as a volunteer in the regiment of an officer acquaintance, stationed a short distance outside Petrograd. There was some not unnatural hesitation before I received an answer, due to the necessity of considering the personality of the regimental commissar – a strong Communist who wished to have the regiment despatched to perform its revolutionary duty against Kolchak's armies. But at the critical moment this individual was promoted to a higher divisional post, and the commander in getting nominated to his regiment a commissar of shaky communistic principles, who ultimately developed anti-Bolshevist sympathies almost as strong as his own. How my commander, a Tsarist officer, who detested and feared the Communists, was forced to serve in the Red army I will explain later.

Despite his ill-concealed sympathies, however, this gentleman won Trotzky's favour in an unexpected and remarkable manner. Being instructed to impede an advance of the forces of the 'White' general, Yudenitch, by the destruction of strategic bridges, he resolved to blow up the wrong bridge, and, if possible, cut off the Red retreat and assist the White advance. By sheer mistake, however, the company he despatched to perform the task blew up the right bridge, thus covering a precipitate Red retreat and effectually checking the White advance.

For days my commander secretly tore his hair and wept, his mortification rendered the more acute by the commendation he was obliged for the sake of appearances to shower upon his men, whose judgment had apparently been so superior to his own. His chagrin reached its height when he received an official communication from army headquarters applauding the timely exploit, while through the Communist organization he was formally invited to join the privileged ranks of the Communist Party! In the view of my commander no affront could have been more offensive than this unsought Bolshevist honour. He was utterly at a loss to grasp my point of view when I told him what to me was obvious, namely, that no offer could have been more providential and that he ought to jump at it. Though inside Russia the approaching White armies were often imagined to be a band of noble and chivalrous crusaders, certain information I had received as to the disorganization prevailing amongst them aroused my misgivings, and I was very doubtful whether my commander's error had materially altered the course of events. The commissar, who did not care one way or the other, saw the humour of the situation. He, too, urged the commander to smother his feelings and see the joke, with the result that the would-be traitor to the pseudo-proletarian cause became a Communist, and combining his persuasions with those of the commissar, succeeded in keeping the regiment out of further action for several weeks. The confidence they had won made it easy to convince army headquarters that the regiment was urgently required to suppress uprisings which were feared in the capital. When disturbances did break out, however, the quelling of them was entrusted to troops drafted from the far south or east, for it was well known that no troops indigenous to Petrograd or Moscow could be relied upon to fire on their own population.

I had hitherto evaded military service as long as possible,

fearing that it might impede the conduct of my intelligence work. The contrary proved to be the case, and for many reasons I regretted I had not enlisted earlier. Apart from greater freedom of movement and preference over civilians in application for lodging, amusement, or travelling tickets, the Red soldier received rations greatly superior both in quantity and quality to those of the civilian population. Previous to this time I had received only half a pound of bread daily and had had to take my scanty dinner at a filthy communal eating-house, but as a Red soldier I received, besides a dinner and other odds and ends not worth mentioning, a pound and sometimes a pound and a half of tolerably good black bread, which alone was sufficient, accustomed as I am to a crude diet, to subsist on with relative comfort.

The commander was a good fellow, nervous and sadly out of place in 'the party', but he soon got used to it and enjoyed its many privileges. He stood me in good stead. Repeatedly detailing me off to any place I wished to go to, on missions he knew were lengthy (such as the purchase of automobile tyres which were unobtainable, or literature of various kinds) I was able to devote my main attention as before to the political and economic situation.

As a Red soldier, I was sent to Moscow and there consulted with the National Centre, the most promising of the political organizations whose object was to work out a programme acceptable to the Russian people as a whole. On account of its democratic character this organization was pursued by the Bolshevist Government with peculiar zeal, and was finally unearthed, and its members, of whom many were Socialists, shot.* From Moscow also I received regularly copies of the

---

* The Bolsheviks assert that I lent the National Centre financial assistance. This is unfortunately untrue, for the British Government had furnished me with no funds for such a purpose. I drew the Government's attention to the existence of the National Centre, but the latter was suppressed by the Reds too early for any action to be taken.

summaries on the general situation that were submitted to the Soviet of People's Commissars. The questions I was instructed in messages from abroad to investigate covered the entire field of soviet administration, but I do not plan to deal with that huge subject here. It is the present and the inscrutable future that fascinate me rather than the past. I will speak only of the peasantry, the army, and 'the party'. For it is on the ability or inability of the Communists to control the army that the stability of the Bolshevist regime in considerable measure depends, while the future lies in the lap of that vast inarticulate mass of simple peasant toilers, so justly termed the Russian Sphinx.

Chapter XI

The Red Army

The day I joined my regiment I donned my Red army uniform, consisting of a khaki shirt, yellow breeches, putties, and a pair of good boots which I bought from another soldier (the army at that time was not issuing boots), and a gray army overcoat. On my cap I wore the Red army badge — a red star with a mallet and plough imprinted on it.

This could not be said to be the regular Red army uniform, though it was as regular as any. Except for picked troops, smartly apparelled in the best the army stores could provide, the rank and file of recruits wore just anything, and often had only bast slippers in place of boots. There is bitter irony and a world of significance in the fact that in 1920, when I observed the Red army again from the Polish front, I found many of the thousands who deserted to the Poles wearing British uniforms which had been supplied, together with so much war material, to Denikin.

'*Tovarishtch Kommandir*,' I would say on presenting myself before my commander, '*pozvoltye dolozhitj* ... Comrade Commander, allow me to report that the allotted task is executed.'

'Good, comrade So-and-so,' would be the reply, 'I will hear your report immediately,' or: 'Hold yourself in readiness at such and such an hour tomorrow.'

The terminology of the former army, like the nomenclature of many streets in the capitals, has been altered and the word 'commander' substituted for 'officer'. When we were alone I did not say 'Comrade Commander' (unless facetiously) but called him 'Vasili Petrovitch', and he addressed me also by Christian name and patronymic.

'Vasili Petrovitch,' I said one day, 'what made you join the Red army?'

'You think we have any option?' he retorted. 'If an officer doesn't want to be shot he either obeys the mobilization order or flees from the country. And only those can afford to take flight who have no family to leave behind.' He drew a bulky pocket-book from his pocket, and fumbling amongst the mass of dirty and ragged documents, unfolded a paper and placed it before me. 'That is a copy of a paper I was made to fill in and sign before being given a Red commission. We all have to sign it, and if you were discovered here I should have signed away my wife's life as well as my own.'

The paper was a typewritten blank, on which first the name, rank in the old army, present rank, regiment, abode, etc., had to be filled in in detail. Then followed a space in which the newly mobilized officer gave an exhaustive list of his relatives, with their ages, addresses, and occupations; while at the bottom, followed by a space for signature, were the following words: *I hereby declare that I am aware that in the event of my disloyalty to the Soviet Government my relatives shall he arrested and deported.*

Vasili Petrovitch spread out his hands, shrugging his shoulders.

'I should prefer to see my wife and my little daughters shot,' he said, bitterly, 'rather than that they be sent to a Red concentration camp. I am supposed to make my subordinates sign these declarations, too. Pleasant, isn't it? You know, I suppose,' he added, 'that appointment to a post of any responsibility is now made conditional upon having relatives near at hand who may be arrested?' (This order had been published in the press.) 'The happiest thing nowadays is to be friendless and destitute, then you cannot get your people shot. Or else act on the Bolshevist principle that conscience, like liberty, is a "bourgeois prejudice". Then you can work for *No. 2 Goróhovaya* and make a fortune.'

Not only my commander but most of the men in my unit talked like this amongst themselves, only quietly, for fear of

Bolshevist spies. One little fellow who was drafted into the regiment was uncommonly outspoken. He was a mechanic from a
factory on the Viborg side of the city. His candour was such
that I suspected him at first of being a *provocateur*, paid by the
Bolsheviks to speak ill of them and thus unmask sympathizers.
But he was not that sort. One day I overheard him telling the
story of how he and his fellows had been mobilized.

'As soon as we were mobilized,' he said, 'we were chased
to all sorts of meetings. Last Saturday at the *Narodny Dom* [the
biggest hall in Petrograd] Zinoviev spoke to us for an hour and
assured us we were to fight for workmen and peasants against
capitalists, imperialists, bankers, generals, landlords, priests, and
other bloodsucking riff-raff. Then he read a resolution that
every Red soldier swears to defend Red Petrograd to the last
drop of blood, but nobody put up his hand except a few in the
front rows who had, of course, been put there to vote "for".
Near me I heard several men growl and say, "Enough! we aren't
sheep, and we know what sort of freedom you want to use us as
cannon fodder for." Son of a gun, that Zinoviev!' exclaimed the
little man, spitting disgustedly; 'next day – what do you think? –
we read in the paper that ten thousand newly mobilized soldiers
had passed a resolution unanimously to defend what Zinoviev
and Lenin call the "Workers' and Peasants' Government"!'
Few people ventured to be so outspoken as this, for everybody
feared the four or five Communists who were attached to the
regiment to eavesdrop and report any remarks detrimental to
the Bolsheviks. One of these Communists was a Jew, a rare
occurrence in the rank and file of the army. He disappeared
when the regiment was moved to the front, doubtless having
received another job of a similar nature in a safe spot in the
rear. The only posts in the Red army held in any number by
Jews are the political posts of commissars. One reason why
there appear to be so many Jews in the Bolshevist administration is that they are nearly all employed in the rear, particularly
in those departments (such as of food, propaganda, public

economy) which are not concerned in fighting. It is largely to the ease with which Jewish Bolsheviks evade military service, and the arrogance some of them show toward the Russians whom they openly despise, that the intense hatred of the Jew and the popular belief in Russia that Bolshevism is a Jewish 'put-up' are due. There are, of course, just as many Jews who oppose the Bolsheviks, and many of these are lying in prison. But this is not widely known, for like Russian anti-Bolsheviks they have no means of expressing their opinions.

‡

Leo Bronstein, the genius of the Red army, now universally known by his more Russian-sounding pseudonym of Trotzky, is the second of the triumvirate of 'Lenin, Trotzky, and Zinoviev', who guide the destinies of the Russian and the World revolution. That the accepted order of precedence is not 'Trotzky, Lenin, and Zinoviev' must be gall and worm-wood to Trotzky's soul. His first outstanding characteristic is overweening ambition; his second – egoism; his third – cruelty; and all three are sharpened by intelligence and wit of unusual brilliancy. According to his intimate associates of former days, his nature is by no means devoid of cordiality, but his affections are completely subordinated to the promotion of his ambitious personal designs, and he casts off friends and relatives alike, as he would clothing, the moment they have served his purpose.

A schoolmate, prison-companion, and political colleague of Trotzky, Dr Ziv, who for years shared his labours both openly and secretly, travelled with him to exile, and was associated with him also in New York, thus sums up his character:

'In Trotzky's psychology there are no elements correspond-ing to the ordinary conceptions of brutality or humanity. In place of these there is a blank... Men, for him, are mere units – hundreds, thousands, and hundreds of thousands of units – by means of which he may satisfy his *Wille zur Macht*. Whether this end is to be achieved by securing for those multitudes conditions of supreme happiness or by mercilessly crushing or exterminating them, is for Trotzky an unessential detail, to be determined not by sympathies or antipathies but by the accidental circumstances of the moment.'

The same writer throws some interesting light on how Bronstein chose his pseudonym. His present assumed name of 'Trotzky' was that of the senior jailer of the Tsarist prison-house at Odessa, where Bronstein and Dr Ziv were incarcerated. The latter describes this jailer as 'a majestic figure, leaning on his long sabre and with the eagle eye of a field-marshal surveying his domain and feeling himself a little tsar'. The motive impelling Trotzky to use a pseudonym is peculiar. 'To call himself Bronstein would be once and for all to attach to himself the hated label designating his Jewish origin, and this was the very thing that he desired everyone to forget as quickly and thoroughly as possible.' This estimation is the more valuable in that the writer, Dr Ziv, is himself a Jew.

The creation and control of a huge militarist machine has hitherto afforded full and ample scope for the exercise of Trotzky's superhuman energy and indomitable will. Regarding the Russian peasants and workers as cattle and treating them as such, he naturally strove at an early date, by coercion or by flattering and alluring inducements, to persuade the trained Tsarist officer staff, with whose technical knowledge he could not dispense, to serve the Red flag. The ideas of a 'democratic army' and 'the arming of the entire proletariat' the demand for which, together with that for the constituent assembly, had served to bring Trotzky and his associates to power, were discarded the moment they had served their purpose.

The same measures were introduced to combat wholesale robbery and pillage – an inevitable phenomenon resulting from Bolshevist agitation – as were employed by the Tsarist army, and with even greater severity. Soldiers' committees were soon suppressed. The 'revolutionary' commanders of 1918, untrained and unqualified for leadership, were dismissed and supplanted by 'specialists' – that is, officers of the Tsarist army, closely watched, however, by carefully selected Communists.

The strength of the Red army now undoubtedly lies in its officer staff. As the indispensability of expert military knowledge became more and more apparent, the official attitude toward Tsarist officers, which was one of contempt and hostility as bourgeois, became tempered with an obvious desire to conciliate. The curious phenomenon was observable of a ribald Red press, still pandering to mob-instincts, denouncing all Tsarist officers as 'counter-revolutionary swine', while at the same time Trotzky, in secret, was tentatively extending the olive branch to these same 'swine', and addressing them in tones of conciliation and even respect. Officers were told that it was fully understood that, belonging to 'the old school', they could not readily acquiesce in all the innovations of the 'proletarian' regime, that it was hoped in course of time they would come to adapt themselves to it, and that if in the meantime they would 'give their knowledge to the revolution' their services would be duly recognized.

'We found it difficult to believe it was Trotzky talking to us,' an officer said to me after the extraordinary meeting of commissars and naval specialists of the Baltic fleet, at which Trotzky abolished the committee system and restored the officers' authority. My friend participated at the meeting, being a high official in the admiralty. 'We all sat round the table in expectation, officers at one end and the Communist commissars at the other. The officers were silent, for we did not know why we had been called, but the commissars, all dressed in leathern jerkins, sprawled in the best chairs, smoking and spitting, and laughing loudly. Suddenly the door opened and Trotzky entered. I had never seen him before and was quite taken aback. He was dressed in the full uniform of a Russian officer with the sole exception of epaulettes. The dress did not suit him, but he held himself erect and leader-like, and when we all stood to receive him the contrast between him and the commissars, whom he himself had appointed, was striking.

When he spoke we were thunderstruck – and so were the commissars – for turning to our end of the table he addressed us not as "Comrades" but as "Gentlemen", thanked us for our services, and assured us he understood the difficulties, both moral and physical, of our situation. Then he suddenly turned on the commissars and to our amazement poured forth a torrent of abuse just such as we are accustomed nowadays to hear directed against ourselves. He called them skulking slackers, demanded to know why they dared sit in his presence with their jerkins all unbuttoned, and made them all cringe like dogs. He told us that the ship committees were abolished; that thenceforward the commissars were to have powers only of political control, but none in purely naval matters. We were so dumbfounded that I believe, if Trotzky were not a Jew, the officers would follow him to a man!'

The position of officers was grievous indeed, especially of such as had wives and families. Flight with their families was difficult, while flight without their families led to the arrest of the latter the moment the officer's absence was noted. Remaining in the country their position was no better. Evasion of mobilization or a default in service alike led to reprisals against their kith and kin. Trotzky's approaches were not an effort to make them serve – that was unavoidable – but to induce them to serve well. Alone his persuasions might have availed little. But with the passage of time the bitter disappointment at continued White failures, and growing disgust at the effect of Allied intervention, coming on top of constant terror, drove many to desperate and some to genuine service in the Red ranks, believing that only with the conclusion of war (irrespective of defeat or victory) could the existing regime be altered. I believe that the number of those who are genuinely serving, under a conviction that the present order of things is a mere passing phase, is considerably larger than is generally supposed outside Russia.

One of the most pitiable sights I have ever witnessed was the arrest of women as hostages because their menfolk were suspected of anti-Bolshevist activities. One party of such prisoners I remember particularly because I knew one or two of the people in it. They were all ladies, with the stamp of education and refinement – and untold suffering – on their faces, accompanied by three or four children, who I presume had refused to be torn away. In the hot summer sun they tracked through the streets, attired in the remnants of good clothing, with shoes out at heel, carrying bags or parcels of such belongings as they were permitted to take with them to prison. Suddenly one of the women swooned and fell. The little party halted. The invalid was helped to a seat by her companions, while the escort stood and looked on as if bored with the whole business. The guards did not look vicious, and were only obeying orders. When the party moved forward one of them carried the lady's bag. Standing beneath the trees of the Alexander Garden I watched the pitiful procession, despair imprinted on every face, trudge slowly across the road and disappear into the dark aperture of *No. 2 Goróhovaya.*

Meanwhile their husbands and sons were informed that a single conspicuous deed on their part against the White or counter-revolutionary armies would be sufficient to secure the release of their womenfolk, while continued good service would guarantee them not only personal freedom, but increased rations and non-molestation in their domiciles. This last means a great deal when workmen or soldiers may be thrust upon you without notice at any time, occupying your best rooms, while you and your family are compelled to retire to a single chamber, perhaps only the kitchen.

Such duress against officers showed an astute understanding of the psychology of the White armies. A single conspicuous deed for the Bolsheviks by an officer of the old army was sufficient to damn that officer for ever in the eyes of the Whites, who appeared to have no consideration for the sore and often hopeless position in which those officers were placed. It was this that troubled my commander after his accidental destruction of the right bridge. I am told that General Brusilov's son was shot by Denikin's army solely because he was found in the service of the Reds. The stupidity of such conduct on the part of the Whites would be inconceivable were it not a fact.

The complete absence of an acceptable programme alternative to Bolshevism, the audibly whispered threats of landlords that in the event of a White victory the land seized by the peasants should be restored to its former owners, and the lamentable failure to understand that in the anti-Bolshevist war politics and not military strategy must play the dominant role, were the chief causes of the White defeats. This theory is borne out by all the various White adventures, whether of Kolchak, Denikin, or Wrangel, the course of each being, broadly speaking, the same. First the Whites advanced triumphantly, and until the character of their regime was realized they were hailed as deliverers from the Red yoke. The Red soldiers deserted to them in hordes and the Red command was thrown into consternation. There was very little fighting considering the vast extent of front. Then came a halt, due to incipient disaffection amongst the civil population in the rear. Requisitioning, mobilization, internecine strife, and corruption amongst officials, differing but little from the regime of the Reds, rapidly alienated the sympathies of the peasantry, who revolted against the Whites as they had against the Reds, and the position of the White armies was made untenable. The first sign of yielding at the front was the signal for a complete reversal of fortune. In some cases this process was repeated more than once, the final result being a determination on the part of the peasantry to hold their own against Red and White alike.

Most Russian émigrés now admit not only that warring against the so-called Soviet Republic has served above all else to consolidate the position of the Bolshevist leaders, but also that the failure of the anti-Bolsheviks was due largely to their own deficient administration. But there are many who continue to lay the blame on anyone's shoulders rather than their own, and primarily upon England – a reproach which is not entirely unjustified, though not for quite the same reason as these critics suppose. For while the Allies and America all participated in military intervention, it was England who for the longest time, and at greatest cost to herself, furnished the counter-revolution with funds and material. Her error and that of her associates lay in making no effort to control the political, i.e., the most important, aspect of the counter-revolution. England appeared to assume that the moral integrity of Kolchak, Denikin, and Wrangel, which has never been called in question by any serious people, was a gauge of the political maturity of these leaders and of the governments they brought into being. Herein lay the fundamental misjudgement of the situation. The gulf that yawns between the White leaders and the peasantry is as wide as that between the Communist party and the Russian people. Not in Moscow, but in the camps of the White leaders were sown the seeds of the disasters that befell them, and this was apparent neither to England nor to any other foreign power.

By the end of 1919 the higher military posts in the Red army, such as those of divisional-, artillery-, and brigade-commanders, were held almost exclusively by former Tsarist generals and colonels. The Bolsheviks are extremely proud of this fact, and frequently boast of it to their visitors. These officers are treated with deference, though as known anti-Bolsheviks they are closely watched, and their families are granted considerable privileges.

In lower ranks there is a predominance of 'Red' officers, turned out from the Red cadet schools where they are instructed by Tsarist officers. Few of the Red cadets are men of education. They are, however, on the whole, strong supporters of the soviet regime. But civilians and even private soldiers also find their way by good service to positions of high responsibility, for the Red army offers a field for advancement not, as in the White armies, according to rank, 'blood', or social standing, but primarily for talent and service. Merit is the only accepted standard for promotion. Common soldiers have become expert regimental commanders, artillery officers, and cavalry leaders. In many cases the formerly unknown opportunities which are now offered them make of such people convinced supporters of the present regime, of whose courage and determination there can be no doubt. Granted that the individual, whatever his real political convictions, signs on as a member of the Communist party, any clever adventurer who devotes his talent to the Red army can rise to great heights and make for himself a brilliant career. Had the Russian people really been fired by revolutionary enthusiasm or devotion to their present rulers, the Red army would, under the system introduced by Trotzky, have rapidly become not merely a formidable but an absolutely irresistible military force.

‡

But the Russian people are not and never will be fired by enthusiasm for the Communist revolution. As long as the White armies were permeated by the landlord spirit there was indeed an incentive to defend the land, an incentive exploited to the full by the Bolsheviks in their own favour. I witnessed a striking instance of this on the northwest front. One of the generals of the White army operating against Petrograd issued an order to the peasant population to the effect that 'this year the produce of the land might be reaped and sold by those who had sown and tilled it [that is, by the peasants who had seized it], but next year the land must be restored to its rightful owners [that is, the former landlords]'. Needless to say, the effect was suicidal, although this same general had been welcomed upon his advance three weeks before with unprecedented rejoicings. Moreover, this particular order was republished by the Bolsheviks in every paper in Soviet Russia and served as powerful propaganda amongst the peasant soldiers on every front.

In November, 1920, I talked to soldiers fresh from the Red ranks in the northern Ukraine. I found peasants, who were willing enough to join insurgents, feared to desert to Wrangel's army. Asked why they had not deserted on the southern front, they replied with decision and in surprising unison: '*Rangelya baimsya*'; which was their way of saying: 'We are afraid of Wrangel.' And this in spite of Wrangel's much-vaunted land law, which promised the land to the peasants. But *behind* Wrangel they knew there stood the landlords.

But the first campaign of the Red army against a non-Russian foe, Poland, which did not threaten the peasants' possession of the land, resulted in complete collapse at the very height of Red power. And this is the more significant in that quite an appreciable degree of anti-Polish national feeling was aroused in Russia, especially amongst educated people, and was exploited by the Bolsheviks to strengthen their own position. But there was one striking difference between the Red and the Polish armies, which largely accounted for the outcome of the war. Badly officered as the Poles were by incompetent, selfish, or corrupt officers, the rank and file of the Polish army was fired even in adversity by a spirit of national patriotism unseen in Europe since the first days of the Great War. It only required the drafting in of a few French officers, and the merciless weeding out of traitors from the Polish staff, to make of the Polish army the formidable weapon that swept the Red hordes like chaff before it. In the Red army, on the other hand, the situation was precisely the reverse. The Reds were officered by commanders who were either inspired by anti-Polish sentiment, or believed, as the Communist leaders assured them, that the revolutionary armies were to sweep right across Europe. But the rank and file were devoid of all interest in the war. Thus they only advanced as long as the wretchedly led Poles retreated too rapidly to be caught up, and the moment they met organized resistance the Russian peasants either fled, deserted, or mutinied in their own ranks.

The Polish victory effectually dispelled the myths of peasant support of the revolution and the invincibility of the Red army, but beyond that it served no useful purpose as far as Russia is concerned. Rather the contrary, for by temporarily aligning Russian intellectuals on the side of the Communists it served even more than the civil wars to consolidate the position of the Soviet Government.

The terror that prevails in the Red army, and which is, when all is said and done, the measure most relied upon by the Soviet Government to ensure discipline, leads at times to extraordinary and apparently inexplicable episodes. In September, 1920, I witnessed the retaking of the fortress of Grodno by the Poles. As I watched the shells falling over the trenches on the outskirts of the town I thought of the wretches lying in them, hating the war, hating their leaders, and merely waiting till nightfall to creep out of the city. Though it was said that Grodno was defended by some of the best Red regiments the retreat was precipitate. But a day or two later near Lida they unexpectedly turned and gave battle. Trotzky was, or had recently been in that sector, and had ordered that ruthless measures be taken to stay the flight. One Polish division was suddenly attacked by five Red divisions. Four of the latter were beaten, but the last, the 21st, continued to fight with savage fury. Three times they bore down in massed formation. It came to a hand-to-hand fight in which the Poles were hard pressed. But after the third attack, which fortunately for the Poles was weaker, an entirely unforeseen and incomprehensible event occurred. The soldiers of the 21st Soviet division killed every one of their commissars and Communists and came over to the Poles in a body with their guns!

It would seem at such times as if conscious human intelligence were completely numbed. Impelled by despair, people act like automatons, regardless of danger, knowing that worse things await them (and especially their kith and kin) if they are detected in attempted disloyalty. People may, by terror, be made to fight desperately for a thing they do not believe in, but there comes after all a breaking point.

‡

The organs of terror in the army are Special Departments of

the Extraordinary Commission, and Revolutionary Tribunals. The methods of the Extraordinary Commission have been described. In the army to which my regiment belonged the order for the formation of revolutionary tribunals stated that they 'are to be established in each brigade area, to consist of three members, and to carry out on the spot verdicts of insubordination, refusal to fight, flight or desertion by complete units, such as sections, platoons, companies, etc.' Sentences (to death inclusively) were to be executed immediately. Verdicts might also be conditional; that is, guilty units might be granted an opportunity to restore confidence in themselves by heroic conduct and thus secure a reversal of the verdict. At the same time, 'separate specially reliable units are to be formed of individuals selected from steady units, whose duty will be to suppress all insubordination. These selected units will also execute the sentences of death'.

Desertion from the Red army is not difficult, but if one lives in or near a town one's relatives pay. Desertion, as what the Bolsheviks call a 'mass-phenomenon', is combated by special Commissions for Combating Desertion, established in every town and large village and at frontier points. The mere abundance of these commissions is indicative of the prevalence of desertion. Their agents hang about the outskirts of towns, at crossroads, frontier stations, etc., prodding truckloads of hay or looking under railroad cars. If the identity of a deserter is established but he cannot be ferreted out, the property of his relatives is confiscated and they are liable to be arrested unless they expose him or until he returns voluntarily.

The peasantry sometimes try to organize desertion. Pickets are posted to give warning of the approach of punitive detachments. In Ukrainia, where the peasants show more vigour and capacity for self-defence against the Communists than in the north, villagers organize themselves into armed bands led by sub-officers of the old army and effectively hold the punitive detachments at bay for considerable periods.

The mobilization of peasants is at times so difficult a proce-
dure that when a regiment has been gathered it is often sent
down to the front in sealed cars. Arms are rarely distributed
until the moment to enter the fray, when a machine gun is
placed behind the raw troops, and they are warned that they
have the option either of advancing or being fired on from the
rear. At the same time provincial districts are cautioned that
every village in which a single deserter is discovered will be
burned to the ground. However, though several such orders
have been published, I do not know of a case in which the
threat has been put into execution.

Mobilization of town-workers is naturally easier, but here
also subterfuge has sometimes to be resorted to. In Petrograd
I witnessed what was announced to be a 'trial' mobilization;
that is, the workers were assured that they were not going to
the front and that the trial was only to be practice for an emergency. The result was that the prospective recruits, glad of an
extra holiday plus the additional bread ration issued on such
occasions, turned up in force (all, of course, in civilian clothes)
and the trial mobilization was a great success. A portion of the
recruits were taken to the Nicholas Station and told they were
going out of town to manoeuvre. Imagine their feelings when
they discovered that they were locked into the cars, promptly
despatched to the front, and (still in civilian clothes) thrust
straight into the firing line!

Every Red army man is supposed to have taken the following oath;

I, a member of a labouring people and citizen of the Soviet
Republic, assume the name of warrior of the Workers' and
Peasants' Army. Before the labouring classes of Russia and of
the whole world I pledge myself to bear this title with honour,
conscientiously to study the science of war, and as the apple
of my eye defend civil and military property from spolia-
tion and pillage. I pledge myself strictly and unswervingly to

observe revolutionary discipline and perform unhesitatingly all orders of the commanders appointed by the Workers' and Peasants' Government. I pledge myself to refrain and to restrain my comrades from any action that may stain and lower the dignity of a citizen of the Soviet Republic, and to direct my best efforts to the sole object of the emancipation of all workers. I pledge myself at the first call of the Workers' and Peasants' Government to defend the Soviet Republic from all dangers and assault on the part of her foes, and to spare neither my energies nor life in the struggle for the Russian Soviet Republic, for the cause of Socialism and the fraternity of peoples. If with evil intent I infringe this my solemn oath may my lot be universal contempt and may I fall a victim to the ruthless arm of revolutionary law.

Very few Red army men have any recollection of having taken this oath, which is reserved for officers or for propagandist purposes. If it is taken by the common soldiers at all it is read out to whole battalions at a time and they are told when to raise their hands.

The method of administering justice followed by the Revolutionary Tribunals is primitive. The judges are guided by no rules, instructions, or laws, but solely by what is known as 'revolutionary conscience'. The fact that the judges are often illiterate does not affect the performance of their functions, for since none but ardent Communists are admitted to these posts, their revolutionary consciences are *ipso facto* bound always to be clear.

The malpractices of these courts reached such a pitch that late in 1920 the Bolsheviks, after abolishing all jurisprudence at the universities, were actually combing out from the ranks of the army all such as had technical knowledge of Tsarist law, offering them posts as legal 'specialists', as had already been done with military, industrial, and agricultural experts.

The Bolsheviks discriminate minutely between their regiments, which are classed as reliable, semi-reliable, and doubtful.

The backbone of the army is composed of regiments which consist purely of convinced Communists. These units, called by such names as the 'Iron Regiment', the 'Death Regiment', the 'Trotzky Regiment', etc., have acted up to their names and fight with desperate ferocity. Reliance is also placed in non-Russian regiments, Lettish, Bashkir, Chinese troops, etc., though their numbers are not large. The total number of Communists being exceedingly small, they are divided up and distributed amongst the remaining regiments in little groups called 'cells'. The size of a cell averages about 10 per cent of the regiment. It is this political organization of the Red army for purposes of propaganda and political control which is its most interesting feature, distinguishing it from all other armies. Isolated as the soldiers are from their homes, unhabituated in many cases by nearly seven years of war from normal occupations, and provisioned visibly better than civilians, it is felt that under military conditions the peasant will be most susceptible to Communist propaganda.

The system of political control is as follows. Side by side with the hierarchy of military commanders there exists a corresponding hierarchy of members of the Communist party, small numerically, but endowed with far-reaching powers of supervision. These branches of the Communist party extend tentacularly to the smallest unit of the army, and not a single soldier is exempt from the omnipresent Communist eye. The responsible Communist official in a regiment is called the Commissar, the others are called 'political workers', and constitute the 'cell'. In my own unit, numbering nearly 200 men, there were never more than half a dozen Communists or 'political workers', and they were regarded with hatred and disgust by the others. Their chief duty obviously was to eavesdrop and report suspicious remarks, but their efforts were crowned with no great success because the commissar, to whom the Communists reported, was a sham Communist himself and a personal friend of my commander.

In other regiments in Petrograd with which I was in touch it was different. I particularly remember one commissar, formerly a locksmith by trade. He had had an elementary education and was distinguished by a strange combination of three marked traits: he was an ardent Communist, he was conspicuously honest, and he was an inveterate toper. I will refer to him as comrade Morozov. Knowing that drunkenness was scheduled as a 'crime unworthy of a Communist', Morozov tried to cure himself of it, a feat which should not have been difficult considering that vodka has been almost unobtainable ever since the Tsar prohibited its production and sale at the beginning of the Great War. But Morozov nevertheless fell to vodka every time there was a chance. On the occasion of the wedding of a friend of his who was a speculator (and a genuine speculator) in foodstuffs, he invited two or three regimental companions, one of whom I knew well, to the feast. Although Petrograd was starving, there was such an abundance of good things at this repast and such a variety of wines and spirits, extracted from cellars known only to superior 'speculators' who supplied important people like commissars, that it lasted not only one night, but was continued on the morrow. Morozov disappeared from his regiment for three whole days and would undoubtedly have lost his post and, in the event of the full truth leaking out, have been shot, had not his friends sworn he had had an accident.

Yet Morozov could not have been bribed by money and would have conscientiously exposed any 'speculator' he found in his regiment. He was thoroughly contrite after the episode of the marriage-feast. But it was not the wanton waste of foodstuffs that stirred his conscience, nor his connivance and participation in the revels of a 'speculator', but the fact that he had failed in his duty to his regiment and had only saved his skin by dissembling. His sense of fairness was remarkable for a Communist. At the elections to the Petrograd Soviet to which he was a candidate for his regiment, he not only permitted but positively insisted that the voting be by secret ballot – the only case of secret voting that I heard of. The result was that he was genuinely elected by a large majority, for apart from this quite unusual fairness he was fond of his soldiers and consequently popular. His intelligence was rudimentary and may be described as crudely locksmithian. An eddy of fortune had swept him to his present pinnacle of power, and judging others by himself he imagined the soviet regime was doing for everyone what it had done for him. Possessing no little heart but very little mind, he found considerable difficulty in reconciling the ruthless attitude of the Communists toward the people with his own more warm-hearted inclinations, but the usual Jesuitical argument served to still any inner questionings – namely, that since the Communists alone were right, all dissentients must be 'enemies of the State' and he was in duty bound to treat them as such.

During the six or eight weeks that I had the opportunity to study the figure of Morozov after his appointment as regimental commissar, a perceptible change came over him. He grew suspicious and less frank and outspoken. Though he would scarcely have been able to formulate his thoughts in words, it was clear that the severity with which any criticism, even by Communists, of political commands from above was deprecated, and the rigid enforcement within and without the party of iron discipline, differed greatly from the prospect of proletarian brotherhood which he had pictured to himself. At the same time he could not escape from these shackles except by becoming an 'enemy of the State', and, like all Communists, he finally attributed the non-realization of his dreams to the insidious machinations of the scapegoats designated by his superiors, namely, to the non-Bolshevist Socialists, the Mensheviks and Socialist-Revolutionaries, who must be exterminated wholesale.

Morozov's responsibilities, like those of all commissars, were heavy. Though in purely military affairs he was subordinate to the regimental commander, he none the less was made responsible for the latter's loyalty and answered equally with him for discipline in the ranks; besides which the responsibility for all political propaganda (regarded by the Government as of paramount importance) and even for accuracy of army service rested upon him. A regimental commissar's responsibilities are, in fact, so great that he can rarely guarantee his own security without having recourse to spying provocation, and 'experimental denunciation'.

Even Morozov had to resort to questionable strategy of this nature to forestall possible treachery in others for which he would have been held responsible. Having been informed by a member of his 'cell' that the conduct of a junior officer gave rise to misgivings, he had a purely fictitious concrete charge drawn up for no other reason than to see how the officer would react when it was brought against him. It was found, as was not unnatural, that the original complaint of the 'political worker' was due to sheer spite, and that nothing had been further from the mind of the young officer, who was of a mild disposition, than to conspire against the all-powerful commissar. Anonymous written denunciations of individuals, charging them with counter-revolutionary activities, are of frequent occurrence, and commissars, terrified for their own safety, prefer to err at the cost of the wrongly accused rather than risk their own positions through leniency or over-scrupulous attention to justice.

There is an intermediate grade between a 'cell' leader and a commissar, known as a political guide. The latter has not the authority of a commissar but represents a stepping stone to that dignity. Political guides have duties of investigation and control, but their chief task is to rope in the largest possible number of neophytes to the Communist party. The whole power of the Bolshevist Government is founded on the diligence, zeal, and – it must be added – unscrupulousness of these various Communist officials. All sorts of instructions and propaganda pamphlets and leaflets are received by the 'cells' in enormous quantities, and they have to see that such literature is distributed in the ranks and amongst the local population. It is read but little, for the soldiers and peasants are sick of the constant repetition of worn-out propagandist phraseology. It was hoped originally that by the never-ending repetition of the words 'vampires', 'bourgeois', 'class-struggle', 'blood-sucking capitalists and imperialists', and so forth, some at least of the ideas presented would sink into the listeners' minds and be taken for good coinage. But the results are almost negligible. It says much for the latent intelligence of the Russian peasant and worker that in spite of it all the membership of 'the party' is no more than some half million, half of whom would be anything but Communists if they could. Propagandist leaflets are used principally for wrapping herrings up in and making cigarettes of, for *mahorka* (the pepper-like tobacco beloved of the Russian soldier) is still issued in small quantities.

The only aspect of the above propaganda in which positive results have been obtained is the rousing of hatred and revenge for everything 'bourgeois'. The word *bourgeois* is as foreign to the Russian language as it is to the English, and the average Russian soldier's conception of 'bourgeois' is simply everything that is above his understanding. But by cleverly associating the idea of 'bourgeois' with that of opulence and landed possessions, Bolshevist agitators have made great play with it.

Yet even this has cut less deep than might have been expected, considering the effort expended. Propaganda on a wide scale is possible only in the towns and the army, and the army is after all but a very small percentage of the whole peasantry. The vast majority of the peasants are home in their villages, and Bolshevist propaganda and administration reach no farther than a limited area bordering either side of Russia's sparse network of railways.

Every Communist organization throughout Russia has to present periodical reports to headquarters on the progress of its labours. It goes without saying that, fearful of strict censure, such reports are invariably drawn up in the most favourable light possible. Particularly is this the case in the army. If the membership of a 'cell' does not increase, the supervising commissar or political guide will be asked the reason why. He will be publicly hauled over the coals for lack of energy, and unless his labours fructify he is liable to be lowered to an inferior post. Thus it is in the interest of Communist officials to coax, cajole, or even compel soldiers to enter the ranks of the party. The statistics supplied are compiled at headquarters and summaries are published. It is according to these statistics that the membership of the Communist party is a little more than half a million, out of the 120 or 130 million inhabitants of Soviet Russia.

‡

Another feature of the Red army which is worthy of note is the group of organizations known as 'Cultural-Enlightenment Committees', which are entrusted with the work of entertaining and 'enlightening' the soldiers. Being partly of an educational character the collaboration of non-Communists on these committees is indispensable, though rigid Communist control renders free participation by intellectuals impossible. There is also a lack of books. A department at headquarters in which Maxim Gorky is interested deals with the publication of scientific and literary works, but compared with the deluge of propagandist literature the work of his department is nil. The cultural-enlightenment committees arrange lectures on scientific subjects, dramatic performances, concerts, and cinema shows. The entertainments consist chiefly in the staging of 'proletarian' plays, written to the order of the department of propaganda. From the artistic standpoint these plays are exceedingly bad – unmitigated Bolshevist atrocities – but their strong point is that they represent the class-struggle in a vivid and lurid light. As no one would go to see them alone, other plays, usually farces, or musical items are thrown in by way of attraction. Propagandist speeches by Lenin, Trotzky, Zinoviev and others, reproduced on gramophones, are sometimes reeled off in the intervals. Schools of reading and writing are attached to some cultural-enlightenment committees.

In my regiment we had no cultural-enlightenment committee. Not existing for purposes of control they were not so
universal as the 'cells', but depended to some extent for their
establishment upon the enterprise of the commissar. Living,
however, mostly in Petrograd, I came in touch through friends
with other regiments than my own, and attended several entertainments got up by cultural-enlightenment committees, until I
knew the propagandist speeches, which were always the same,
almost by heart. Let me describe just one such meeting. It was
in the regiment of which Morozov was commissar. At this
particular meeting I was to have functioned as amateur accompanist and should have done so if one of the singers, from
a Petrograd theatre, had not unexpectedly brought a professional with her.* The organizer of this entertainment, though
he played but little part in the performance, deserves a word
of mention. As a sailor, of about 20 years of age, he differed
greatly from his fellows. He was not ill-favoured in looks, unintelligent but upright, and occupied the post of chairman of the

---

* In such company I was regarded as an invalid, suffering in body
and mind from the ill-treatment received at the hands of a capitalistic government. The story ran that I was born in one of the
Russian border provinces, but that my father, a musician, had been
expelled from Russia for political reasons when I was still young.
My family had led a nomadic existence in England, Australia, and
America. The outbreak of the war found me in England, where I
was imprisoned and suffered cruel treatment for refusal to fight.
Bad food, brutality, and hungerstriking had reduced me physically and mentally, and after the revolution I was deported as an
undesirable alien to my native land. The story was a plausible one
and went down very well. It accounted for mannerisms and any
deficiency in speech. It also relieved me of the necessity of participation in discussions, but I took care that it should be known
that there burned within me an undying hatred of the malicious
government at whose hands I had suffered wrong.

Poor Committee of a house where I was an habitual visitor. I will refer to him as Comrade Rykov. Like Morozov, Rykov had had only an elementary education and knew nothing of history, geography, or literature. History for him dated from Karl Marx, whom he was taught to regard rather as the Israelites did Moses; while his conception of geography was confined to a division of the world's surface into Red and un-Red. Soviet Russia was Red, capitalistic countries (of which he believed there were very few) were White; and 'white' was an adjective no less odious than 'bourgeois'. But Rykov's instincts were none the less good and it was with a genuine desire to better the lot of the proletariat that he had drifted into 'the party'. Under the Tsarist regime he had suffered maltreatment. He had seen his comrades bullied and aggrieved. The first months of the revolution had been too tempestuous, especially for the sailors, and the forces at issue too complex, for a man of Rykov's stamp to comprehend the causes underlying the failure of the Provisional Government. To him the Soviet Government personified the Revolution itself. A few catch-phrases, such as 'dictatorship of the proletariat', 'tyranny of the bourgeoisie', 'robber-capitalism', 'Soviet emancipation' completely dominated his mind and it seemed to him indisputably just that the definition of these terms should be left absolutely to the great ones who had conceived them. Thus Rykov, like most Communists, was utterly blind to inconsistencies. The discussion by the highest powers of policy, especially foreign, of which the rest of the world hears so much, passed over them completely. Rykov accepted his directions unhesitatingly from 'those who knew'. He never asked himself why the party was so small, and popular discontent he attributed, as he was told to do, to the pernicious agitation of Mensheviks and Socialist-Revolutionaries, who were but monarchists in disguise: Rykov was the type of man the Bolsheviks were striving their utmost to entice into the Communist party. He had three supreme recommendations: he was an untiring worker, his genuinely good motives would serve to popularize the party, and he never thought. It is independent thinkers the Bolsheviks cannot tolerate. Rykov, like a good Communist, accepted the dogma laid down from above and that was the alpha and omega of his creed. But when it came to doing something to improve the lot of his fellows and, incidentally, to lead them into the true Communist path, Rykov was all there. In other realms he would have made an ideal Y. M. C. A. or Salvation Army worker, and it was not surprising whenever it was a question of amusing or entertaining the soldiers that he was in great demand.

The hall was decorated with red flags. Portraits of Lenin, Trotzky, Zinoviev, and of course of Karl Marx, wreathed in red bunting and laurels, decorated the walls. Over the stage hung a crude inscription painted on cardboard: 'Long live the Soviet Power', while similar inscriptions, 'Proletarians of all countries, unite', and 'Long live the World Revolution', were hung around. The audience, consisting of the regiment and numerous guests, sat on wooden forms and disregarded the exhibited injunction not to smoke.

The entertainment commenced with the singing of 'The Internationale', the hymn of the World Revolution. The music of this song is as un-Russian, unmelodious, banal, and uninspiring, as any music could possibly be. To listen to its never-ending repetition on every possible and impossible occasion is not the least of the inflictions which the Russian people are compelled to suffer under the present dispensation. When one compares it with the noble strains of the former national anthem, or with the revolutionary requiem which the Bolsheviks have happily not supplanted by any atrocity such as 'The Internationale' but have inherited from their predecessors, or with national songs such as *Yeh-Uhnem* or for that matter with any Russian folk-music, then 'The Internationale' calls up a picture of some abominable weed protruding from the midst of a garden of beautiful and fragrant flowers.

'The Internationale' was sung with energy by those in the audience who knew the words, and the accompanist made up with bombastic pianistic flourishes for the silence of those who did not.

Nothing could have afforded a more remarkable contrast than the item that followed. It was an unaccompanied quartet by four soldiers who sang a number of Russian folk-songs and one or two composed by the leader of the four. If you have not listened to the Russian peasants of a summer evening singing to accompany their dances on the village green, you cannot know exactly what it meant to these peasant soldiers, cooped in their city barracks, to hear their songs re-sung. The singers had studiously rehearsed, the execution was excellent, the enthusiasm they aroused was unbounded, and they were recalled again and again. They would probably have gone on endlessly had not the Jewish agitator, who was acting as master of ceremonies and who had to make a speech later, announced that they must get along with the programme. The contrast between Bolshevism and Russianism could never have been more strikingly illustrated than by this accidental sequence of 'The Internationale' followed by Russian folk-songs. The former was an interpretation in sound of all the drab, monotonous unloveliness of the supposedly proletarian regime, the latter an interpretation in music of the unuttered yearnings of the Russian soul, aspiring after things unearthly, things beautiful, things spiritual.

There followed a selection of songs and romances by a lady singer from one of the musical-comedy theatres, and then rose the agitator. The job of a professional agitator is a coveted one in Red Russia. A good agitator is regarded as a very important functionary, and receives high pay. Coached in his arguments and phraseology in the propagandist schools of the capitals, he has nothing whatever to do but talk as loudly and as frequently as possible, merely embellishing his speeches in such a way as to make them forceful and, if possible, attractive. He requires no logic, and consequently no brains, for he is guaranteed against heckling by the Bolshevist system of denouncing

political opponents as 'enemies of the State' and imprisoning
them. Thus the entire stock-in-trade of a professional agitator
consists of 'words, words, words', and the more he has of them
the better for him.

The youth who mounted the stage and prepared to harangue
the audience was nineteen years of age, of criminal past (at
this very time he was charged by the Bolsheviks themselves
with theft), and possessed of pronounced Hebrew features. His
complexion was lustrous, his nose was aquiline and crooked,
his mouth was small, and his eyes resembled those of a
mouse. His discourse consisted of the usual exhortations to
fight the landlord Whites. He was violent in his denunciation
of the Allies, and of all non-Bolshevist Socialists. His speech
closed somewhat as follows:

'So, comrades, you see that if we give in to the Whites all
your land will go back to the landowners, all the factories to the
money makers, and you will be crushed again under the yoke of
the murderous bankers, priests, generals, landlords, police, and
other hirelings of bourgeois tyranny. They will whip you into
slavery, and on the bleeding backs of you, your wives, and your
children they will ride themselves to wealth. We Communists
only can save you from the bloody rage of the White demons.
Let us defend Red Petrograd to the last drop of our blood!
Down with the English and French imperialist bloodsuckers!
Long live the proletarian World Revolution!'

Having ended his speech he signalled to the accompanist to
strike up 'The Internationale'. Then followed another strange
contrast, one of those peculiar phenomena often met with in
Russia, even in the Communist party. A modest, nervous, and
gentle-looking individual whom I did not know, as different
from the previous speaker as water from fire, made a strangely
earnest speech, urging the necessity of self-education as the
only means of restoring Russia's fallen fortunes. At the admission of fallen fortunes the Jew looked up with displeasure. He
had sung the glories of the Red administration and the exploits

of the Red army. It was not enough, said the speaker, that Russia had won the treasured Soviet Power – that, of course, was an inestimable boon – but until the people dragged themselves out of the morass of ignorance they could not profit by its benefits. The masses of Russia, he urged, should set strenuously to work to raise themselves culturally and spiritually, in order to fit themselves for the great task they were called upon to perform, namely, to effect the emancipation of the workers of all the world.

'The Internationale' was not sung when he concluded. There was too much sincerity in his speech, and the bombastic strains of that ditty would have been sadly out of place. The rest of the programme consisted of two stage performances, enacted by amateurs, the first one a light comedy, and the second a series of propagandist tableaux, depicting the sudden emancipation of the worker by the Soviet Power, heralded by an angel dressed all in red. In one of these Comrade Rykov proudly participated. In the concluding tableau the Red angel was seen guarding a smiling workman and his family on one side, and a smiling peasant and family on the other, while the audience was invited to rise and sing 'The Internationale'.

Of conscious political intelligence in the cultural-enlightenment committees there is none, nor under 'iron party discipline' can there possibly be any. All Communist agitators repeat, parrot-like, the epithets and catch-phrases dictated from above. None the less, despite their crudity and one-sidedness, these committees serve a positive purpose in the Red army. By the provision of entertainment the savagery of the soldiery has been curbed and literacy promoted. If they were non-political and run by intelligent people with the sole object of improving the minds of the masses they might be made a real instrument for the furtherance of education and culture. At present they are often grotesque. But representing an 'upward' trend, the cultural-enlightenment committees form a welcome contrast to the majority of Bolshevist institutions.

‡

Our survey of the essential features of the Red army is now complete and may be summed up as follows:

1. A military machine, with all the attributes of other armies but differing in terminology. Its strength at the close of 1920 was said to be about two million, but this is probably exaggerated.

2. A concomitant organization, about one tenth in size, of the Communist party, permeating the entire army, subjected to military experts in purely military decisions, but with absolute powers of political and administrative control, supplemented by 'Special Departments' of the Extraordinary Commission, Revolutionary Tribunals, and Special Commissions for Combating Desertion.

3. A network of Communist-controlled propagandist organizations called Cultural-Enlightenment Committees, whose object is the entertainment and education of the soldiers.

Tractable, docile, and leaderless though the Russian people are, the machine which has been built up in the Red army is still a monument to the inflexible will and merciless determination of its leader, Trotzky. Its development has been rapid and is perhaps not yet complete. Trotzky would make of it an absolutely soul-less, will-less, obedient instrument which he may apply to whatsoever end he thinks fit. Unless a popular leader appears, the army is Trotzky's as long as he can feed it.

There are those who have long believed an internal military coup to be imminent, organized by old-time generals such as Brusilov, Baluev, Rattel, Gutov, Parsky, Klembovsky and others, whose names are associated with the highest military posts in Soviet Russia. Three things militate against the early success of such a coup. First, the experience of internal conspiracies shows it to be next to impossible to conspire against the

Extraordinary Commission. Secondly, the memory of White administrations is still too fresh in the minds of the common soldier. Thirdly, these generals suffer from the same defect as Wrangel, Denikin, and Kolchak, in that they are not politicians and have no concrete programme to offer the Russian people.

The local popularity of peasant leaders such as the 'little fathers' Balahovitch in Bielorusia and Makhno in Ukrainia, who denounce Bolsheviks, Tsars, and landlords alike, shows that could a bigger man than these be found to fire the imagination of the peasantry on a nation-wide scale the hoped-for national peasant-uprising might become a reality. Until such a figure arises it is not from outside pressure or internal militarist conspiracies, but in the very heart and core of the Communist Party, that we must look for the signs of decay of Bolshevism. Such signs are already coming to light, and must sooner or later lead to cataclysmic developments – unless they are forestalled by what Pilsudski, the socialist president of the Polish Republic, foresees as a possibility. Pilsudski spent many years in exile in Siberia under the Tsar for revolutionary agitation and knows Russia through and through. He foresees the possibility that the entire Russian population, maddened with hunger, disease, and despair, may eventually rise and sweep down on western Europe in a frantic quest for food and warmth. Such a point will not be reached as long as the peasant, successfully defying Bolshevist administration, continues to produce sufficient for his own requirements. It needs, however, but some severe stress of nature, such as the droughts which periodically visit the country, to reduce the people to that condition. Will anything be able to stop such an avalanche? Should it ever begin, the once so ardently looked-for Russian steam roller will at last have become an awful, devastating reality.

Chapter XII

'The Party' and the People

If I were asked what feature of the Communist regime I regarded as, above all, the most conspicuous, the most impressive, and the most significant, I should say without hesitation the vast spiritual gulf separating the Communist party from the Russian people. I use the word 'spiritual' not in the sense of 'religious'. The Russian equivalent, *duhovny*, is more comprehensive, including the psychological, and everything relating to inner, contemplative life, and ideals.

History scarcely knows a more flagrant misnomer than that of 'government of workers and peasants'. In the first place the Bolshevist Government consists not of workers and peasants but of typical intellectual bourgeois. In the second, its policy is categorically repudiated by practically the entire Russian nation, and it rides the saddle only by bullying the workers and peasants by whom it purports to have been elected. The incongruity between Russian national ideals and the alien character of the Communists naturally will not be apparent to outsiders who visit the country to study the Bolshevist system from the very viewpoint which least of all appeals to the Russian, namely, the possibility of its success as a *socialist* experiment. But those foreign socialist enthusiasts who adhere to Bolshevist doctrines are presumably indifferent to the sentiments of the Russian people, for their adherence appears to be based on the most un-Russian of all aspects of those doctrines, namely, their internationalism. And this un-Russian, international aspect of Bolshevism is admittedly its prime characteristic.

There is a sense of course in which the psychology of all peoples is becoming increasingly international, to the great benefit of mankind. No one will deny that half our European troubles are caused by the chauvinistic brandishing of national flags and quarrels about the drawing of impossible frontier lines. But these are the antics of a noisy few – 'Bolsheviks of the right' – and do not reflect the true desire of peoples, which is for peace, harmony, and neighbourliness. Not so the immediate aspirations until the present time of the Bolsheviks, whose first principle is world-wide civil war between classes, and whose brandishing of the red flag surpasses that of the most rabid western chauvinists. Theirs is not true internationalism. Like their claim to represent the Russian people, it is bogus.

The gulf between 'the party' and the people yawns at every step, but I will only mention one or two prominent instances. The most important institution established by the Bolsheviks is that known as the 'Third International Workers' Association', or briefly, the 'Third International'. The aim of this institution is to reproduce the Communist experiment in all countries. The First International was founded in 1864 by Karl Marx. It was a workers' association not world-revolutionary in character. Its sympathy, however, with its Commune discredited it, and it was followed by the Second, which confined itself to international labour interests. The Third International was founded in Moscow in the first week of March, 1919, amid circumstances of great secrecy by a chance gathering of extreme socialists from about half a dozen of the thirty European states, leavened with a similar number of Asiatics. Subsequently a great meeting was held, at which the Second, called the 'yellow' International because it is composed of moderates, was declared defunct and superseded by the 'real', that is, the Communist, International.

The next day this group of unknown but precocious individuals came to their headquarters at Petrograd, 'the Metropolis of the World Revolution'. I went to meet them at the Nicholas railway station. The mystery that enshrouded the birth of the Third International rendered it impossible to be duly impressed with the solemnity of the occasion, and although I had not

come either to cheer or to jeer, but simply to look on, I could
not but be struck by the comicality of the scene. The day was
frosty, and for nearly two hours the members of the Third
International, standing bareheaded on a specially constructed
tribune, wasted time saying exactly the same things over and
over again, their speeches being punctuated by the cacophony
of three badly directed bands. In spite of their luxurious fur
coats the delegates shivered and their faces turned blue. They
did not at all look the desperadoes I had half anticipated. Some
of them were even effeminate in appearance. Only Zinoviev,
the president, with his bushy dishevelled hair, looked like an
unrepentant schoolboy amid a group of delinquents caught
red-handed in some unauthorized prank.

The orators, with chattering teeth, sang in divers tongues
the praises of the Red regime. They lauded the exemplary order
prevailing in Russia and rejoiced at the happiness, contentment,
and devotion to the Soviet Government which they encountered at every step. They predicted the immediate advent of the
world revolution and the early establishment of Bolshevism in
every country. They all perorated their lengthy orations with
the same exclamations: 'Long live the Third International!';
'Down with the bourgeoisie!'; 'Long live socialism!' (by which
they meant Bolshevism), etc., and no matter how many times
these same slogans had been shouted already, on each occasion they were retranslated at length, with embellishments, and
to the musical accompaniment of the inevitable 'Internationale'.

The position of the Third International in Russia and
its relation to the Soviet Government are not always easy to
grasp. The executives both of the International and of the
Government are drawn from the Communist party, while every
member of the Government must also be a member of the
Third International. Thus, though technically not inter-change-
able, the terms Soviet Government, Third International, and
Communist party merely represent different aspects of one
and the same thing. It is in their provinces of action that they

differ. The province of the Third International is the whole world, including Russia: that of the present Soviet Government is Russia alone. It would seem as if the Third International, with its superior powers and scope and with firebrands like Zinoviev and Trotzky at its helm, must override the Moscow government. In practice, however, this is not so. For the hard logic of facts has now proved to the Moscow government that the theories which the Third International was created to propagate are largely wrong and impracticable, and they are being repudiated by the master mind of Lenin, the head of the home government. Thus two factions have grown up within the Communist party: that of Lenin, whose interests for the time are centred in Russia and who would sacrifice world-revolutionary dreams to preserve Bolshevist power in one country; and that of the Third International, which throws discretion to the winds, standing for world revolution for ever and no truck with the bourgeoisie of capitalistic states. Hitherto the majority in the party have swung to the side of Lenin, as is not unnatural, for very few rank-and-file Communists really care about the world revolution, having no conception of what it implies. And if they had, they would probably support him more heartily still.

At the very moment when the Third International was haranguing for its own satisfaction outside the Nicholas station, very different things were happening in the industrial quarters of the city. There, the workers, incensed by the suppression of free speech, of freedom of movement, of workers' coopera-tion, of free trading between the city and the villages, and by the ruthless seizure and imprisonment of their spokesmen, had risen to demand the restoration of their rights. They were led by the men of the Putilov iron foundry, the largest works in Petrograd, at one time employing over forty thousand hands. The Putilov workers were ever to the fore in the revolution-ary movement. They led the strikes which resulted in the revolution of March, 1917. Their independent bearing, their

superior intelligence and organization, and their efforts to
protest against Bolshevist despotism, aroused the fears and
hatred of the Communists, who quite rightly attributed this
independent attitude to the preference of the workers for the
non-Bolshevist political parties.

The dispute centred round the Bolshevist food system which
was rapidly reducing the city to a state of starvation. Hoping the
storm would blow over, the Bolshevist authorities allowed it for
a time to run its course, endeavouring to appease the workers
by an issue of rations increased at the expense of the rest of
the population. The latter measure only intensified the workers'
indignation, while the hesitation of the Bolsheviks to employ
force encouraged them in their protests. Unauthorized meetings and processions increased in frequency, the strikes spread
to every factory in the city, speakers became more violent, and
all sorts of jokes were made publicly at the expense of the
Bolsheviks. Ambling in the industrial quarters I saw a party of
men emerge from a plant singing 'The Marseillaise' and cheering. At the same time they carried a banner on which was rudely
imprinted the following couplet:

Dolai Lenina s koninoi,
Daitje tsarya s svininoi,

which being interpreted means: 'Down with Lenin and horse-
flesh, give us a tsar and pork!'

As the disturbances developed, typewritten leaflets began
to be distributed containing resolutions passed at the various
meetings. One of these leaflets was the resolution passed
unanimously by 12,000 workers (at that time the entire staff) of
the Putilov works, demanding that the task of provisioning be
restored to the former cooperative societies. The language of
the resolution was violent, the Bolshevist leaders were referred
to as bloody and hypocritical tyrants, and demands were also
put forward for the cessation of the practice of torture by the

Extraordinary Commission and for the immediate release of numerous workers' representatives.

I knew of this resolution the day of the meeting, because some friends of mine were present at it. The proceedings were enthusiastic in the extreme. The Bolsheviks did not mind that much, however, because they were careful that nothing about it should get into the press. But when the typed resolutions spread surreptitiously with alarming rapidity, in exactly the same way as in December, 1916, the famous speech of Miliukoff against Rasputin in the Duma was secretly distributed from hand to hand, then the Bolsheviks saw things were going too far and took urgent measures to suppress the unrest without any further delay.

One Sunday between thirty and forty street cars full of sailors and guards, the latter of whom spoke a language that workers who encountered them declared was not Russian, arrived in the vicinity of the Putilov works and occupied all the entrances. During the next three days between three and four hundred men were arrested, while in those cases where the workers were not to be found their wives were taken in their stead. This process is always simple enough for the workers are not allowed to possess arms. It is significant that amongst those arrested at one of the shipping yards were two men who had declared at a meeting that even the English parliament was superior to the Soviets as the Bolsheviks ran them. These two were amongst those who were subsequently shot. When after returning to England I recounted this incident to the Committee on International Affairs of the British Labour Party, the gentleman on my right (I do not know his name) found nothing better to exclaim than, 'Serve 'em right.'

The uproar over the arrest of the workers, and especially of their wives, was terrific. The resolutions having spread all over the city, you could already hear people whispering to each other with furtive joy that there was shortly to be a general insurrection, that Zinoviev and others were preparing to take flight, and so on. In the course of three weeks things became so bad that it was deemed advisable to call Lenin from Moscow in the hope that his presence would overawe the workers, and a great Communist counter-demonstration was organized at the *Narodny Dom*.

The *Narodny Dom* (House of the People) is a huge palace built for the people by the late Tsar. Before the war it used to be very difficult, owing to the system of *abonnements*, to obtain tickets to the state theatres, of which the Marinsky Opera and the Alexandrinsky Theatre were the chief; so the Tsar, at his own expense, built this palace and presented it to the people. Besides numerous varieties, it contained a large theatre where the same dramatic works were produced as in the state theatres, and the biggest opera house in Russia, where the Russian peasant Shaliapin, the greatest operatic singer and actor the world has yet seen, sang regularly to huge audiences of six or eight thousand lower middle class and working people. In the days when I was a student of the Conservatoire of Petrograd, eking out a living by teaching English, I often used to frequent the *Narodny Dom* opera. There was free admission to a portion of the hall, while the most expensive seats were at cinematograph prices. The inevitable deficit was made up out of the state exchequer. Over the porch of the building was an inscription: *From the Tsar to his people*. When the Bolsheviks came into power they removed this inscription, and also abolished the name of 'House of the People', changing it to 'House of Rosa Luxembourg and Karl Liebknecht'. Containing the largest auditorium in Russia, this building is now frequently used for special celebrations. As a rule, on such occasions only the Communist élite and special delegates are admitted. The common people to whom the Tsar presented the palace are refused admission.

On the evening of the great Communist counter-demonstration against the Petrograd strikers, machine guns barred the entrance to what was once the House of the People, and the approaches bristled with bayonets. The former Tsar, when last he visited it, drove up in an open carriage. Not so the new 'Tsar', the president of the workers' republic, whose moment of arrival was a secret and who arrived literally hedged round with a special bodyguard of Red cadets.

The audience was a picked one, consisting of the principal Communist organs of the city and delegates of organizations such as trade unions, teachers, and pupils, selected by the Communists. I got in with a ticket procured by my manager. When Lenin emerged on to the stage, the audience rose as one man and greeted him with an outburst of vociferous applause lasting several minutes. The little man, who has such a hold on a section of his followers, advanced casually to the footlights. His oriental features betrayed no emotion. He neither smiled, nor looked austere. Dressed in a plain drab lounge suit, he stood with his hands in his pockets, waiting patiently till the cheering should subside. Was he indifferent to the welcome, or was he secretly pleased? He showed no sign and at length held up his hand to indicate that there had been enough of it.

The orators of the revolution – and they are indeed great orators – all have their distinctive style. That of Trotzky, with poised, well-finished, well-reasoned phrases, is volcanic, fierily hypnotic : that of Zinoviev, torrential, scintillating with cheap witticisms, devoid of original ideas, but brilliant in form and expression; that of Lunacharsky, violent, yet nobly and pathetically impressive, breathing an almost religious fervour. Lenin differs from all of these. He knows and cares for no rhetorical cunning. His manner is absolutely devoid of all semblance of affectation. He talks fast and loudly, even shouts, and his gesticulations remind one of the tub-thumping demagogue. But he possesses something the others do not possess. Cold and calculating, he is not actuated to the extent Zinoviev and Trotzky are by venom against political opponents and the bourgeoisie. On the contrary, despite his speeches, which are often nothing more than necessary pandering to the cruder instincts of his colleagues, Lenin (himself an ex-landlord) has never ceased to believe not only that the Russian bourgeoisie as a class are necessary to the state, but that the entire Russian peasantry is and always will be a class of small property-owning farmers with the psychology of the *petit bourgeois*. True, in 1918 the attempt was made, chiefly through the medium of committees of the village poor, to thrust Communism upon the peasantry by force. But it was soon relinquished and Lenin headed the retreat. Astonishingly ignorant of world events and completely out of harmony with western workers, Lenin has maintained his position in Russia simply by his understanding of this single trait of the Russian peasant character and by repeatedly conceding to it – even to the complete temporary repudiation of communistic principles.

In all other respects Lenin is a dogmatic disciple of Karl Marx, and his devotion to the cause of the world revolution is tempered only by the slowly dawning realization that things in the western world are not exactly as enthusiastic Communists describe. But Lenin's better understanding of the mind of the Russian peasant gives him an advantage over his fellows in presenting his case to his followers, bringing him a little nearer to actualities; so that his speech, while laboured, abstruse, and free from rhetorical flourish, is straightforward and, to his little-thinking Communist audiences, carries persuasion that he must be right. But the 'right' refers not to ethics, which does not enter into Bolshevist philosophy, but only to tactics.

On the occasion I am describing also Lenin spoke mainly of tactics. The vicious Mensheviks and Socialist-revolutionaries had agitated in the factories and persuaded the workers to down tools and make preposterous demands which were incompatible with the principles of the workers' and peasants' government. The chief ground of complaint was the Bolshevist food commissariat. The workers were hungry. Therefore the workers must be fed and the revolt would subside. A heroic effort must be made to obtain food for the factories. So the government had decided to stop the passenger traffic on every railroad in Russia for the space of three weeks, in order that all available locomotives and every available car and truck might be devoted to the sole purpose of transporting forced supplies of food to the northern capital.

Of the results of these so-called 'freight weeks' little need be said beyond the fact that the experiment was never repeated on account of its complete failure to solve the problem. For though the government supplies did indeed very slightly increase, the population in the end was much hungrier than before for the very simple reason that the stoppage of the passenger traffic materially interfered with the ebb and flow of 'sackmen', upon whose illicit and risky operations the public relied for at least half, and the better half, of their food supplies!

The workers' revolt subsided, not through the better feeding of the men, but because they were effectually reduced to a state of abject despair by the ruthless seizure of their leaders and the cruel reprisals against their wives and families, and because this moment was chosen by the authorities to remove a large draft of workers to other industrial centres in the interior, thus reducing their numbers. Still, on the occasion of Lenin's visit, the workers did make a final attempt to assert themselves. A delegation from the largest factories was sent to present their demands, as set forth in resolutions, to the president in person at the *Narodny Dom*. But the delegation was refused admission. They returned, foiled, to their factories and observed to their comrades that 'it was easier to approach the Tsar Nicholas than it was to gain access to the president of the "Soviet Republic"'. What, I wondered, would the Third International have thought of such words?

‡

After the experiment of the 'freight weeks', the next expedient resorted to, when the selfsame demands were again presented, was a strangely inconsistent but an inevitable one. It was a partial concession of freedom to 'sackmen'. After long and loud

clamouring, a certain percentage of workers were granted the
right to journey freely to the provinces and bring back two
poods (72 lbs.) of bread per head. Thus they got the nickname
of two-pooders and the practice was called 'two-pooding'.
As everyone strove to avail himself of the right the railroads
not unnaturally became terribly congested, but the measure
nevertheless had the desired effect. Not only was there almost
immediately more bread but the price fell rapidly. The workers travelled to the grain-growing districts, came to terms with
the villagers who willingly gave up to them what they hid from
Bolshevist requisitioners, and journeyed back, jealously clutching their sacks of bread. I happened to be travelling to Moscow
at this time and the sight of swarms of wretched 'two-pooders',
filling all the cars and clambering on the roofs and buffers, was a
pitiful one indeed. But just at the moment when it seemed as if
a genuine solution of the food problem in the capitals had been
found 'two-pooding' was summarily cut short by government
edict on the ground that the congestion of the railways rendered
impossible the transport of the government's supplies.

For over a year more the Bolsheviks strove their utmost to
stave off the inevitable day when it would no longer be possible to forbid the right of free trading. As the feud between
themselves and the peasants deepened, and the difficulty of
provisioning increased, the government sought by one palliative after another to counteract the effects of their own food
policy. But recently, in the spring of this year, the fateful step
was taken. Against considerable opposition from his followers
Lenin publicly repudiated the communistic system of forced
requisitions and with certain restrictions restored the principle
of freedom in the buying and selling of food.

This step was a policy of desperation but it is the most
important event since the Bolshevist *coup d'état* in November,
1917. For it is a repudiation of the fundamental plank of
the Communist platform, the first principle of which is the
complete suppression of all free trading, private business

initiative, and individual enterprise. There is no limit to the possibilities opened up by this tragic necessity – as it must seem to the Communists. But having taken it, however reluctantly, why do they not release their opponents from prison and invite their cooperation – those opponents whose chief protest was against the stupidity of the Bolshevist food system?

The explanation is that with the Bolshevist leaders the welfare of the workers and peasants, and of humanity in general, is completely subservient to the interest of the Communist party, and this attitude is inspired not so much by selfish motives as by an amazingly bigoted conviction that the Bolshevist interpretation of Marxian dogma is the sole formula that will ultimately lead to what they regard as the 'emancipation of all workers'. Astonishing as it may seem in these days, when the better elements of mankind are struggling to temper prejudice with reason, theory to the Bolsheviks is all in all, while facts are only to be recognized when they threaten the dictatorship of the party. Thus the concession of freedom of trade to the peasantry does not imply any yielding of principle, but merely adaptation to adverse conditions, a step 'backward', which must be 'rectified' the moment circumstances permit. That is why Bolshevist sophists have been talking themselves blue since Lenin's announcement in the endeavour to prove to home and foreign followers that the chameleon has not and never will change its colour. 'Free trading,' they say, 'is only a temporary un-avoidable evil.' Temporary? But can anyone who believes in human nature conceive of a possible return to the system Lenin has discarded?

‡

One day there occurred in Petrograd a startling event that would have made foreign protagonists of proletarian dictatorship, had they been present, sit bolt upright and diligently scratch their heads.

A re-registration of the party had taken place, the object being to purge its ranks of what were referred to as ' undesirable elements' and 'radishes', the latter being a happy epithet invented by Trotzky to designate those who were red only on the outside. A stringent condition of re-entry was that every member should be sponsored for his political reliability, not only upon admission but in perpetuity, by two others. Such were the fear and suspicion prevailing even within the ranks of the party. The result was that, besides those who were expelled for misdemeanours, many Communists, disquieted by the introduction of so stringent a disciplinary measure, profited by the re-registration to retire, and the membership was reduced by more than 50 per cent. A total of less than 4,000 was left out of a population of 800,000.

Immediately after the purge there were districts of the 'metropolis of the world revolution' where scarcely a Communist was left. The central committee had been prepared to purge the party of a certain number of undesirables, but the sudden reduction by over half was a totally unexpected blow. Its bitterness was enhanced by the fact that only three weeks earlier, by means of threats, bribes, trickery, and violence, the Communists had secured over 1,100 out of 1,390 seats at the elections to the Petrograd Soviet, which result they were holding up to the outside world as indicative of the spreading influence of Bolshevism.

The vitally urgent problem arose of how to increase the party membership. With this end in view a novel and ingenious idea was suddenly conceived. It was resolved to make an appeal for party recruits *amongst the workers!* Amazing though it may seem, according to their own utterances the Communists leaders thought of this course only as a last resort. To the outsider this must seem almost incredible. Even in Russia it seemed so at first, but on second thoughts it appeared less strange. For ever since the murder in 1918 of the Jewish commissars Volodarsky and Uritzky, the former by unknown workmen and the latter

by a Socialist-Revolutionary Jew, the Communists had come
to regard the workers on the whole as an unreliable element,
strongly under Menshevist and Socialist-Revolutionary influence. The small section that joined the Bolsheviks were elevated
to posts of responsibility, and thus became detached from the
masses. But a larger section, openly adhering to anti-Bolshevist
parties, were left, and the persecution to which their spokesmen
were constantly subjected only enhanced their prestige in the
workers' eyes.

Of whom, then, had the Communist party consisted for
the first two years of the Red regime? The question is not easy
to answer, for the systems of admission have varied as much
as the composition of the party itself. The backbone of the
rank and file was originally formed by the sailors, whom I heard
Trotzky describe during the riots of July, 1917, as 'the pride
and glory of the revolution'. But a year or so later there was
a good sprinkling of that type of workman who, when he is
not a Communist, is described by the Communists as 'workman bourgeois'. Though the latter were often self-seekers and
were regarded by the workers in general as snobs, they were a
better element than the sailors, who with few exceptions were
ruffians. Further recruits were drawn from amongst people of
most varied and indefinite type – yardkeepers, servant girls,
ex-policemen, prison warders, tradesmen, and the petty bourgeoisie. In rare instances one might find students and teachers,
generally women of the soft, dreamy, mentally weak type, but
perfectly sincere and disinterested. Most women Communists
of the lower ranks resembled ogresses.

In early days membership of the party, which rapidly came
to resemble a political aristocracy, was regarded as an inestimable privilege worth great trouble and cost to obtain. The
magic word *Communist* inspired fear and secured admission and
preference everywhere. Before it every barrier fell. Of course
endless abuses arose, one of which was the sale of the recommendations required for membership. As workers showed no

inclination to join, it was self-seekers for the most part who got in, purchasing their recommendations by bribes or for a fixed sum and selling them in their turn after admission. These were the 'undesirables' of whom the leaders were so anxious to purge the party.

Various expedients were then devised to filter applicants. Party training schools were established for neophytes, where devotion to 'our' system was fanned into ecstasy while burning hatred was excited toward every other social theory whatsoever. The training schools were never a brilliant success, for a variety of reasons. The instruction was only theoretical and the lecturers were rarely able to clothe their thoughts in simple language or adapt the abstruse aspects of sociological subjects to the mentality of their audiences, consisting of very youthful workers or office employees lured into attendance by an extra half pound of bread issued after each lecture. The course was irksome, involving sacrifice of leisure hours, and the number of *ideiny* ('idealistic') applicants was too small to permit rigorous discipline. The training schools were gradually superseded by Communist clubs, devoting their attention to concerts and lectures, resembling the cultural-enlightenment committees in the army.

Another deterrent to 'radishes' was devised by establishing three degrees for professing converts:

1. Sympathizers.
2. Candidates.
3. Fully qualified Communists.

Before being crowned with the coveted title of 'member of the Communist party', neophytes had to pass through the first two probationary stages, involving tests of loyalty and submission to party discipline. It was the prerogative only of the third category to bear arms. It was to them that preference was given in all appointments to posts of responsibility.

One source there is, upon which the Bolsheviks can rely for new drafts with some confidence. I refer to the Union of Communist Youth. Realizing their failure to convert the present generation, the Communists have turned their attention to the next and established this Union which all school children are encouraged to join. Even infants, when their parents can be induced or compelled to part with them, are prepared for initiation to the Union by concentration in colonies and homes, where they are fed on preferential rations at the expense of the rest of the population, and clothed with clothing seized from children whose parents refuse to be separated. It is the object of these colonies to protect the young minds from pernicious non-Communist influence and so to instil Bolshevist ideology that by the time they reach adolescence they will be incapable of imbibing any other. According to Bolshevist admissions many of these homes are in an appalling state of insanitation, but a few are kept up by special efforts and exhibited to foreign visitors as model nurseries. It is still too early to estimate the success of this system. Personally I am inclined to think that, when not defeated by the misery of insanitation and neglect, the propagandist aims will be largely counteracted by the silent but inevitably benevolent influence of the self-sacrificing intellectuals (doctors, matrons, and nurses) whose services cannot be dispensed with in the running of them. The tragedy of the children of Soviet Russia is in the numbers that are thrown into the streets. But the Union of Communist Youth, consisting of adolescents, with considerable license permitted them, with endless concerts, balls, theatre parties and excursions, supplementary rations and issues of sweetmeats, processioning, flag-waving, and speechmaking at public ceremonies, is still the most reliable source of recruits to the Communist party.

It will be readily realized that the party consisted of a heterogeneous medley of widely differing characters, in which genuine toilers were a minority. When the novel suggestion was made of inviting workers to join, this fact was admitted with laudable candour. The Bolshevist spokesmen frankly avowed they had completely forgotten the workers, and a great campaign was opened to draw them into the party. 'The watchword "Open the party doors to the workers",' wrote *Pravda* on July 25, 1919, 'has been forgotten. Workers get "pickled" as soon as they join' – which meant they become Communists and entirely lose their individuality as workers. Zinoviev wrote a long proclamation to toilers explaining who the Communists were, and their objects.

'The Bolshevist party,' said he, 'was not born a year or two ago. Our party has behind it more than one decade of glorious activity. The best workers of the world called themselves Communists with pride... The party is not a peculiar sect, it is not an aristocracy of labour. It consists also of workers and peasants – only more organized, more developed, knowing what they want and with a fixed programme. The Communists are not the masters, in the bad sense of that word, of the workers and peasants, but only their elder comrades, able to point out the right path... Recently we have purged our ranks. We have ejected those who in our opinion did not merit the grand honour of being called Communists. They were mostly not workers but people more or less of the privileged classes who tried to "paste" themselves on to us because we are in power... Having done this we open wide the door of the party to people of labour... All honest labourers may enter it. If the party has defects let us correct them together... We warn everyone that in our party there is iron discipline. You must harden yourself and at the call of the party take up very hard work. We call all who are willing to sacrifice themselves for the working-class. Strengthen and help the only party in the world that leads the workers to liberty!'

With all formalities such as probationary stages removed, and diffident candidates magnanimously assured that if only they joined they could learn later what it was all about, the membership of the party in the northern capital rose in three months to 23,000. This was slightly less than could have been mustered, prior to the purging, by combining members, sympathizers, candidates, and the Union of Communist Youth. The figures in Moscow were approximately the same.

The above remarks apply to the rank and file. Intellectuality in the party has always been represented largely, though by no means exclusively, by Jews, who dominate the Third International, edit the Soviet journals, and direct propaganda. It must never be forgotten, however, that there are just as many Jews who are opposed to Bolshevism, only they cannot make their voice heard. I find that those who warn against a coming pogrom of Jews as a result of the evils of Bolshevism are liable often to meet with the reception of a Cassandra. Unfortunately, I fear such an occurrence to be inevitable if no modifying foreign influence is at hand in the country, and it will be fanned by old-régimists the world over. It will be a disaster, because Jews who have become assimilated into the Russian nation may play a valuable part in the reconstruction of the country. There are many who have already played leading roles in Russia's democratic institutions, such as the cooperative societies and land and town unions, which the Bolsheviks have suppressed.

The higher orders of the party, whether Jew or Russian, consist of the same little band of devotees, a few hundred strong, who before the revolution were, still are, and presumably ever will be the Bolshevist party proper. They in their turn are subjected to the rigid dictatorship of the central party committee, which rules Russia absolutely through the medium of the Council of People's Commissars.

As it became increasingly evident that the only elements who of their own free will and in considerable numbers would willingly join the party were 'undesirables', while a large proportion even of those workers who were coaxed into it were but indifferent Communists, the tendency grew to make of the party a closed corporation subject to merciless discipline, the members of which though enjoying material privileges should have no will of their own, while undesirables should be deterred

by the imposition upon all members of arduous duties. Such
is the position in the capitals at the present time. The 'iron party
discipline' is needed also for another reason besides that of
barring black sheep. With demoralization, famine, and misery
on the increase, insubordinate whisperings and questions are
arising, even within the party, especially since the exacerbating
factor of war has disappeared. These questionings are growing
in force and affect the highest personages in the state. Trotzky,
for instance, no longer able to satisfy his insatiable ambition,
is showing an inclination to branch out on a line all his own
in opposition to the moderate and compromising tendencies
of Lenin. The feud between them has been relieved temporarily by assigning to Trotzky a dominant role in the promotion
of the world revolution while Lenin controls domestic affairs.
But the arrangement is necessarily temporary. The characters
of the two men, except under stress of war, are as incompatible
as their respective policies of violence and moderation.

The number of Communists being relatively so infini-
tesimal, how is it that today on every public and supposedly
representative body there sits an overwhelming and triumphant
Communist majority? Let me very briefly describe the election
and a single meeting of the Soviet of Petrograd whose sittings
I attended.

There are people who still ask: What exactly is a 'soviet'?
– and the question is not unnatural considering that the
Bolsheviks have been at pains to persuade the world that there
is an indissoluble connection between *Soviet* and *Bolshevism*.
There is, however, absolutely no essential association whatsoever between the two ideas, and the connection that exists in
the popular mind in this and other countries is a totally falla-
cious one. The Russian word *soviet* has two meanings: 'counsel'
and 'council'. When you ask advice you say, 'Please give me
soviet,' or 'can you *soviet* me what to do?' Dentists have on their
notices: 'Painless extractions. Soviet gratis.' There was a State
Soviet (in the sense of 'council') in the constitution of the Tsar.

It was the upper house, corresponding to the Senate or the House of Lords. It was a reactionary institution and resembled the Bolshevist Soviets in that only certain sections of the community had a voice in elections to it.

According to the original idea, even as propounded at one time by the Bolsheviks, the political soviet or council should be a representative body to which all sections of the working community (whether of hand or brain) should have an equal right to vote. These Soviets should elect superior ones (borough, county, provincial, etc.), until a central soviet is constructed, electing in its turn a cabinet of People's Commissars, responsible to a periodically convened Congress. This system exists on paper at this day, but its validity in working is completely nullified by the simple process of preventing any but Communists from entering the lowest soviet – the only one that is in direct contact with the people. This restraint is often effected by force, but the franchise law in any case is limited and has the effect of disenfranchising four out of every five peasants. A few non-Bolsheviks none the less generally manage to get elected, although at risk of gross molestation; but they are regarded by the Communists as intruders and can exert no influence in politics.

One might ask why the Bolsheviks, suppressing all free soviets, maintain the farce of elections at all, since they cause a lot of bother. 'Soviets', however, in some form or other, even fictitious, are indispensable in order that the government may continue to call itself for propagandist purposes the 'Soviet' Government. If the soviet or freely elected council system did work unshackled in Russia today, Bolshevism would long ago have been abolished. In fact one of the demands frequently put forward during strikes is for a restoration, side by side with the free cooperative societies, of the soviet system which is now virtually suppressed. Paradoxical though it be, Bolshevism is in reality the complete negation of the soviet system. It is by no means impossible that the downfall of the Communists may

result in a healthy effort to set the Soviets in some form at work
for the first time. If this book served no other purpose than to
impress this vitally important fact upon the reader, I should feel
I had not written in vain.

Whenever it is possible, that is, whenever no serious opposition to a Communist candidate is expected, the Bolsheviks
allow an election to take its normal course, except that the
secret ballot has been almost universally abolished. Before they
rose to power the secret ballot was a carding principle of the
Bolshevist programme. The argument, so typical of Bolshevist
reasoning, now put forward in justification of its abolition,
is that secret voting would be discrepant in a proletarian republic that has become 'free'.

For this reason, the number of Communists who are elected
without opposition is very considerable, and, strangely enough,
it is upon the bourgeoisie, engaged in the multifarious clerical
tasks of the over-burdened bureaucratic administration, that
the authorities are able to rely for least opposition. Employees
of the government offices mostly miss the elections if they
can, and if they cannot, acquiesce passively in the appointment
of Communists, knowing that the proposal of opponents will
lead, at the least, to extreme unpleasantness. A partial explanation of this docility and the general inability of the Russian
people to assert themselves is to be found in sheer political
inexperience, for the halcyon days of March, 1917, before
the Bolsheviks returned, were the only time they have known
liberty. But at the elections of that period there was little or no
controversy, and in any case political experience is not to be
acquired in the short space of a few weeks.

I will cite but one instance of election in a thoroughly
bourgeois institution. The return by the Marinsky Opera of a
Communist delegate to the Petrograd Soviet was given prominence in the Bolshevist press, and having at one time been
connected with this theatre I was interested to elucidate the
circumstances. On the election day, of all the singers, orchestra,

chorus, and the large staff of scene-shifters, mechanics, attend-
ants, caretakers, etc., numbering several hundred people, not
half a dozen appeared. So the election was postponed till
another day, when the Communist 'cell', appointed to control
the election, brought in a complete outsider, whom they
'elected' as delegate from the theatre. The staff were completely
indifferent and unaware until afterwards that any election had
taken place!

Not to the passive bourgeoisie but to the active workers do
the Bolsheviks look for opposition in the cities. It is to counteract and forcibly prevent non-Bolshevist propaganda in the
workshops that their chief energies are devoted. The elections
I am describing were noteworthy because they followed immediately upon a fresh outburst of strikes, particularly affecting
the railwaymen and street-car workers. At one of the tramway
parks bombs had been thrown killing one worker and wound-
ing three Communists.

Only one meeting at each factory or other institution
was permitted and the printed instructions stated it must be
controlled by Communists who were to put forward their
candidates first. Everywhere where there had been disturbances
guards were introduced to maintain order during the meeting,
and spies of the Extraordinary Commission were sent to note
who, if anyone, raised their hand against the Communist candidates. At the Obuhov works the workers were told straight that
any who voted against the Communists would be dismissed
without the right of employment elsewhere. At the Putilov
works the election meeting was held without being announced
so that scarcely any one was present. Next day the Putilov men
heard to their amazement that they had unanimously elected
some twenty Communists to the soviet!

In the district where I was living the Jewish agitator of whom
I have spoken was entrusted with the conduct of a much-
advertised house-to-house campaign to impress the workers
and especially their wives with the virtues of the Communists.

The reception he received was by no means universally cordial and the ultimate triumph of the Communists was to him a matter of considerable relief. It goes without saying, this was the only kind of canvassing. All non-Communist parties being denounced as counter-revolutionary, the entire populace, except for a few intrepid individuals, who courageously proclaimed their adherence to non-Bolshevist socialist parties, sheltered behind the title of 'non-partisan', and having no programme to put forward but anti-Communist, put none forward at all. To put one forward was impossible anyway, for the printing press, the right of free speech, and the right to use firearms (which played a great part) were confined exclusively to Communists.

But at this particular election the Bolsheviks forgot the women workers, who turned out to be unexpectedly obstreperous. In one factory on the Vasili Island where mostly women were employed, the Communists were swept off the platform and the women held their own meeting, electing eight non-partisan members. In several smaller workshops the Communists suffered unexpected defeat, perhaps because all the available arms were concentrated in the larger factories, and the ultimate outcome of the elections, though the Communists of course were in the majority, was a reduction of their majority from 90 to 82 per cent.

On the opening day of the Soviet, armed with the mandate of a guest from my regiment, I made my way to the famous Tauride Palace, now called 'Palace of Uritzky', the seat of the former Duma. I pictured to myself, as I entered the building, the memorable days and nights of March, 1917. There was no such enthusiasm now as there had been then. No, there was war, war between a Party and the People. Machine guns fixed on motor-cycles were posted threateningly outside the porch and a company of Reds defended the entrance.

The meeting was scheduled for 5 o'clock, so knowing soviet practices I strolled in about quarter to six, counting on still having time on my hands before there would be anything doing.

Speaking of unpunctuality, I remember an occasion in 1918 when I had to make a statement to the Samara soviet on some work I was engaged in. I wished to secure a hall for a public lecture on science by an American professor. I received an official invitation to appear at the soviet at 5 p.m. to explain my object in detail. I attended punctually. At 5:30 the first deputy strolled in and, seeing no one there, asked me when the sitting would begin.

'I was invited for 5 o'clock,' I replied.

'Yes,' he said, 'five o'clock – that's right,' and strolled out again. At 6 three or four workmen were lounging about, chatting or doing nothing to pass the time.

'Do you always start so unpunctually?' I asked one of them. 'If you have lived so long in Russia,' was the good-natured retort, 'you ought to know us by now.' At 7 everybody was in evidence except the chairman. That dignitary appeared at 7:15 with the apology that he had 'stopped to chat with a comrade in the street.'

Today's soviet meeting at Petrograd, scheduled for 5, began at 9, but there were extenuating circumstances. The still-discontented workmen had been invited during the day to listen to Zinoviev who strove to pacify them by conceding their furlough, which on account of the war had been cancelled. The soviet deputies wandered up and down the lobbies and corridors, while the workmen streamed out talking heatedly or with looks of gloom on their faces.

The hall within the palace has been altered with improvements. The wall behind the tribune where the portrait of the Tsar used to hang has been removed and a deep alcove made, seating over 100 people, where the executive committee and special guests sit. The executive committee numbers 40 people and constitutes a sort of cabinet, doing all the legislation. Its members are always Communists. The Soviet proper never takes part in legislation. By its character, and especially by the manner in which its sittings are held, it is impossible that it should. The number of deputies is over 1,300, an unwieldy body in which discussion is difficult in any case, but to make it completely impossible numerous guests are invited from other organizations of a Communist character. By this means the audience is doubled. And one must still add the chauffeurs, street-car conductors, and general servants of the building who also find their way in. Everybody takes part in the voting, no discrimination being made between members and bidden or unbidden guests.

At 9 all was ready for the soviet to open. By sitting three at a desk there were seats for about 2,000 people. The others stood at the back or swarmed into the balcony. Sailors were very conspicuous. The day was warm and the air was stifling. Around the walls hung notices: 'You are requested not to smoke.' In spite of this, half way through the meeting the room was full of smoke. Together with others I doffed my coat and, removing my belt, pulled up my shirt and flapped it up and down by way of ventilation. Performed *en gros* this operation was hardly conducive to the purification of the atmosphere.

I secured a seat at the back whence I could see everything. My neighbour was a woman, a dishevelled little creature who seemed much embarrassed at her surroundings. Every time anyone rose to speak she asked me who it was. While we waited for proceedings to begin she confided, in answer to my question, that she was a guest, like myself. 'I signed on recently as a "sympathizer",' she said.

Suddenly there was a burst of applause. A well-known figure with bushy hair and Jewish features entered and strolled nonchalantly up to the tribune. 'That is Zinoviev,' I said to my neighbour, but she knew Zinoviev.

A bell rang and silence ensued.

'I pronounce the Fourth Petrograd Soviet open,' said a tall man in clothes of military cut who stood at the right of the president's chair. 'That is Evdokimov, the secretary,' I said to my companion, to which she replied profoundly, 'Ah!'

An orchestra stationed in one corner of the hall struck up 'The Internationale'. Everyone rose. Another orchestra up in the balcony also struck up 'The Internationale', but two beats later and failed to catch up. You listened and sang with the one you were nearest to.

'At the instance of the Communist party,' proceeded Evdokimov in a clear voice, 'I propose the following members to be elected to the executive committee.' He read out forty names, all Communists. 'Those in favour raise hands.' A sea of hands rose. 'Who is against?' To the general excitement a number of hands were raised – an unheard-of event for many a month. 'Accepted by large majority,' exclaimed the secretary.

'The Communist party,' he continued, 'proposes the following to be elected to the presidium.' He read the names of seven Communists, including his own. About half a dozen hands were raised against this proposal, to the general amusement.

'The Communist party proposes comrade Zinoviev to be president of the soviet,' proceeded the secretary in heightened tones. There was a storm of applause. One single hand was raised in opposition and was greeted with hilarious laughter. Zinoviev advanced to the presidential chair and the orchestras struck up 'The Internationale'. The election of the executive committee, the presidium, and the president had occupied less than five minutes.

Opening his speech with a reference to the recent elections, Zinoviev exulted in the fact that of the 1,390 members a thousand were fully qualified members of the Communist party while many others were candidates. 'We were convinced,' he exclaimed, 'that the working class of Red Petrograd would remain true to itself and return only the best representatives to the soviet, and we were not mistaken.' After defining the tasks of the new soviet as the defence and provisioning of the city he spoke of the strikes, which he attributed to agents of the Allies and to the Mensheviks and Socialist-Revolutionaries. It was perhaps not such a bad thing, he said in effect, that some

rascal Mensheviks and Socialist-Revolutionaries had got into
the soviet, for it would be the easier to catch them if they
were on the side of the counter-revolutionaries. Continuing,
he praised the Red army and the Baltic fleet and concluded, as
usual, with a prediction of early revolution in western Europe.
'Comrades,' he cried, 'the tyrannous governments of the west
are on the eve of their fall. The bourgeois despots are doomed.
The workers are rising in their millions to sweep them away.
They are looking to us, to the Red proletariat, to lead them to
victory. Long live the Communist International!'

He ended amid tremendous cheering. During his speech
'The Internationale' was played three times and at its conclusion twice more.

Then Zinoviev proposed a novel motion. He invited discussion. There was a distinct tendency in view of the increase of
the non-partisan element in the soviet to invite the latter's cooperation – under strict control, of course, of the Communists.
The permission of discussion, however, was easy to understand
when the next speaker announced by the president declared
himself to be an ex-Menshevik now converted to Communism.
His harangue was short and ended with a panegyric of the
Bolshevist leaders. He was followed by an anarchist, who was
inarticulate, but who roundly denounced the 'thieves of the
food department'. His speech was punctuated by furious howls
and whistling, particularly on the part of the sailors. None
the less he introduced an anti-Communist resolution which
was scarcely audible and for which a few hands were raised.
Zinoviev repeatedly called for order but looked pleased enough
at the disturbance. The anarchist sat down amid a storm of
laughter and booing. Zinoviev then closed the discussion.

There then approached the tribune a business-like looking
little man, rather stout, round-shouldered, and with a black
moustache. 'This is Badaev, commissar of food,' I said to my
neighbour. Sitting in front of us were two young soldiers who
seemed to treat the general proceedings with undue levity. When

the plump Badaev mounted the tribune they nudged each other and one of them said, referring to the graded categories into which the populace is divided for purposes of provisioning: 'Look! what a tub! Ask him what food category he belongs to' – at which little pleasantry they both giggled convulsively for several minutes.

Badaev spoke well but with no oratorical cunning. He said the food situation was deplorable, that speculation was rife, and mentioned decrees which should rectify defects. Badaev could hardly be called a logician. Though the soup was bad, he said in effect, the Communist provisioning apparatus would be the most perfect in the world. He admitted abuses in the communal kitchens. Communists, he acknowledged regretfully, were as bad as the others. 'You must elect controllers for the eating-houses,' he said, 'but you must never let them stay long in one job. They have a knack of chumming up with the cook, so you must always keep them moving.'

There were several other speakers who all sang the praises of the Communist party and the good judgment of the electorate. At first attentive, after midnight the audience became languid. Periodically 'The Internationale' was played. Toward the end many people lolled over the desks with their heads on their arms. Like schoolchildren, they were not allowed to leave before the end except upon some valid pretext.

At last 'The Internationale' was played for the very last time while the men did up their loosened belts and donned their coats. The audience streamed out into the cool summer air. My head ached violently. I walked along to the quay of the Neva. The river was superb. The sky-line of the summer night was tinged with delicate pink, blue, and green. I looked at the water and leaning over the parapet laid my throbbing temples against the cold stone.

A militiaman touched my arm. 'Who are you?' he demanded.

'I come from the soviet.'

'Your mandate?'

I showed it. 'I am going home,' I added.

He was not a rough-looking fellow. I had a strange impulse to exclaim bitterly: 'Comrade, tell me, how long will this revolution last?' But what was the good? Though everybody asks it, this is the one question nobody can answer.

My path lay along the beautiful river. The stream flowed fast – faster than I walked. It seemed to me to be getting ever faster. It was like the Revolution – this river – flowing with an inexorable, ever swifter, endless tide. To my fevered fancy it became a roaring torrent tearing all before it, like the rapids of Niagara; not, however, like those, snowy white, but Red, Red, Red.

Chapter XIII

Escape

Flight from the prison of 'Soviet' Russia was as difficult a matter for me as for any Russian anxious to elude pursuit and escape unobserved. Several designs failed before I met with success. According to one of these I was to be put across the Finnish frontier secretly, but officially, by the Bolshevist authorities as a foreign propagandist, for which I was fitted by my knowledge of foreign languages. I was already in possession of several bushels of literature in half a dozen tongues which were to be delivered at a secret address in Finland. Fighting, however, unexpectedly broke out on the Finnish frontier, the regiment through which the arrangements were being made moved, and the plan was held up indefinitely. Before it could be renewed I had left Petrograd.

Another scheme was devised by a friend of mine, occupying a prominent position at the Admiralty, at the time when the British fleet was operating in the gulf of Finland. On a certain day a tug was to be placed at the disposal of this officer for certain work near Cronstadt. The plan he invented was to tell the captain of the tug that he had been instructed to convey to the shores of Finland a British admiral who had secretly visited Petrograd to confer with the Bolsheviks. At midnight the tug would be alongside the quay. My friend was to fit me out in sailor's uniform and I was to pose as the disguised British admiral. Then, instead of stopping at Cronstadt, we should steam past the fort and escape, under the soviet flag and using soviet signals, to Finland. If the captain smelt a rat a revolver would doubtless quiet his olfactory nerve. But two days before the event, the famous British naval raid on Cronstadt was made and several Russian ships were sunk. My friend was ordered there at once to assist in reorganization, and I – well, I failed to become an admiral. The most exciting of these unsuccessful efforts ended with shipwreck in a fishing boat in the gulf. At a house where I was staying there had been a search, the object of which was to discover the source of Allied intelligence, and I escaped by throwing a fit (previously rehearsed in anticipation of an emergency) which so terrified the searchers that they left me alone. But I was forced subsequently to flee out of the city and hide for some nights in a cemetery. Having got wind of my difficulties, the British Government sought to effect my rescue by sending U-boat chasers nearly up to the mouth of the Neva to fetch me away. These boats were able to run the gauntlet of the Cronstadt forts at a speed of over 50 knots. A message informed me of four nights on which a chaser would come, and I was to arrange to meet it at a certain point in the sea at a stipulated hour. The difficulties were almost insurmountable, but on the fourth night I succeeded, with a Russian midshipman, in procuring a fishing boat and setting out secretly from a secluded spot on the northern shore. But the weather had been bad, a squall arose, our boat was unwieldy and rode the waves badly. My companion behaved heroically and it was due to his superior seamanship that the boat remained afloat as long as it did. It was finally completely overwhelmed, sinking beneath us, and we had to swim ashore. The rest of the night we spent in the woods, where we were fired on by a patrol but eluded their vigilance by scrambling into a scrubby bog and lying still till daylight.

Then one day my commander informed me that he had orders to move our regiment to the front. After a moment's consideration I asked if he would be able to send some of his soldiers down in small detachments, say of two or three, to which he replied, 'Possibly.' This intelligence set me thinking very hard. In a minute I leaned over to him and in a low tone said something which set him, too, thinking very hard. A smile gradually began to flicker round his lips and he very slowly closed one eye and reopened it.

'All right,' he said, 'I will see to it that you are duly "killed".'

Thus it came to pass that on a Sunday evening two or three days before the regiment left Petrograd I set out with two companions, detailed off to join an artillery brigade at a distant point of the Latvian front near Dvinsk. The Baltic State of Latvia was still at war with Soviet Russia. My companions belonged to another regiment but were temporarily transferred. They were both fellows of sterling worth who had stood by me in many a scrape, and both wished to desert and serve the Allies, but feared they might be shot as Communists by the Whites. So I had promised to take them with me when I went. One was a giant over six feet high, a law student, prize boxer, expert marksman, a Hercules and sportsman in every sense and a boon companion on an adventure such as ours. The other was a youth, cultured, gentle, but intrepid, who luckily knew the strip of country to which we were being sent.

The first night we travelled for eleven hours in the lobby of a passenger car. The train was already packed when we got on, people were sitting on the buffers and roofs, but having some muscle between us we took the steps by storm and held on tight.

I was the fortunate one on top. The lobby might have contained four comfortably, but there were already nine people in it, all with sacks and baggage. About half an hour after the train started I succeeded in forcing the door open sufficiently to squeeze half in. My companions smashed the window and, to the horror of those within, clambered through it and wedged themselves downwards. Treating the thing, in Russian style, as a huge joke, they soon overcame the profanity of the opposition. Eventually I got the other half of me through the door, it shut with a slam, and we breathed again.

Next day we slept out on the grass at a junction station. The second night's journey was to take us to the destination

mentioned on our order papers, and in the course of it we had
a curious experience. About 3 in the morning we noticed that
the train had been shunted on to a siding, while muffled cries
in the stillness of the night showed that something unusual
was happening. One of my companions, who reconnoitred,
brought the most unwelcome intelligence that the train was
surrounded and was going to be searched. On the previous day,
while resting at the junction station, we had been encountered
by a shady individual clearly belonging to the local Committee
for Combating Desertion, who questioned us repeatedly
regarding our duties and destination. The recollection of this
incident gave rise in our minds to a fear that we might be the
objects of the search, and this suspicion became intensified
with all three of us to the force of a terrible conviction when,
after a second reconnoitre, we learned that our car was the
particularly suspected one. We occupied with two other men
a half compartment at the end of a long second-class coach,
but conversation with our fellow travellers failed to give us any
clue as to their business. The problem which faced us was, how
to dispose of three small packets we were carrying, containing
maps, documents, and personal papers of my own, all of the
most incriminating nature. They were concealed in a bag of
salt, through the sides of which the packets slightly protruded.
The bag of salt would most certainly be opened to see what
was in it. Our first idea was to throw it out of the window, but
this could not be done unobserved because our two unknown
travelling companions occupied the seats nearest the window.
So in the pitch darkness we thrust them, loose, under the seat,
where they would of course be discovered but we would say
desperately that they were not ours. This was just done when
the door opened and a man with a candle put his head in and
asked: 'Where are you all going?' It turned out that we were
all leaving the train at Rezhitsa. 'Rezhitsa?' said the man with
the candle, 'Good. Then at Rezhitsa we will put prisoners
in here.'

I will not attempt to describe the hour of suspense that followed. Calmly though my two friends resigned themselves to what appeared to be an inevitable fate, I was quite unable to follow their example. I, personally, might not be shot – not at once at any rate – but should more likely be held as a valuable hostage, whom the Soviet Government would use to secure concessions from the British. But my two faithful companions would be shot like dogs against the first wall, and though each of us was cognizant from the outset of the risk, when the fatal moment came and I knew there was absolutely nothing could save them the bitterness of the realization was past belief.

Compartment by compartment the train was searched. The subdued hubbub and commotion accompanying the turning out of passengers, the examination of their belongings, and the scrutiny of seats, racks, and cushions, gradually approached our end of the coach. From the other half of our compartment somebody was ejected and someone else put in in his stead. A light gleamed through the chink in the partition. We strained our ears to catch the snatches of conversation. Though our unknown travelling companions were invisible in the darkness, I felt that they too were listening intently. But nothing but muffled undertones came through the partition. The train moved forward, the shuffling in the corridors continuing. Then suddenly our door was rudely slid open. Our hearts stood still. We prepared to rise to receive the searchers. The same man with the candle stood in the doorway. But all he said on seeing us again was, 'Ach – yes!' in a peevish voice, and pushed the door to. We waited in protracted suspense. Why did nobody come? The whole train had been searched except for our half compartment. There was silence now in the corridor and only mutterings came through the partition. The pallid dawn began to spread. We saw each other in dim outline, five men in a row, sitting motionless in silent, racking expectation. It was light when we reached Rezhitsa. Impatiently we remained seated

while our two unknown companions moved out with their
things. We had to let them go first, before we could recover the
three packages that had slid under the seat. As if in a dream,
we pushed out with the last of the crowd, moved hastily along
the platform, and dived into the hustling mass of soldiers and
peasant men and women filling the waiting room. Here only we
spoke to each other. The same words came – mechanically and
drily, as if unreal: '*They overlooked us!*'

Then we laughed.

An hour later we were ensconced in a freight train which
was to take us the last ten miles to the location of our artillery
brigade. The train was almost empty and the three of us had a
box-car to ourselves. A couple of miles before we reached our
destination we jumped off the moving train, and, dashing into
the woods, ran hard till we were sure there was no pursuit. The
younger of my companions knew the district and conducted
us to a cottage where we gave ourselves out to be 'Greens' –
neither Reds nor Whites. The nickname of 'green guards' was
applied to widespread and irregular bands of deserters both
from the Red and White armies, and the epithet arose from the
fact that they bolted for the woods and hid in great numbers
in the fields and forests. The first 'Greens' were anti-Red, but a
dose of White regime served to make them equally anti-White,
so that at various times they might be found on either side or
none. It was easy for them to maintain a separate roving existence, for the peasantry, seeing in them the truest protagonists
of peasant interests, fed, supported, and aided them in every
way. Under leaders who maintained with them terms of *cama-
raderie* it was not difficult to make disciplined forces out of the
unorganized Greens. Not far from the point where we were, a
band of Greens had turned out a trainload of Reds at a wayside
station and ordered 'all Communists and Jews' to 'own up'.
They were shown up readily enough by the other Red soldiers
and shot on the spot. The remainder were disarmed, taken into
the station, given a good feed, and then told they might do as

they liked – return to the Reds, join the Whites, or stay with the Greens – 'whichever they preferred'.

Our humble host fed us and lent us a cart in which we drove toward evening to a point about two miles east of Lake Luban, which then lay in the line of the Latvian front. Here in the woods we climbed out of the cart and the peasant drove home. The ground round Lake Luban is very marshy, so there were but few outposts. On the map it is marked as impassable bog. When we got near the shore of the lake we lay low till after dark and then started to walk round it. It was a long way, for the lake is about sixteen miles long and eight or ten across. To walk in the woods was impossible, for they were full of trenches and barbed wire and it was pitch-dark. So we waded through the bog, at every step sinking half way up to the knees and sometimes nearly waist-deep. It was indeed a veritable slough of despond. After about three hours, when I could scarcely drag one leg after the other any farther through the mire, and drowning began to seem a happy issue out of present tribulation, we came upon a castaway fishing boat providentially stranded amongst the rushes. It was a rickety old thing, and it leaked dreadfully, but we found it would hold us if one man bailed all the time. There were no oars, so we cut boughs to use in their stead, and, with nothing to guide us but the ever kindly stars, pushed out over the dark and silent rush-grown waters and rowed ourselves across to Latvia.

The romantic beauty of September dawn smiled on a world made ugly only by wars and rumours of wars. When the sun rose our frail bark was far out in the middle of a fairy lake. The ripples, laughing as they lapped, whispered secrets of a universe where rancour, jealousies, and strife were never known. Only away to the north the guns began ominously booming. My companions were happy, and they laughed and sang merrily as they punted and bailed. But my heart was in the land I had left, a land of sorrow, suffering, and despair; yet a land of contrasts, of hidden genius, and of untold possibilities; where barbarism and saintliness live side by side, and where the only treasured law, now trampled underfoot, is the unwritten one of human kindness. 'Someday,' I meditated as I sat at the end of the boat and worked my branch, 'this people will come into their own.' And I, too, laughed as I listened to the story of the rippling waters.

Chapter XIV

Conclusion

As I put pen to paper to write the concluding chapter of this book the news is arriving of the affliction of Russia with one of her periodical famine scourges, an event which cannot fail to affect the country politically as well as economically. Soviet organizations are incompetent to cope with such a situation. For the most pronounced effect both on the workers and on the peasantry of the communistic experiment has been to eliminate the stimulus to produce, and the restoration of liberty of trading came too late to be effective. A situation has arisen in which Russia must make herself completely dependent for rescue upon the countries against which her governors have declared a ruthless political war.

The Communists are between the devil and the deep sea. To say 'Russia first' is equivalent to abandoning hope of the world revolution, for Russia can only be restored by capitalistic and bourgeois enterprise. But neither does the prospect of refusing all truck with capitalists, preserving Russia in the position of world-revolutionary citadel, offer any but feeble hopes of world-revolutionary success. For the gulf between 'the party' and the Russian people, or as Lenin has recently expressed it in a letter to a friend in France[*], 'the gulf between the governors and the governed', is growing ever wider. Many Communists show signs of weakening faith. Bourgeois tendencies, as Lenin observes, 'are gnawing more and more at the heart of the party'. Lastly and most terrible, the proletarians of the West, upon whom the Bolsheviks from their earliest moments

---

[*] Published in the *New York Times*, August 24, 1921.

based all their hopes, show no sign whatever of fulfilling the constantly reiterated Bolshevist prediction that they would rise in their millions and save the only true proletarian government from destruction.

Alas, there is but one way to bridge the gulf dividing the party from the people. It is for Russian Communists to cease to be first Communists and then Russians, and to become Russians and nothing else. To expect this of the Third International, however, is hopeless. Its adherents possess none of the greatness of their master, who, despite subsequent casuistic tortuosities, has demonstrated the ability, so rarely possessed by modem politicians, honestly and frankly to confess that the policy he had inaugurated was totally wrong. The creation of the Third International was perhaps inevitable, embodying as it does the essentials of the Bolshevist creed, but it was a fatal step. If the present administration lays any claim to be a *Russian* government, then the Third International is its enemy. Even in June, 1921, at the very time when the Soviet Government was considering its appeal to western philanthropy, the Third International was proclaiming its insistence on an immediate world revolution and discussing the most effective methods of promoting and exploiting the war which Trotzky declared to be inevitable between Great Britain and France, and Great Britain and the United States! But there *are* Communists who are willing to put Russia first, overshadowed though they often be by the International; and the extent to which the existing organized administration may be utilized to assist in the alleviation of suffering and a bloodless transition to sane government depends upon the degree in which Communist leaders unequivocally repudiate Bolshevist theories and become the nearest things possible to patriots.

There are many reasons why, in the event of a modification of regime, the retention of some organized machine, even that established by the Communists, is desirable. In the first place there is no alternative ready to supplant it. Secondly, the soviet system has existed hitherto only in name, the Bolsheviks have never permitted it to function, and there is no evidence to prove that such a system of popular councils properly elected would be a bad basis for at least a temporary system of administration. Thirdly, Bolshevist invitations to non-Bolshevist experts to function on administrative bodies, especially in the capitals, began as I have already pointed out at an early date. For one reason or other, sometimes under compulsion, sometimes voluntarily, many of these invitations have been accepted. Jealously supervised by the Communist party, experts who are anything but Communists hold important posts in government departments. They will obviously be better versed in the exigencies of the internal situation than outsiders. To sweep away the entire apparatus means to sweep away such men and women with it, which would be disastrous. It is only the purely political organizations – the entire paraphernalia of the Third International and its department of propaganda, for instance, and, of course, the Extraordinary Commission – that must be consigned bag and baggage to the rubbish heap.

I have always emphasized the part silently and self-sacrificingly played by a considerable section of the intellectual class who have never fled from Russia to harbours of safety, but remained to bear on their backs, together with the mass of the people, the brunt of adversity and affliction. These are the great heroes of the revolution, though their names may never be known. They will be found amongst teachers, doctors, nurses, matrons, leaders of the former cooperative societies, and so forth, whose one aim has been to save whatever they could from wreckage or political vitiation. Subjected at first to varying degrees of molestation and insult, they stuck it through despite all, and have never let pass an opportunity to alleviate distress. Their unselfish labours have restored even some of the soviet departments, particularly such as are completely non-political in character, to a state of considerable efficiency. This is no indication of devotion to Bolshevism, but rather of devotion to the people despite Bolshevism. I believe the number of such disinterested individuals to be much larger than is generally supposed and it is to them that we must turn to learn the innermost desires and needs of the masses.

I will cite in this connection a single instance. There was formed just previous to the Great War an organization known as the League for the Protection of Children, which combined a number of philanthropic institutions and waged war on juvenile criminality. As a private non-State and bourgeois institution its activities were suppressed by the Bolsheviks, who sought to concentrate all children's welfare work in Bolshevist establishments, the atmosphere of which was political and the objects propagandist. The state of these establishments varies, some being maintained by special effort in a condition of relative cleanliness, but the majority, according to the published statements of the Bolsheviks, falling into a condition of desperate insanitation and neglect. In any case, toward the close of 1920, the Bolsheviks were constrained, in view of ever-increasing juvenile depravity and demoralization, to appeal to the remnants of the despised bourgeois League for the Protection of Children to investigate the condition of the children of the capitals and suggest means for their reclamation. The report submitted by the League was appalling in the extreme. I am unable to say whether the recommendations suggested were accepted by the rulers, but the significance lies in the fact that, notwithstanding persecution, the League has contrived to maintain some form of underground existence through the worst years of oppression, and its leaders are at hand, the moment political freedom is re-established, to recommence the work of rescuing the children or to advise those who enter the country from abroad with that benevolent object.

The fact that the Russian people, unled, unorganized, and coerced, are growing indifferent to politics, but that the better and educated elements amongst them are throwing themselves into any and every work, economic or humanitarian, that may stave off complete disaster, leads to the supposition that if any healthy influence from outside, in the form of economic or philanthropic aid, is introduced into Russia, it will rally round it corresponding forces within the country and strengthen them. This indeed has always been the most forceful argument in favour of entering into relations with Bolshevist Russia. The fact that warring against the Red regime has greatly fortified its power is now a universally recognized fact; and this has resulted not because the Red armies, as such, were invincible, but because the politics of the Reds' opponents were selfish and confused, their minds seemed askew, and their failure to propose a workable alternative to Bolshevism served to intensify the nausea which overcomes the Russian intellectual in Petrograd and Moscow whenever he is drawn into the hated region of party politics. So great indeed is the aversion of the bourgeois intellectual for politics that he may have to be pushed back into it, but he must first be strengthened physically and the country aided economically.

Whether the intervention should be of an economic or philanthropic character was a year ago a secondary question. The Bolshevist regime being based almost entirely on abnormalities, it needed but the establishment of any organization on normal lines for the latter ultimately to supersede the former. Now, however, the intervention must needs be humanitarian. Soviet Russia has resembled a closed room in which some foul disease was developing, and which other occupants of the house in the interests of self-protection tightly closed and barred lest infection leak out. But infection has constantly leaked out, and if it has been virulent it is only because the longer and tighter the room was barred, the fouler became the air within! This was not the way to purify the chamber, whose use everyone recognized as indispensable. We must unbolt the doors, unbar the windows, and force in the light and air we believe in. Then, the occupants being tended and the chamber thoroughly cleansed, it will once again become habitable.

Is it too late to accomplish this vast humanitarian task? Is
the disaster so great that the maximum of the world's effort
will be merely a palliative? Time will show. But if the Russian
dilemma has not outgrown the world's ability to solve it, Russia
must for years to come be primarily a humanitarian problem, to
be approached from the humanitarian standpoint.

There are many who fear that even now the faction of the
Third International will surely seek to exploit the magnanimity
of other countries to its own political advantage. Of course
it will! The ideals of that institution dictate that the appeal
to western philanthropy shall conceal a dagger such as was
secreted behind the olive branch to western capitalism. Has not
the Third International to this day persistently proclaimed its
intention to conspire against the very governments with which
the Bolsheviks have made, or are hoping to make, commercial
contracts, and from which they now beg philanthropic aid? But
the Third International, I believe, has a bark which is much
worse than its bite. Our fear of it is largely of our own creation. Its lack of understanding of the psychology of western
workers is amazing, and its appeals are astonishingly illogical.
To kill it, let it talk.

The essential impotence of the Third International is
fully recognized by those little nations that were once part of
Russia. Having thrown off the yoke of revolution, they have
long sought to open economic intercourse with their unlov-
able eastern neighbour. True, their attitude is inspired in part
by apprehension of those who would compel them forcibly
to renew the severed tie rather than allow them to reunite
voluntarily with Russia when the time shall mature; but their
desire for normal intercourse is based primarily on the conviction that the communistic experiment would rapidly succumb
under any normal conditions introduced from outside. Nothing
will undermine Bolshevism so effectually as kindness, and
the more non-political, disinterested, and all-embracing that
kindness, the greater will be its effect. With the supplanting

of the spirit of political bigotry by that of human sympathy many rank-and-file Communists, attracted to the party in their ignorance by its deceptive catch-phraseology and the energy, resolution, and hypnotic influence of its leaders, will realize with the rest of Russia and with the whole world that Bolshevism is politically a despotism, economically a folly, and as a democracy a stupendous delusion, which will never guide the proletarian ship to the harbour of communistic felicity. Misgivings are often expressed in liberally minded circles that reaction might undo all that has been achieved since that historic moment when Nicholas II signed the deed of abdication from the Russian throne. 'Reaction', in these days of loose terminology, is as abused a word as 'bourgeois', 'proletariat', or 'soviet'. If it means stepping backward, a certain amount of healthy reaction in Russia is both desirable and inevitable. Are not retrogression and progress at times identical? No man, having taken the wrong turning, can advance upon his pilgrimage until he returns to the cross-roads. But the Russian nation has undergone a psychological revolution more profound than any visible changes, great though these be, and the maximum of possible reaction must still leave the country transformed beyond recognition. This would still be the case even if the sum-total of revolutionary achievements were confined to the decrees promulgated during the first month after the overthrow of the Tsar. We need not fear healthy reaction.

No power on earth can deprive the peasant of the land now acquired, in the teeth of landlord and Bolshevik alike, on a basis of private ownership. By strange irony of fate, the Communist regime has made the Russian peasant still less communistic than he was under the Tsar. And with the assurance of personal possession, there must rapidly develop that sense of responsibility, dignity, and pride which well-tended property always engenders. For the Russian loves the soil with all his heart, with all his soul, and with all his mind. His folk-songs are full of affectionate descriptions of it. His plough and

his harrow are to him more than mere wood and iron. He loves
to think of them as living things, as personal friends. Barbaric
instincts have been aroused by the Revolution, and this simple
but exalted mentality will remain in abeyance as long as those
continue to rule who despise the peasant's primitive aspirations
and whose world-revolutionary aims are incomprehensible to
him. A veiled threat still lies behind ambiguous and inconsistent
Bolshevist protestations. When this veiled threat is eliminated
and the peasant comes fully into his own I am convinced that
he will be found to have developed independent ideas and an
unlooked for capacity for judgment and reflection which will
astonish the world, and which with but little practice will thoroughly fit him for all the duties of citizenship.

Shortly after the Baltic republic of Lithuania had come to
terms with Soviet Russia, one of the members of the Lithuanian
delegation who had just returned from Moscow told me the
following incident. In discussing with the Bolsheviks, out of
official hours, the internal Russian situation, the Lithuanians
asked how, in view of the universal misery and lack of liberty,
the Communists continued to maintain their dominance. To
which a prominent Bolshevist leader laconically replied: 'Our
power is based on three things: first, on Jewish brains; secondly,
on Lettish and Chinese bayonets; and thirdly, on the crass
stupidity of the Russian people.'

This incident eminently betrays the true sentiments of
the Bolshevist leaders toward the Russians. They despise the
people over whom they rule. They regard themselves as of
superior type, a sort of cream of humanity, the 'vanguard
of the revolutionary proletariat', as they often call themselves.
The Tsarist Government, except in its final degenerate days,
was at least Russian in its sympathies. The kernel of the
Russian tragedy lies not in the brutality of the Extraordinary
Commission, nor even in the suppression of every form of
freedom, but in the fact that the Revolution, which dawned so
auspiciously and promised so much, has actually given Russia a

government utterly alienated from the sympathies, aspirations, and ideals of the nation.

The Bolshevist leader would find but few disputants of his admission that Bolshevist power rests to large extent on Jewish brains and Chinese bayonets. But his gratitude for the stupidity of the Russian people is misplaced. The Russian people have shown not stupidity but eminent wisdom in repudiating both Communism and the alternative to it presented by the land-lords and the generals. Their tolerance of the Red preferably to the White is based upon the conviction, universal throughout Russia, that the Red is a merely passing phenomenon. Human nature decrees this, but there was no such guarantee against the Whites with the support of the Allies behind them. A people culturally and politically immature like the Russians may not easily be able to embody in a formula the longings that stir the hidden depths of their soul, but you cannot on this account call them stupid. The Bolsheviks are all formula – empty formula – and no soul. The Russians are all soul with no formula. They possess no developed system of self-expression outside the arts. To the Bolshevik the letter is all in all. He is the slave of his shibboleths. To the Russian the letter is nothing; it is only the spirit that matters. More keenly than is common in the western world he senses that the kingdom of heaven is to be found not in politics or creeds of any sort or kind, but simply within each one of us as individuals.

The man who says: 'The Russians are a nation of fools,' assumes a prodigious responsibility. You cannot call a people stupid who in a single century have raised themselves from obscurity to a position of pre-eminence in the arts, literature, and philosophy. And whence did this galaxy of geniuses from Glinka to Scriabine and Stravinsky, or such as Dostoievsky, Turgeniev, Tolstoy, and the host of others whose works have so profoundly affected the thought of the last half-century – whence did they derive their inspiration if not from the common people around them? The Russian nation, indeed, is

not one of fools, but of potential geniuses. But the trend of
their genius is not that of western races. It lies in the arts and
philosophy and rarely descends to the more sordid realms of
politics and commerce.

Yet, in spite of a reputation for unpracticalness, the
Russians have shown the world at least one supreme example
of economic organization. It is forgotten nowadays that Russia
deserves an equal share in the honours of the Great War. She
bore the brunt of the first two years of it and made possible
the long defence of the western front. And it is forgotten (if
ever it was fully recognized) that while corruption at Court
and treachery in highest military circles were leading Russia to
perdition, the provisioning of the army and of the cities was
upheld heroically, with chivalrous self-sacrifice, and with astonishing proficiency, by the one great democratic and popularly
controlled organization Russia has ever possessed, to wit, the
Union of Cooperative Societies. The almost incredible success
of the Russian cooperative movement was due, I believe, more
than anything else to the spirit of devotion that actuated its
leaders. It is futile to point, as some do, to exceptional cases of
malpractices. When an organization springs up with mushroom
growth, as did the Russian cooperatives, defects are bound to
arise. The fact remains that by the time the Revolution came,
the Russian cooperative societies were not only supplying the
army but also providing for the needs of almost the entire
nation with an efficiency unsurpassed in any other country.

The Bolsheviks waged a ruthless and desperate war against
public cooperation. The Cooperative Unions represented an
organ independent of the State and could therefore not be
tolerated under a Communist regime. But, like religion, cooperation could never be completely uprooted. On the contrary,
their own administration being so incompetent, the Bolsheviks
have on many occasions been compelled to appeal to what
was left of the cooperative societies to help them out, especially in direct dealings with the peasantry. So that, although

free cooperation is entirely suppressed, the shell of the former great organization exists in a mutilated form, and offers hope for its resuscitation in the future when all cooperative leaders are released from prison. There are many ways of reducing the Russian problem to simple terms, and not the least apt is a struggle between Cooperation and Coercion.

A deeper significance is attached in Russia to the word 'Cooperation' than is usual in western countries. The Russian Cooperative Unions up to the time when the Bolsheviks seized power by no means limited their activities to the mere acquisition and distribution of the first necessities of life. They had also their own press organs, independent and well-informed, they were opening scholastic establishments, public libraries and reading rooms, and they were organizing departments of Public Health and Welfare. Russian Cooperation must be understood in the widest possible sense of mutual aid and the dissemination of mental and moral as well as of physical sustenance. It is a literal application on a wide social scale of the exhortation to do unto others as you would that they should do to you. This comprehensive and idealistic movement was the nearest expression yet manifested of the Russian social ideal, and I believe that, whatever the outward form of the future constitution of Russia may be, in essence it will resolve itself into a Cooperative Commonwealth.

There is one factor in the Russian problem which is bound to play a large part in its solution, although it is the most indefinite. I mean the power of emotionalism. Emotionalism is the strongest trait of the Russian character and it manifests itself most often, especially in the peasantry, in religion. The calculated efforts of the Bolsheviks to suppress religion were shattered on the rocks of popular belief. Their categorical prohibition to participate in or attend any religious rites was ultimately confined solely to Communists, who when convicted of attending divine services are liable to expulsion from the privileged ranks for 'tarnishing the reputation of the party'. As

regards the general populace, to proclaim that Christianity is
'the opium of the people' is as far as the Communists now
dare go in their dissuasions. But the people flock to church
more than ever they did before, and this applies not only to the
peasants and factory-hands but also to *the* bourgeoisie, who it
was thought were growing indifferent to religion. This is not
the first time that under national affliction the Russian people
have sought solace in higher things. Under the Tartar yoke they
did the same, forgetting their material woes in the creation
of many of those architectural monuments, often quaint and
fantastic but always impressive, in which they now worship. I
will not venture to predict what precisely may be the outcome
of the religious revival which undoubtedly is slowly developing,
but will content myself with quoting the words of a Moscow
workman, just arrived from the Red capital, whom I met in
the northern Ukraine in November, 1920. 'There is only one
man in the whole of Russia,' said this workman, 'whom the
Bolsheviks fear from the bottom of their hearts and that is
Tihon, the Patriarch of the Russian Church.'

‡

A story runs of a Russian peasant, who dreamt that he was
presented with a huge bowl of delicious gruel. But, alas, he was
given no spoon to eat it with. And he awoke. And his mortification at having been unable to enjoy the gruel was so great that
on the following night, in anticipation of a recurrence of the
same dream, he was careful to take with him to bed a large
wooden spoon to eat the gruel with when next it should appear.

The untouched plate of gruel is like the priceless gift of
liberty presented to the Russian people by the Revolution. Was
it, after all, to be expected that after centuries of despotism,
and amid circumstances of world cataclysm, the Russian nation
would all at once be inspired with knowledge of how to use
the new-found treasure, and of the duties and responsibilities

that accompany it? But I am convinced that during these dark years of affliction the Russian peasant is, so to speak, fashioning for himself a spoon, and when again the dream occurs, he will possess the wherewithal to eat his gruel. Much faith is needed to look ahead through the black night of the present and still see dawn ahead, but eleven years of life amongst all classes from peasant to courtier have perhaps infected me with a spark of that patriotic love which, despite an affectation of pessimism and self-deprecation, does almost invariably glow deep down in the heart of every Russian. I make no excuse for concluding this book with the oft-quoted lines of 'the people's poet', Tiutchev, who said more about his country in four simple lines than all other poets, writers, and philosophers together. In their simplicity and beauty the lines are quite untranslatable, and my free adaptation to the English, which must needs be inadequate, I append with apologies to all Russians:

Umom Rossii nie poniatj,
Arshinom obshchym nie izmieritj,
U niei osobiennaya statj –
V Rossiu mozhno tolko vieritj.

Seek not by Reason to discern
The soul of Russia: or to learn
Her thoughts by measurements designed
For other lands. Her heart, her mind.
Her ways in suffering, woe, and need.
Her aspirations and her creed.
Are all her own –
Depths undefined.
To be discovered, fathomed, known
By Faith alone.

Also published by Biteback

OPERATION GARBO
THE PERSONAL STORY OF THE MOST SUCCESSFUL SPY OF WORLD WAR II

NIGEL WEST & JUAN PUJOL GARCÍA

Garbo was the British codename of Juan Pujol García, perhaps the most influential spy of the Second World War. By feeding false information to the Germans on the eve of the D-Day landings he ensured Hitler held troops back that might otherwise have defeated the Normandy landings. This allowed the Allied push against the Nazis in Europe to begin. Amazingly, Garbo's cover was never broken and he remains the only person ever to have been awarded both the British MBE and the German Iron Cross. After the war Garbo faked his own death and fled to Venezuela with a mistress, where he later opened a book store. Ironically, his family in Spain only found out he was still alive when this book was published, Garbo having failed to realise it would also be translated into Spanish.

288pp paperback, £9.99

Available from all good bookshops
www.bitebackpublishing.com

Also published by Biteback

GREEK MEMORIES

COMPTON MACKENZIE

Greek Memories, due to be published in November 1932, included secret letters and documents, named serving SIS officers, exposed the cover used by agents in foreign capitals and revealed the real name of the wartime chief of the British Secret Service – Mansfield Cumming. This was a step too far for the authorities. Compton Mackenzie was hauled before the courts and *Greek Memories* was banned.

Greek Memories was eventually re-published in 1939, stripped of all controversial material, but the original remained banned. Now, for the first time, here is Mackenzie's memoir as it should have been told – uncensored, unrestricted and with no holds barred.

480pp paperback, £14.99

Available from all good bookshops
www.bitebackpublishing.com

Also published by Biteback

THE BLETCHLEY PARK CODEBREAKERS

EDITED BY RALPH ERSKINE & MICHAEL SMITH

The British codebreakers at Bletchley Park are now believed to have shortened the duration of the Second World War by up to two years. During the dark days of 1941, as Britain stood almost alone against the the Nazis, this remarkable achievement seemed impossible. This extraordinary book, originally published as *Action This Day*, includes descriptions by some of Britain's foremost historians of the work of Bletchley Park, from the breaking of Enigma and other wartime codes to the invention of modern computing, and its influence on Cold War codebreaking. Crucially, it features personal reminiscences and very human stories of wartime codebreaking from former Bletchley Park codebreakers themselves. This edition includes new material from one of those who was there, making *The Bletchley Park Codebreakers* compulsive reading.

512pp paperback, £12.99